AWS Certified Big Data - Specialty

Technology Workbook

www.ipspecialist.net

Document Control

Proposal Name	:	AWS Big Data - Specialty
Document Version	:	Version 1
Document Release Date	:	15th May - 2019
Reference	:	BDS - C00

Feedback:
If you have any comments regarding the quality of this book, or otherwise alter it to better suit your needs, you can contact us through email at info@ipspecialist.net
Please make sure to include the book's title and ISBN in your message.

About IPSpecialist

IPSPECIALIST LTD. IS COMMITTED TO EXCELLENCE AND DEDICATED TO YOUR SUCCESS.

Our philosophy is to treat our customers like family. We want you to succeed, and we are willing to do everything possible to help you make it happen. We have the proof to back up our claims. We strive to accelerate billions of careers with great courses, accessibility, and affordability. We believe that continuous learning and knowledge evolution are the most important things to keep re-skilling and up-skilling the world.

Planning and creating a specific goal is where IPSpecialist helps. We can create a career track that suits your visions as well as develop the competencies you need to become a professional Network Engineer. We can also assist you with the execution and evaluation of your proficiency level, based on the career track you choose, as they are customized to fit your specific goals.

We help you STAND OUT from the crowd through our detailed IP training content packages.

Course Features:

- ❖ Self-Paced learning
  - Learn at your own pace and in your own time
- ❖ Covers Complete Exam Blueprint
  - Prep-up for the exam with confidence
- ❖ Case Study Based Learning
  - Relate the content with real life scenarios
- ❖ Subscriptions that suits you
  - Get more and pay less with IPS subscriptions
- ❖ Career Advisory Services
  - Let the industry experts plan your career journey
- ❖ Virtual Labs to test your skills
  - With IPS vRacks, you can evaluate your exam preparations
- ❖ Practice Questions
  - Practice questions to measure your preparation standards
- ❖ On Request Digital Certification
  - On request digital certification from IPSpecialist LTD

About the Authors:

This book has been compiled with the help of multiple professional engineers. These engineers specialize in different fields e.g. Networking, Security, Cloud, Big Data, IoT etc. Each engineer develops content in his/her own specialized field that is compiled to form a comprehensive certification guide.

About the Technical Reviewers:

Nouman Ahmed Khan

AWS-Architect, CCDE, CCIEX5 (R&S, SP, Security, DC, Wireless), CISSP, CISA, CISM, Nouman Ahmed Khan is a Solution Architect working with a major telecommunication provider in Qatar. He works with enterprises, mega-projects, and service providers to help them select the best-fit technology solutions. He also works as a consultant to understand customer business processes and helps select an appropriate technology strategy to support business goals. He has more than 14 years of experience working in Pakistan/Middle-East & UK. He holds a Bachelor of Engineering Degree from NED University, Pakistan, and M.Sc. in Computer Networks from the UK.

Abubakar Saeed

Abubakar Saeed has more than twenty-five years of experience, managing, consulting, designing, and implementing large-scale technology projects, extensive experience heading ISP operations, solutions integration, heading Product Development, Pre-sales, and Solution Design. Emphasizing on adhering to Project timelines and delivering as per customer expectations, he always leads the project in the right direction with his innovative ideas and excellent management skills.

Areeba Tanveer

Areeba Tanveer is an AWS Certified Solution Architect – Associate working professionally as a Technical Content Developer. She holds a Bachelor's of Engineering degree in Telecommunication Engineering from NED University of Engineering and Technology. She also worked as a project Engineer in Pakistan Telecommunication Company Limited (PTCL). She has both the technical knowledge and industry sounding information, which she utilizes effectively when needed.

Syed Hanif Wasti

Syed Hanif Wasti is a Computer Science graduate working professionally as a Technical Content Developer. He is a part of a team of professionals operating in the E-learning and digital education sector. He holds a Bachelor's Degree in Computer Sciences from PAF-KIET, Pakistan. He has completed his training of MCP and CCNA. He has both the technical knowledge and industry sounding information, which he uses efficiently in his career. He previously worked as a Database and Network administrator and obtained a good experience in software development.

Afia Afaq

Afia Afaq works as a Technical Content Developer. She holds a Bachelor of Engineering Degree in Telecommunications Engineering from NED University of Engineering and Technology. She also has worked as an intern in Pakistan Telecommunication Company Limited (PTCL) as well as in Pakistan Meteorological Department (PMD). Afia Afaq uses her technical knowledge and industry sounding information efficiently in her career.

Hira Arif

Hira Arif is an Electrical Engineer Graduate from NED University of Engineering and Technology, working professionally as a Technical Content Writer. Prior to that, she worked as a Trainee Engineer at Sunshine Corporation. She utilizes her knowledge and technical skills profoundly when required.

Free Resources:

With each workbook bought from Amazon, IPSpecialist offers free resources to our valuable customers.

Once you buy this book, you will have to contact us at support@ipspecialist.net or tweet @ipspecialistnet to get this limited time offer without any extra charges.

Free Resources Include:

Exam Practice Questions in Quiz Simulation: IP Specialists' Practice Questions have been developed keeping in mind the certification exam perspective. The collection of these questions from our technology workbooks is prepared keeping the exam blueprint in mind, covering not only important but necessary topics as well. It is an ideal document to practice and revise your certification.

Career Report: This report is a step-by-step guide for a novice who wants to develop his/her career in the field of computer networks. It answers the following queries:

- Current scenarios and future prospects.
- Is this industry moving towards saturation or are new opportunities knocking at the door?
- What will the monetary benefits be?
- Why to get certified?
- How to plan and when will I complete the certifications if I start today?
- Is there any career track that I can follow to accomplish specialization level?

Furthermore, this guide provides a comprehensive career path towards being a specialist in the field of networking and highlights the tracks needed to obtain certification.

IPS Personalized Technical Support for Customers: Good customer service means helping customers efficiently, in a friendly manner. It is essential to be able to handle issues for customers and do your best to ensure they are satisfied. Providing good service is one of the most important things that can set our business apart from the others of its kind.

Great customer service will result in attracting more customers and attain maximum customer retention.

IPS is offering personalized TECH support to its customers to provide better value for money. If you have any queries related to technology and labs, you can simply ask our technical team for assistance via Live Chat or E-mail.

Become an Author & Earn with Us

If you are interested in becoming an author and start earning passive income, IPSpecialist offers "Earn with us" program. We all consume, develop and create content during our learning process, certification exam preparations, and while searching, developing and refining our professional careers. That content, notes, guides, worksheets and flip cards among other material is normally for our own reference without any defined structure or special considerations required for formal publishing.

IPSpecialist can help you craft this 'draft' content into a fine product with the help of our global team of experts. We sell your content via different channels as:

1. Amazon – Kindle
2. eBay
3. LuLu

4. Kobo
5. Google Books
6. Udemy and many 3rd party publishers and resellers

Our Products

Technology Workbooks

IPSpecialist Technology workbooks are the ideal guides to developing the hands-on skills necessary to pass the exam. Our workbook covers official exam blueprint and explains the technology with real life case study based labs. The content covered in each workbook consists of individually focused technology topics presented in an easy-to-follow, goal-oriented, step-by-step approach. Every scenario features detailed breakdowns and thorough verifications to help you completely understand the task and associated technology.

We extensively used mind maps in our workbooks to visually explain the technology. Our workbooks have become a widely used tool to learn and remember the information effectively.

vRacks

Our highly scalable and innovative virtualized lab platforms let you practice the IP Specialist Technology Workbook at your own time and your own place as per your convenience.

Quick Reference Sheets

Our quick reference sheets are a concise bundling of condensed notes of the complete exam blueprint. It is an ideal and handy document to help you remember the most important technology concepts related to the certification exam.

Practice Questions

IP Specialists' Practice Questions are dedicatedly designed from a certification exam perspective. The collection of these questions from our technology workbooks is prepared keeping the exam blueprint in mind covering not only important but necessary topics as well. It is an ideal document to practice and revise your certification.

Content at a glance

Table of Contents

AWS Certifications

AWS Certifications are industry-recognized credentials that validate your technical cloud skills and expertise while assisting you in your career growth. These are one of the most valuable IT certifications right now since AWS has established an overwhelming lead in the public cloud market. Even with the presence of several tough competitors such as Microsoft Azure, Google Cloud Engine, and Rackspace, AWS is by far the dominant public cloud platform today, with an astounding collection of proprietary services that continues to grow.

The two key reasons as to why AWS certifications are prevailing in the current cloud-oriented job market:

- There is a dire need for skilled cloud engineers, developers, and architects – and the current shortage of experts is expected to continue into the foreseeable future.
- AWS certifications stand out for their thoroughness, rigor, consistency, and appropriateness for critical cloud engineering positions.

Value of AWS Certifications

AWS places equal emphasis on sound conceptual knowledge of its entire platform, as well as on hands-on experience with the AWS infrastructure and its many unique and complex components and services.

For Individuals

- Demonstrate your expertise in designing, deploying, and operating highly available, cost-effective, and secured applications on AWS.
- Gain recognition and visibility of your proven skills and proficiency with AWS.
- Earn tangible benefits such as access to the AWS Certified LinkedIn Community, get invited to AWS Certification Appreciation Receptions and Lounges, obtain AWS Certification Practice Exam Voucher and Digital Badge for certification validation, AWS Certified Logo usage and access to AWS Certified Store.
- Foster credibility with your employer and peers.

For Employers

- Identify skilled professionals to lead IT initiatives with AWS technologies.
- Reduce risks and costs to implement your workloads and projects on the AWS platform.
- Increase customer satisfaction.

Types of Certification

Role-based Certification

- *Foundational* - Validate overall understanding of the AWS Cloud. Pre-requisite to achieving Specialty certification or an optional start towards Associate certification.
- *Associate-* Technical role-based certifications. No pre-requisite.
- *Professional-* Highest level technical role-based certification. Relevant Associate certification required.

Specialty Certification

- Validate advanced skills in specific technical areas.
- Require one active role-based certification.

About AWS – Certified Big Data - Specialty Exam

Exam Questions	Multiple choice and multiple answer
Exam Number	BDS-C00
Time to Complete	170 minutes
Available Languages	English, Japanese, Korean, and Simplified Chinese
Exam Fee	300 USD

The AWS Certified Big Data – Specialty exam validates the skills and experience in performing complex big data analyses using AWS technologies. Example concepts you should understand for this exam include:

➢ Implementation of core AWS Big Data services as per basic architectural best practices
➢ Design and maintain Big Data
➢ Automation of data analysis

Recommended AWS Knowledge

- Two or more years of hands-on experience using AWS technologies

- Best practices of AWS security
- Independently define AWS architecture and services and understand how they integrate with each other
- Define and architect AWS big data services and explain how they fit in the data lifecycle of collection, ingestion, storage, processing, and visualization

	Domain	%
Domain 1	Collection	17%
Domain 2	Storage	17%
Domain 3	Processing	17%
Domain 4	Analysis	17%
Domain 5	Visualization	12%
Domain 6	Data Security	20%
Total		100%

Chapter 01: Introduction to Cloud Computing

What is Cloud Computing?

Cloud Computing is the practice of using a network of remote servers hosted on the internet to store, manage and process data rather than using a local server or personal computer. It is the on-demand delivery of computing resources through a cloud service platform with pay-as-you-go pricing.

Advantages of Cloud Computing

1. **Trade capital expense for variable expense**

    Pay only for the resources consumed instead of heavily investing in datacenters and servers before knowing your requirements.

2. **Benefit from massive economies of scale**

    Achieve lower variable costs than you can get on your own. Cloud computing providers, such as Amazon, build their own data centers and achieve higher economies of scale that results in lower prices.

3. **Stop guessing capacity**

    Access as much or as little resources needed instead of buying too much or too little resources by guessing your needs. Scale up and down as required with no long-term contracts.

4. **Increase speed and agility**

    New IT resources are readily available so that you can scale up infinitely with demand. The result is a dramatic increase in agility for the organizations.

5. **Stop spending money on running and maintaining datacenters**

    Eliminates the traditional need for spending money on running and maintaining datacenters, which are managed by the cloud provider.

6. **Go global in minutes**

    Provide lower latency at minimal cost by easily deploying your application in multiple regions around the world.

Types of Cloud Computing

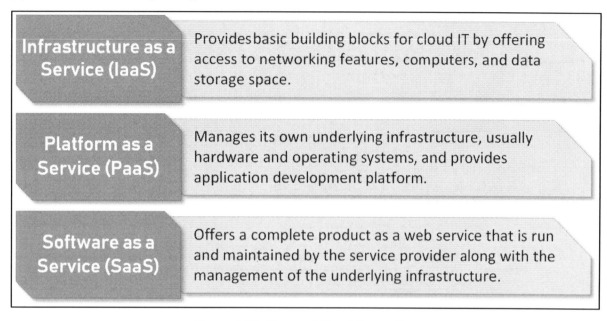

Figure 1-01: Types of Cloud Computing

Cloud Computing Deployments Models

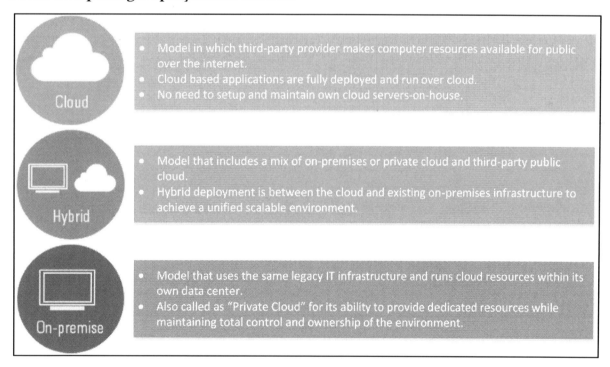

Figure 1-02: Cloud Computing Deployment Model

Amazon Web Services Cloud Platform

Amazon Web Services (AWS) is a secured cloud service platform, offering computing power, database storage, content delivery and other functionality on-demand to help businesses scale and grow. AWS cloud products and solutions can be used to build sophisticated applications with increased flexibility, scalability and reliability.

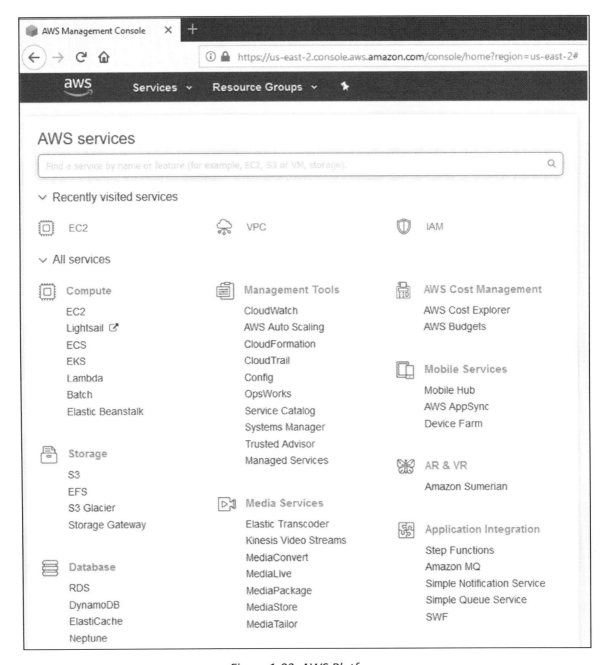

Figure 1-03: AWS Platform

The Cloud Computing Difference

This section compares cloud computing with the traditional environment; it reviews and provides the information to why these new and better practices have emerged.

IT Assets Become Programmable Resources: In a traditional environment, it would take days to weeks depending on the complexity of the environment to setup IT resources such as servers and networking hardware, etc. On AWS, servers, databases, storage, and higher-level application components can be instantiated within seconds. These instances can be used as temporary and disposable resources to meet the actual demand, while only paying for what you have used.

Global, Available, and Unlimited Capacity: With AWS cloud platform you can deploy your infrastructure into different AWS regions around the world. Virtually unlimited on-demand capacity is available to enable future expansion of your IT architecture. The global infrastructure ensures high availability and fault tolerance.

Higher Level Managed Services: Apart from computing resources in the cloud, AWS also provides other higher-level managed services such as storage, database, analytics, application, and deployment services. These services are instantly available to developers, consequently reducing dependency on in-house specialized skills.

Security Built-in: In a non-cloud environment, security auditing would be a periodic and manual process. The AWS cloud provides plenty of security and encryption features with governance capabilities that enable continuous monitoring of your IT resources. Your security policy can be embedded in the design of your infrastructure.

AWS Cloud Economics

Weighing financial aspects of a traditional environment versus the cloud infrastructure is not as simple as comparing hardware, storage, and compute costs. You have to manage other investments, such as:

- Capital expenditures
- Operational expenditures
- Staffing
- Opportunity costs
- Licensing
- Facilities overhead

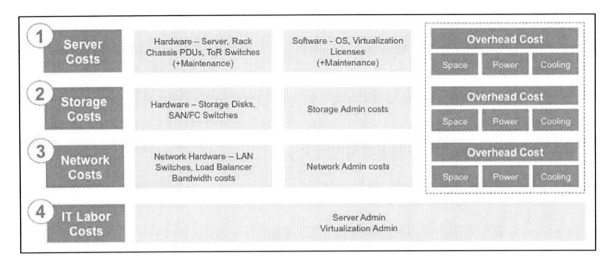

Figure 1-04: Typical Data Center Costs

On the other hand, a cloud environment provides scalable and powerful computing solutions, reliable storage, and database technologies at lower costs with reduced complexity, and increased flexibility. When you decouple from the data center, you are able to:

- **Decrease your TCO**: Eliminate the costs related to building and maintaining data centers or co-location deployment. Pay for only the resources that you have consumed.
- **Reduce complexity**: Reduce the need to manage infrastructure, investigate licensing issues, or divert resources.
- **Adjust capacity on the fly**: Scale resources up and down depending on the business needs using secure, reliable, and broadly accessible infrastructure.
- **Reduce time to market**: Design and develop new IT projects faster.
- **Deploy quickly, even worldwide**: Deploy applications across multiple geographic areas.
- **Increase efficiencies**: Use automation to reduce or eliminate IT management activities that waste time and resources.
- **Innovate more**: Try out new ideas as the cloud makes it faster and cheaper to deploy, test, and launch new products and services.
- **Spend your resources strategically**: Free your IT staff from handling operations and maintenance by switching to a DevOps model.
- **Enhance security**: Cloud providers have teams of people who focus on security, offering best practices to ensure you are compliant.

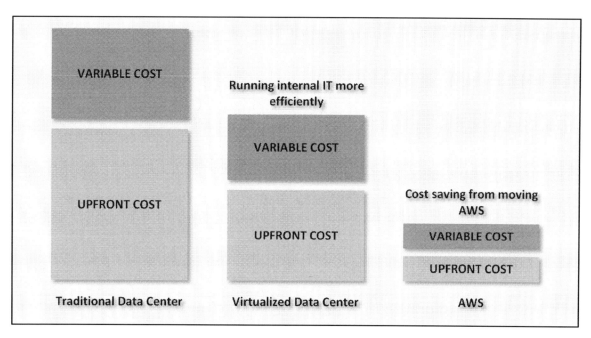

Figure 1-05: Cost Comparisons of Data Centers and AWS

AWS Virtuous Cycle

The AWS pricing philosophy is driven by a virtuous cycle. Lower prices mean more customers are taking advantage of the platform, which in turn results in driving the costs down further.

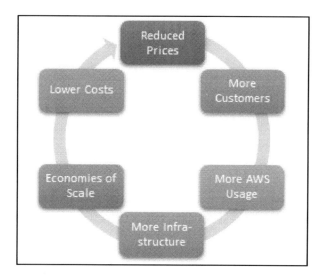

Figure 1-06: AWS Virtuous Cycle

AWS Cloud Architecture Design Principles

A good architectural design should take advantage of the inherent strengths of the AWS cloud-computing platform. Below are the key design principles that need to be taken into consideration while designing.

Scalability

Systems need to be designed in such a way that they are capable of growing and expanding over time with no drop in performance. The architecture needs to be able to take advantage of the virtually unlimited on-demand capacity of the cloud platform and scale in a manner where adding extra resources results in an increase in the ability to serve additional load.

There are generally two ways to scale an IT architecture; vertically and horizontally.

Scale Vertically- Increase specifications such as RAM, CPU, IO, or networking capabilities of an individual resource.

Scale Horizontally- Increase the number of resources such as adding more hard drives to a storage array or adding more servers to support an application.

- Stateless Applications– An application that needs no knowledge of previous interactions and stores no sessions. It can be an application that when given the same input, provides the same response to an end user. A stateless application can scale horizontally since any request can be serviced by any of the available compute resources (e.g., Amazon EC2 instances, AWS Lambda functions). With no session data to be shared, you can simply add more compute resources as needed and terminate them when the capacity is no longer required.

- Stateless Components- Most applications need to maintain some kind of state information, for example, web applications need to track previous activities such as whether a user is signed in or not, etc. A portion of these architectures can be made stateless by storing state in the client's browser using cookies. This can make servers relatively stateless because the sessions are stored in the user's browser.

- Stateful Components – Some layers of the architecture are Stateful, such as the database. You need databases that can scale. Amazon RDS DB can scale up, and by adding read replicas, it can also scale out. Whereas, Amazon DynamoDB scales automatically and is a better choice. It requires the consistent addition of Read Replicas.

- Distributed Processing – Processing of a very large data requires a distributed processing approach where big data is broken down into pieces and have

computing instances work on them separately in parallel. On AWS, the core service that handles this is Amazon Elastic Map Reduce (EMR). It manages a fleet of EC2 instances that work on the fragments of data simultaneously.

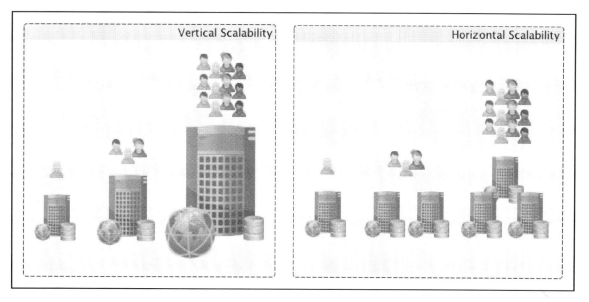

Figure 1-07: Vertical vs. Horizontal Scalability

Disposable Resources Instead of Fixed Servers

In a cloud-computing environment, you can treat your servers and other components as temporary disposable resources instead of fixed components. Launch as many as needed and use as long as you need them. If a server goes down or needs a configuration update, it can be replaced with the latest configuration server instead of updating the old one.

Instantiating Compute Resources- When deploying resources for a new environment or increasing the capacity of the existing system, it is important to keep the process of configuration and coding as an automated and repeatable process to avoid human errors and long lead times.

- <u>Bootstrapping</u>– Executing bootstrapping after launching a resource with the default configuration, enables you to re-use the same scripts without modifications.

- <u>Golden Image</u>– Certain resource types such as Amazon EC2 instances, Amazon RDS DB instances, Amazon Elastic Block Store (Amazon EBS) volumes, etc., can be launched from a golden image, which is a snapshot of a particular state of that resource. This is used in auto-scaling, for example, by creating an Amazon Machine Image (AMI) of a customized EC2 instance; you can launch as many instances as needed with the same customized configurations.

- Hybrid– Using a combination of both approaches, where some parts of the configuration are captured in a golden image, while others are configured dynamically through a bootstrapping action. AWS Elastic Beanstalk follows the hybrid model.

Infrastructures as Code– AWS assets are programmable, allowing you to treat your infrastructure as code. This lets you repeatedly deploy the infrastructure across multiple regions without the need to go and provision everything manually. AWS Cloud Formation and AWS Elastic Beanstalk are the two such provisioning resources.

Automation

One of the design's best practices is to automate whenever possible to improve the system's stability and efficiency of the organization using various AWS automation technologies. These include AWS Elastic Beanstalk, Amazon EC2 Auto recovery, Auto Scaling, Amazon Cloud Watch Alarms, Amazon Cloud Watch Events, AWS Ops Works Lifecycle events and AWS Lambda Scheduled Events.

Loose Coupling

IT systems can ideally be designed with reduced interdependency. As applications become more complex, you need to break them down into smaller loosely coupled components so that the failure of any one component does not cascade down to other parts of the application. The more loosely coupled a system is, the more resilient it is.

Well-Defined Interfaces– Using technology-specific interfaces such as RESTful APIs, components can interact with each other to reduce inter-dependability. This hides the technical implementation detail allowing teams to modify any underlying operations without affecting other components. Amazon API Gateway service makes it easier to create, publish, maintain and monitor thousands of concurrent API calls while handling all the tasks involved in accepting and processing including traffic management, authorization, and accessing control.

Service Discovery– Applications deployed as a set of smaller services require the ability to interact with each other since the services may be running across multiple resources. Implementing Service Discovery allows smaller services to be used irrespective of their network topology details through the loose coupling. In AWS platform service discovery can be achieved through Amazon's Elastic Load Balancer that uses DNS end points; so if your RDS instance goes down and you have Multi-AZ enabled on that RDS database, the Elastic Load Balancer will redirect the request to the copy of the database in the other Availability Zone.

Asynchronous Integration- Asynchronous Integration is a form of loose coupling where an immediate response between the services is not needed, and an acknowledgment of the request is sufficient. One component generates events while the other consumes. Both components interact through an intermediate durable storage layer, not through point-to-point interaction. An example for this is an Amazon SQS Queue. If a process fails while reading messages from the queue, messages can still be added to the queue for processing once the system recovers.

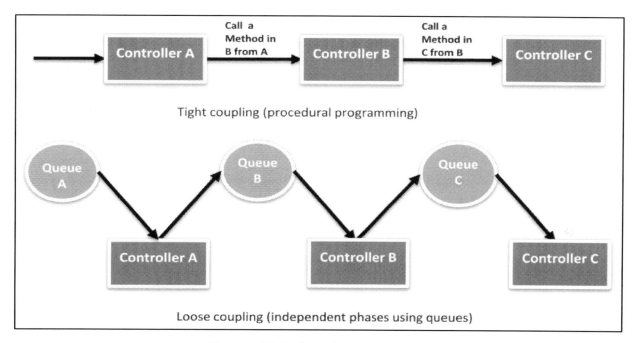

Figure 1-08: Tight and Loose Coupling

Graceful Failure– Increases loose coupling by building applications that handle component failure in a graceful manner. In the event of component failure, this helps to reduce the impact on the end users and increase the ability to progress on offline procedures.

Services, Not Servers

Developing large-scale applications requires a variety of underlying technology components. Best design practice would be to leverage the broad set of computing, storage, database, analytics, application, and deployment services of AWS to increase developer productivity and operational efficiency.

Managed Services- Always rely on services, not severs. Developers can power their applications by using AWS managed services that include databases, machine learning, analytics, queuing, search, e-mail, notifications, and many more. For example, Amazon S3

can be used to store data without having to think about capacity, hard disk configurations, replication, etc. Amazon S3 also provides a highly available static web hosting solution that can scale automatically to meet traffic demand.

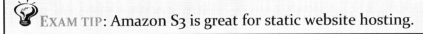

EXAM TIP: Amazon S3 is great for static website hosting.

Server-less Architectures – Server-less architectures reduce the operational complexity of running applications. Event-driven and synchronous services can both be built without managing any server infrastructure. For example, your code can be uploaded to AWS Lambda compute service that runs the code on your behalf. Develop scalable synchronous APIs powered by AWS Lambda using Amazon API Gateway. Lastly combining this with Amazon S3 for serving static content, a complete web application can be produced.

EXAM TIP: For event-driven managed service/server-less architecture, use AWS Lambda. If you want to customize to your own needs, then Amazon EC2 offers flexibility and full control.

Databases

AWS managed database services remove constraints that come with licensing costs and the ability to support diverse database engines. While designing system architecture, keep these different kinds of database technologies in mind:

Relational Databases

- Often called RDBS or SQL databases.
- Consist of normalized data in well-defined tabular structures known as tables, consisting of rows and columns.
- Provide powerful query language, flexible indexing capabilities, strong integrity controls, and ability to combine data from multiple tables fast and efficiently.
- Amazon Relational Database Service (Amazon RDS) and Amazon Aurora.
- *Scalability:* Can scale vertically by upgrading to a larger Amazon RDS DB instance or adding more and faster storage. For read-heavy applications, use Amazon Aurora to horizontally scale by creating one or more Read Replicas.
- *High Availability:* using Amazon RDS Multi-AZ deployment feature creates synchronously replicated standby instance in a different Availability Zone (AZ). In

case of failure of the primary node, Amazon RDS performs an automatic fail over to the standby without manual administrative intervention.

- *Anti-Patterns:* If your application does not need joins or complex transactions, consider a NoSQL database instead. Store large binary files (audio, video, and image) in Amazon S3 and only hold the metadata for the files in the database.

Non-Relational Databases

- Often called NoSQL databases

- The trade off query and transaction capabilities of relational databases for a more flexible data model

- Utilize a variety of data models, including graphs, key-value pairs, and JSON documents

- Amazon DynamoDB

- *Scalability:* Automatically scales horizontally by data partitioning and replication

- *High Availability:* Synchronously replicates data across three facilities in an AWS region to provide fault tolerance in case of a server failure or Availability Zone disruption

- *Anti-Patterns:* If your schema cannot be de-normalized and requires joins or complex transactions, consider a relational database instead. Store large binary files (audio, video, and image) in Amazon S3 and only hold the metadata for the files in the database

> EXAM TIP: In any kind of given scenario, if you have to work on complex transactions or using JOINs, then you should use Amazon Aurora, Amazon RDS, MySQL or any other relational database. However, if you are not, then you should use a non-relational database like Amazon DynamoDB.

Data Warehouse

- A special type of relational database optimized for analysis and reporting of large amounts of data.

- Used to combine transactional data from disparate sources, making them available for analysis and decision-making.

- Running complex transactions and queries on the production database create massive overhead and require immense processing power, hence the need for data warehousing arises.

- Amazon Redshift

- *Scalability:* Amazon Redshift uses a combination of massively parallel processing (MPP), columnar data storage and targeted data compression encoding to achieve efficient storage and optimum query performance. It increases performance by increasing the number of nodes in data warehouse cluster.

- *High Availability:* By deploying production workloads in multi-node clusters, it enables the data written to a node to be automatically replicated to other nodes within the cluster. Data is also continuously backed up to Amazon S3. Amazon Redshift automatically re-replicates data from failed drives and replaces nodes when necessary.

- *Anti-Patterns:* It is not meant to be used for online transaction processing (OLTP) functions, as Amazon Redshift is a SQL-based relational database management system (RDBMS). For high concurrency workload or a production database, consider using Amazon RDS or Amazon DynamoDB instead.

Search

- Search service is used to index and search; it is in both structured and free text format.

- Sophisticated search functionality typically outgrows the capabilities of relational or NO SQL databases. Therefore a search service is required.

- AWS provides two services, Amazon CloudSearch and Amazon ElasticSearch Service (Amazon ES).

- Amazon CloudSearch is a managed search service that requires little configuration and scales automatically; whereas Amazon ES offers an open source API offering more control over the configuration details.

- *Scalability:* Both use data partitioning and replication to scale horizontally.

- *High-Availability:* Both services store data redundantly across Availability Zones.

Removing Single Points of Failure

A system needs to be highly available to withstand any failure of the individual or multiple components (e.g., hard disks, servers, network links, etc.).You should have resiliency built across multiple services as well as multiple Availability Zones to automate recovery and reduce disruption at every layer of your architecture.

Introducing Redundancy - Have multiple resources for the same task. Redundancy can be implemented in either standby or active mode. In standby mode, functionality

is recovered through secondary resource while the initial resource remains unavailable. In active mode, requests are distributed to multiple redundant compute resources when one of them fails.

***Detect Failure*-** Detection and reaction to failure should both be automated as much as possible. Configure health checks and mask failure by routing traffic to healthy endpoints using services like ELB and Amazon Route53. Auto Scaling can be configured to replace unhealthy nodes using the Amazon EC2 autorecovery feature or services such as AWS OpsWorks and AWS Elastic Beanstalk.

***Durable Data Storage*–** Durable data storage is vital for data availability and integrity. Data replication can be achieved by introducing redundant copies of data. The three modes of replication that can be used are: asynchronous replication, synchronous replication, and Quorum-based replication.

- <u>Synchronous replication</u> only acknowledges a transaction after it has been durably stored in both the primary location and its replicas.

- <u>Asynchronous replication</u> decouples the primary node from its replicas at the expense of introducing replication lag.

- <u>Quorum-based replication</u> combines synchronous and asynchronous replication to overcome the challenges of large-scale distributed database systems.

***Automated Multi-Data Center Resilience*–**This is achieved by using the multiple Availability Zones offered by the AWS global infrastructure. Availability Zones are designed to be isolated from failures of the other Availability Zones. For example, a fleet of application servers distributed across multiple Availability Zones can be attached to the Elastic Load Balancing service (ELB). When health checks of the EC2 instances of a particular Availability Zone fail, ELB will stop sending traffic to those nodes. Amazon RDS provides automatic failover support for DB instances using Multi-AZ deployments, while Amazon S3 and Amazon DynamoDB stores data redundantly across multiple facilities.

***Fault Isolation and Traditional Horizontal Scaling*–**Fault isolation can be attained through sharding. Sharding is a method of grouping instances into groups called shards. Each customer is assigned to a specific shard instead of spreading traffic from all customers across every node. Shuffle sharding technique allows the client to try every endpoint in a set of shared resources until one succeeds.

Optimize for Cost

Reduce capital expenses by benefiting from the AWS economies of scale. Main principles of optimizing for cost include:

Right-Sizing- AWS offers a broad set of options for instance types. Selecting the right configurations, resource types and storage solutions that suit your workload requirements can reduce cost.

Elasticity- Implement Auto Scaling to horizontally scale up and down automatically depending upon your need to reduce cost. Automate turning off non-production workloads when not in use. Use AWS managed services wherever possible that helps in taking capacity decisions as and when needed.

Take Advantage of the Variety of Purchasing Options– AWS provides flexible purchasing options with no long-term commitments. These purchasing options can reduce cost while paying for instances. Two ways to pay for Amazon EC2 instances are:

- o **Reserved Capacity**– Reserved instances enable you to get a significantly discounted hourly rate when reserving computing capacity as oppose to On-Demand instance pricing. Ideal for applications with predictable capacity requirements.

- o **Spot Instances** - Available at discounted pricing compared to On-Demand pricing. Ideal for workloads that have flexible start and end times. Spot instances allow you to bid on spare computing capacity. When your bid exceeds the current Spot market price, your instance is launched. If the Spot market price increases above your bid price, your instance will be terminated automatically.

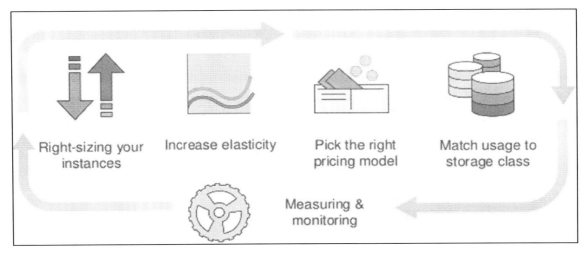

Figure 1-09: Cost Optimization Pillars

Caching

Caching is used to store previously calculated data for future use. This improves application performance and increases the cost efficiency of implementation. A good practice is to implement caching in the IT architecture whenever possible.

Application Data Caching– Application data can be stored in the cache for subsequent requests to improve latency for end users and reduce the load on back-end systems. Amazon ElastiCache makes it easy to deploy, operate, and scale an in-memory cache in the cloud.

Edge Caching– Both static and dynamic content can be cached at multiple edge locations around the world using Amazon CloudFront. This allows content to be served by infrastructure that is closer to viewers, lowering latency and providing high, sustained data transfer rates to deliver large popular objects to end users at scale.

Security

AWS allows you to improve your security in a variety of ways; it also lets the use of security tools and techniques that traditional IT infrastructures implement.

Utilize AWS Features for Defence in Depth–Isolates parts of the infrastructure by building a VPC network topology using subnets, security groups, and routing controls. Sets up web application firewall for protection using AWS WAF.

Offload Security Responsibility to AWS- Security of the underlying cloud infrastructure is managed by AWS; you are only responsible for securing the workloads you deploy in AWS.

Reduce Privileged Access– To avoid a breach of security, reduce privileged access to the programmable resources and servers. For example, defining IAM roles to restrict root level access.

Security as Code -AWS Cloud Formation scripts can be used that incorporate your security policy and reliably deploys it. Security scripts can be re-used among multiple projects as part of your continuous integration pipeline.

Real-Time Auditing– AWS allows you to continuously monitor and automate controls to minimize security risk exposures. Services like AWS Config, Amazon Inspector, and AWS Trusted Advisor continually monitor IT resources for compliance and vulnerabilities. Testing and auditing in real-time are essential for keeping the environment fast and safe.

Mind Map

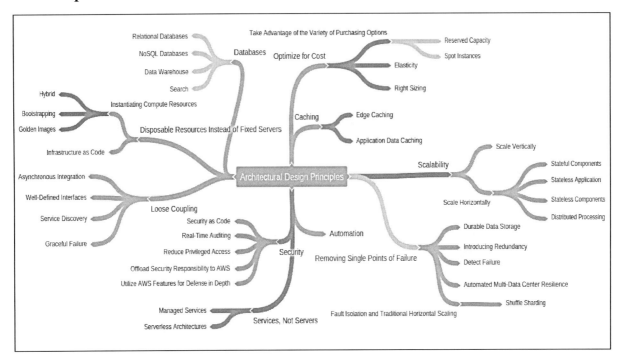

Figure 1-10: Mind Map of Architectural Design Principles

Practice Questions:

1. In AWS, which of the following maps to a separate geographic location?
   A. AWS Region
   B. AWS Datacenter
   C. AWS Edge Location
   D. AWS Availability Zone

2. Which Cloud Computing type is used to provide Basic Building Block for Cloud?
   A. IaaS
   B. SaaS
   C. PaaS
   D. FaaS

3. Which Cloud Computing Type is used as a complete product as a web service?
   A. IaaS
   B. SaaS
   C. PaaS
   D. FaaS

4. Which type of Deployment model includes mixture of on-premises, public third party cloud and private cloud?
   A. Cloud
   B. Hybrid
   C. On-premises
   D. Cloud and Hybrid both

5. In AWS, you have _____ and _____ services to provide continuous monitoring service of resources.
   A. Encryption
   B. AIDA64 Extreme
   C. Rainmeter
   D. Security

6. When you use AWS instead of Traditional environment, then you get _____ benefit. Select any 2 from the followings.

A. Decrease efficiency
B. Increase complexity
C. Deploy quickly
D. Security increases

7. Which phenomenon means "Lower prices mean more customers are taking advantage of the platform", which in turn results in further driving down costs.
   A. Lifecycle
   B. Event cycle
   C. Virtuous cycle
   D. None of the above

8. An application that needs no knowledge of previous interactions and stores no session is termed as _____.
   A. Stateless application
   B. Stateful component
   C. Stateful application
   D. None of the above

9. Implement Auto Scaling to horizontally scale up and down automatically depending upon your need to reduce cost is known as _____.
   A. Caching
   B. Sizing
   C. Elasticity
   D. None of the above

10. Which type of pricing option is ideal for workloads that have flexible start and end times?
    A. Reserved
    B. On-demand
    C. Dedicated
    D. Spot

Chapter 02: Collection

Introduction

This chapter includes the details about the topics related to Kinesis Stream, Kinesis Firehose and the data transformation techniques. This chapter also includes the Amazon SQS, AWS Data Pipeline, and AWS IoT.

Kinesis Stream Introduction

Amazon Kinesis

Amazon Kinesis is a service which is used to process, collect, and analyze real-time and streaming data. Through this platform you can gather, process, and analyze the data; and it helps you to process the streaming of data cost-effectively. Amazon Kinesis contains three different types of services which include Amazon Kinesis Streams, Amazon Kinesis Analytics, and Amazon Kinesis Firehose.

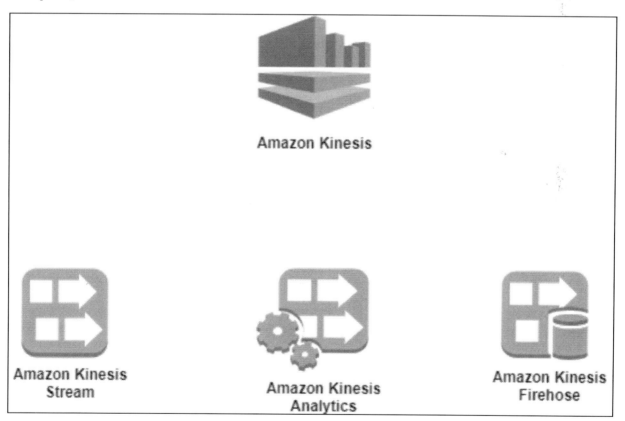

Figure 2-01: Amazon Kinesis with types

Kinesis Stream is used for collecting and processing a large number of data records in real time. Kinesis Analytics is used to process and analyze a large amount of data in real time, whereas Kinesis Firehose is used to load large streaming data into AWS services such as RedShift.

Amazon Kinesis Stream

As it is discussed, Amazon Kinesis is used to collect and process a large stream of data in real time. Essentially you create a data processing which reads the data from Amazon Kinesis Stream as a data record. The process records can then be sent to the dashboard. They are used to generate alerts and dynamically change the pricing or can be used to change the advertising strategy dynamically.

There are some common use cases for Kinesis Stream. The first one is fast logging and other than that, data intake processing is fast in Kinesis Stream. In this, you can have your application pushing data directly into the stream and this could be an application or system log. Another scenario is real-time metrics and reporting. In this, you can use the data which is collected in your stream for analysis and reporting in real time. The data processing application works on metrics and reporting for logs as the data streaming waits to receive patches of the data. Kinesis Stream can also be used for real-time data analytics and complex stream processing which involves a lot of Kinesis Streams in inserting the data from one stream to another stream by using different Kinesis Stream applications.

Benefits of Amazon Kinesis Stream

- Real-time aggregation of data.
- It is used for loading the aggregate data into a data warehouse or map-reduce clusters. Means loading the data into RedShift or EMR.
- Kinesis Stream is also durable and elastic.
- Multiple applications can read data from the stream at the same time. The process can be run in parallel performing different functions on the same data.

Loading Data into Kinesis Stream

In this portion, we will discuss the methods used to load or get data from the Kinesis Stream. In Kinesis Stream, there is a concept of the producer. So, the producer in Kinesis Stream is an application that puts user data record in Kinesis Stream. The Kinesis Producer Library (KPL) allows and simplifies the creation of producer application. The application that gets data from Kinesis Stream is called consumer application, and these consumer applications can be developed by using the Kinesis Client Library (KCL). You

can also use the Kinesis Agent to collect and send data to Kinesis Stream. The Kinesis REST API is also used to put and get a record from the Kinesis Stream over HTTPS.

Kinesis Data Stream High-Level Architecture

The diagram below (Figure 2-02) describes the high-level architecture of the Kinesis Stream. The Producer continually pushes the data into the Kinesis data stream and the consumer processes the data in real time. A consumer such as a custom application that is running on EC2 or Amazon Kinesis Firehose delivery system can store their results using an AWS service such as Amazon DynamoDB, Amazon RedShift, and Amazon S3.

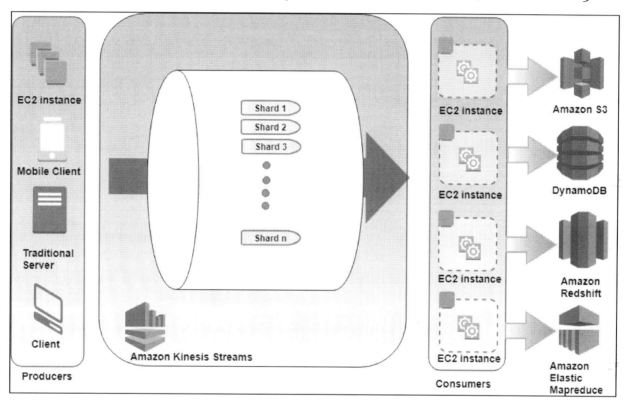

Figure 2-02: Kinesis Data Stream High-Level Architecture

Kinesis Stream Core Concepts

Shard

Shards are uniquely identified groups of a data record within a stream. A Stream is made up of one or more than one shards, each of which provides a fixed amount of capacity. Each shard is capable of supporting up to 5 transactions per second for read, and up to a maximum data read rate of 2 MB per second and up to 1,000 records per second for writes, which includes a maximum total data write rate of 1 MB per second (including partition keys). The capacity of the single shard is 1MB per second of data input. The capacity of the data of your stream is a function of the wide variety of shards which you

specify for the stream. The entire capacity of the stream is the addition of the capacities of its shards. If your data charge increases, you could boom or lower the number of shards allocated to your stream.

In case, you need more capacity; in comparison with the single shard provided capacity. By using Kinesis Stream, you can create multiple shards in a stream. The stream with two shards can give you a total data write rate of 2 MB per second data input and you get a total data read rate of 4 MB per second data output. You get ten transactions per second for read and 2000 records per second for write. If you need to change that, you need to add more shards.

Kinesis Stream supports Resharding. With Resharding, you can dynamically add or remove shards as the data throughput changes. Resharding allows you to adjust the number of shards in your stream to adopt the changes in the rate of the data flow through the stream. Resharding is considered as an advanced operation. Resharding operations are of two types: shard split and shard merge. You divide a single shard into two shards in shard split. Also, you combine two shards into a single shard in shard merge.

Records

A Record is the unit of the data which is stored in the stream. A record consists of a partition key, a sequence number, and data blob. The Partition key allows to group the data by shard and also tells you which shards the data belongs to. The partition key is specified by the application putting the data into the stream.

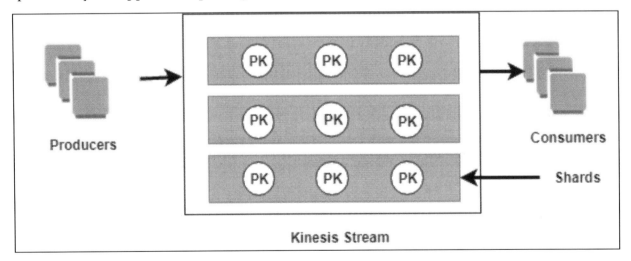

Figure 2-03: Partition Key

You can see the above diagram (Figure 2-03), we have our producers who write data to the Kinesis Stream. Within the stream, we have three shards containing different partition keys in each shard and they are organized by the shard they belong to. The

Sequence Number is the unique identifier for the record inserted into the shard. It is a unique key that identifies data blob. A sequence number is assigned when a producer calls Put Record operation to add the data to a stream. The sequence number is not used to logically separate the data in terms of the shard they have come from. You can only perform this using the partition key. Lastly, the data blob is the actual data that your data producer adds to the stream. The maximum size of the data blob is 1 MB.

Retention Period

The maximum duration after which the data added in the stream is expired. The default retention period is 24 hours by default, and it can be increased to seven days if required. The retention period can be changed through CLI.

Data Producer

Data Producer puts the data records to Kinesis Stream, and this could be something like the web server, a mobile client. There are three ways by which producers put the data record into the Kinesis stream. The first one is Amazon Kinesis Streams API, the second is by using the Amazon Kinesis Producer Library (KPL), and the third is by using the Amazon Kinesis Agent.

Amazon Kinesis Stream API

You can develop producers by using the AWS SDK for Java. Some operations can be used in the stream API. The two operations that add data to the stream are:

- PutRecord (Sends Single data record to the stream at a time.)
- PutRecords (Sends Multiple data records to the stream at a time.)

> **EXAM TIP:** You should use PutRecords for most of the applications because it will give you a higher throughput for your data producer.

Amazon Kinesis Producer Library

The KPL is the configurable library which is used to create producer applications that allow the developers to achieve high-write throughput to a Kinesis Stream. The KPL performs a few different tasks. It helps you to write to one or more Kinesis Streams with an auto-retry configurable mechanism. It also collects records to write multiple records to multiple shards per requests. It allows you to aggregate the user records to increase payload size. It also increases the Kinesis Client Library to de-aggregate the records.

You are not allowed to use KPL if your producer application cannot incur an additional processing delay. The Record Max Buffered Time parameter generates this additional delay in the library, and it sets the maximum amount of time a record spends being

buffered before it sends to Kinesis Stream. A larger value for this parameter results in better performance but can delay the records. Setting it too low can negatively impact the throughput.

The KPL supports two types of batching and batching helps you to use shard efficiently and also helps you with better throughputs. Performing a single action on multiple items refers to as Batching. This reduces the effort of repeatedly acting on each item.

The KPL supports two types of batching:

- Aggregation: Storing multiple records within a single Kinesis Data Streams record.
- Collection: Using the API operation PutRecords to send multiple Kinesis Data Streams records to one or more shards in your Kinesis data stream.

The difference between aggregation and collection is that collection is working with groups of stream records and batching them to reduce HTTP requests whereas aggregation allows you to combine multiple user records into a single stream record to efficiently use the shards.

The PutRecord operation sends multiple requests to your stream as per HTTP request for the applications that require higher throughput. However, with the PutRecord operation, note that a single record failure does not stop the processing of the subsequent records in the PutRecord call. Despite the failure of the single record, if other records in the PutRecord API is successful, HTTP code of status 200 is also returned. So, for partial PutRecord result method in the KPL can be used to detect individual record failures and retry the Put based on the HTTP status code.

Amazon Kinesis Agent

Amazon Kinesis Agent can be used as the data producer. It is a standalone java software application that offers an easier way to collect and send data into the stream. You can install the Kinesis Agent on web servers, log servers, and database servers. You can download and install the agents from GitHub on your EC2 instance. The Kinesis Agent can also monitor multiple directories for files and write to multiple streams. The agent will allow you to pre-process the data before it is sent to Kinesis Stream and this includes the conversion of multi-line records into a single line, convert from delimiter to JSON format and convert a record from a log format to a JSON format.

Data Consumers

Data Consumer gets a data record from shards in the Kinesis Stream and processes the data. These consumers are also known as the Kinesis Stream application. You can develop a consumer application for Kinesis Stream by using the Kinesis Client Library (KCL). The purpose of the KCL is to consume the data from Kinesis Stream and then process that

data. Then, it uses the Kinesis Connector Library to send the data to Redshift or S3 or DynamoDB. The KCL handles a lot of complex tasks for example load balancing across multiple instances responding to instance failures, checkpoints in processing records, and reacting on any Resharding, etc. You can develop a KCL consumer using Java, Node.js, .NET, Python and Ruby. The KCL handles checkpointing. It tracks the record that is already being processed in the shard and it does this by using DynamoDB. In case if a worker fails, KCL will restart the processing of the shard at last known processed record.

Similarly, you can also run your consumer application by running it on EC2 instance under an Auto-Scaling group to replace failed instances and handle additional loads. The KCL automatically load balances the record processing across many instances. It also supports the de-aggregation of records that were aggregated with the KPL.

For each Kinesis Stream application, the Kinesis Client uses a unique DynamoDB table for each application to track application state. Because the KCL utilizes the name of the streams application to create DynamoDB table, so use unique application names in KCL. Each row in the DynamoDB table represents a shard, and the hash key is the shard ID.

The DynamoDB table created by KCL has 10 RCU and 10 WCU. It is possible that this capacity is not enough and you may experience provisioned throughput exceptions. This can happen if an application does frequent checkpointing or your stream has too many shards. Add more provisioned throughput to the DynamoDB table to resolve this issue.

> **EXAM TIP:** Amazon Kinesis Stream is used for any scenario where you are streaming a large number of data that needs to be processed quickly, and you have a requirement to build a custom application to process and analyze streaming data.

Kinesis Stream Emitting Data to AWS Services

At the beginning of the chapter, we have already discussed the producer, Shards, retention period and consumers. In this topic, we will discuss how data is emitted to other AWS services. Consumers can emit data to S3, DynamoDB, Elasticsearch, Redshift, and EMR. To emit the data to other services the consumer needs Kinesis Client Library (KCL) as well as Kinesis Connector Library. You can create a Lambda function to automatically read batches and records of your Kinesis Stream and process them if the records detected in the stream. Those records then sent to S3, DynamoDB or RedShift. The good thing about using Lambda is that the stream can be called frequently to see if there are new records.

Since multiple applications can consume data from the stream, you might have a case where some other data may be sent to services like RedShift, but the rest of the data may be archiving in S3 and use object lifecycle process to archive into the glacier. Data in the stream could be sent to DynamoDB. This may be a use case where you have some gaming application or some application where you need dashboard and collect metrics in real time — if you need to make the data from the stream searchable, then send this data to Elasticsearch using the KCL. Another use case with Redshift. The data is being added to data warehouses.

Use Cases	
S3	Archiving Data
DynamoDB	Metrics
Elasticsearch	Search and Index
Redshift	Micro Batch Loading
EMR	Process and Analyse Data
Lambda	Automate Emitting Data

Table 2-01: Use Cases of AWS Data Processing Services

Kinesis Connector Library

Kinesis Connector Library is used to emit data to certain services. The Connector library is Java-based, and you would use it to develop your consumer application along with the Kinesis Client Library. The Connector library has connectors for DynamoDB, Redshift, S3, and Elasticsearch. The Kinesis Connector application is a pipeline for how records from Amazon Kinesis Stream will be handled. So, with the connector library pipeline records are retrieved from the stream then transformed according to a user-defined data model. Then buffered for batch processing and then emitted to the appropriate AWS service. We start with the Kinesis Stream.

Every Amazon Kinesis connector application is a pipeline that determines how records from an Amazon Kinesis Stream could be treated. Records are retrieved from the stream, converted consistently with a user-defined data model, buffered for batch processing, after which emitted to the right AWS service.

A connector pipeline makes use of the following interfaces:

- Kinesis Connector Pipeline: The implemented pipeline.

- ITransformer: Defines the transformation of information from the Amazon Kinesis Stream so one can match the consumer-defined information model. Consists of methods for custom serializer/deserializers.
- IFilter: IFilter defines a method for excluding the irrelevant records from the processing.
- IBuffer: IBuffer defines a machine for batching the records that are going to be processed. The application specifies three thresholds: number of records, overall bytes be counted, and time. When the thresholds are crossed, the buffer is flushed, and the information is emitted to the destination.
- IEmitter: Defines a technique that makes client calls to different AWS services and persists the information saved within the buffer. The records can also be forwarded to another Amazon Kinesis Stream.

S3- Emitter Class

S3-Emitter Class is the Connector Library tool which includes the implementation for using Amazon S3. This class is used to write down the buffer contents to a single document in Amazon S3. The report name is decided with the aid of the Amazon Kinesis sequence numbers of the primary and last document within the buffer.

Kinesis Firehose

Amazon Kinesis Firehose is a fully managed service used to collect and load streaming data in near real-time into S3, Redshift, and Elasticsearch. You can then use existing BI (business intelligence) tools, and dashboards that you already have set up with Redshift; so, get the data into Redshift and analyze the data using BI tools. Kinesis Firehose is highly available and durable. The data is replicated across AWS regions. Firehose is a fully managed service, and it can automatically scale to meet your throughput requirements and requires no administration. This service also handles sharding and Monitoring. Firehose can process the data by reducing the amount of storage in S3 if that is the destination of your data. This will help you in reducing the cost. With firehose, you can also encrypt the data before it is loaded. You can create a firehose delivery scheme in the Management Console or by using the API.

Key Concept

Consider an example of a web server which is collecting logs. In this case, we have some web servers (Producers), and these producers generate logs which send data to a Kinesis Firehose delivery stream in the form of Records. Each record can be as large as 1000KB. For each delivery stream, you will set a buffer size or buffer interval. Firehose buffer incoming streaming data to a certain size of a certain period before delivering it to S3 or

Elasticsearch. The buffer size can be selected from 1MB to 128MB or buffer interval of 60 to 900 seconds. The condition which is satisfied first, it triggers the data delivery to S3 or Elasticsearch. From the firehose delivery stream, the data is then put into S3 and then using the Copy Command; Redshift can pull the data from S3 for analysis. After the data has been pulled into Redshift, you can use the object lifecycle path to archive the data into Glacier.

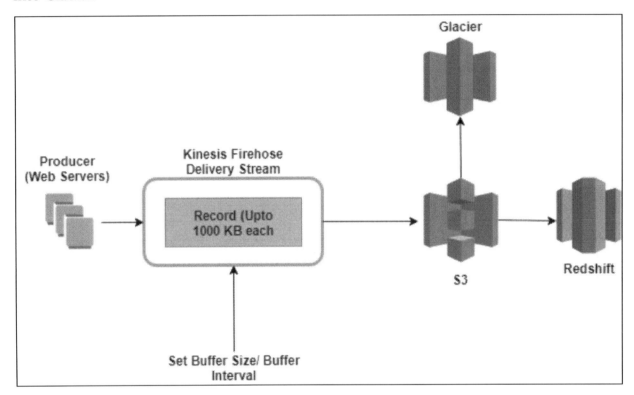

Figure 2-04: Loading data into Kinesis Stream

There are a couple of methods that are used for loading the data into the Kinesis Firehose delivery stream. Firstly, you can use the Kinesis Agent, or you can use the AWS SDK.

Amazon Kinesis Agent

The Kinesis Agent is the standalone Java software application that allows you to collect and send data to the Firehose. You can install it on Linux based web servers, log servers or database web servers. After downloading and installing the agent, you can configure it to monitor the files and send new data to your firehose delivery stream. The Agent is capable of handling file rotation; it will handle checkpointing and also retry a path failure. The Agent will also help in CloudWatch metrics. The Agent can pre-process the records from the monitored files before sending them to your delivery stream. This involves converting the multi-line record to a single line, converting from delimiter to JSON format and converting a record from a log format to JSON format.

AWS SDK

You can use the firehose API to send data to the firehose delivery stream using the AWS SDK. The Firehose API offers two operations for sending data to your firehose delivery stream.

- PutRecord
- PutRecordBatch

PutRecord sends one data record within one call, and PutRecordBatch can send multiple data records within one call.

Transferring Data Using Lambda

Firehose can invoke a Lambda function to transform incoming data and then deliver the transformed data to S3, RedShift or Elasticsearch. And you can enable the firehose data transformation when you create your delivery stream.

Introducing Firehose Data Transformations

With the Firehose data transformation function, you can now specify a Lambda function that can carry out variations immediately on the flow, when you create a delivery stream.

While you permit Firehose data transformation, Firehose buffers incoming data and invokes the specified Lambda characteristic with each buffered batch asynchronously. The transformed records are despatched from Lambda to Firehose for buffering and then delivered to the destination spot. You could additionally pick out to permit source report backup, which returned up all untransformed data on your S3 bucket concurrently at the same time as handing over transformed records to the destination spot.

To get you began, AWS provides the following Lambda blueprints which are available on their documentation, you could adapt to fit your wishes:

- Apache Log to JSON
- Apache Log to CSV
- Syslog to JSON
- Syslog to CSV
- General Firehose Processing

Data Transformation Flow

Firehose will buffer incoming data up to 3 MB or the buffering size specified in the delivery stream. Firehose will then invoke the specified Lambda function with each buffered batch asynchronously. The transformed data is then sent from Lambda to

firehose for buffering. The transformed data is then sent to the destination when the specified buffering size and the buffering interval is reached.

Parameters for Transformation

Some parameters are required for the transformation. So, Lambda must contain these parameters. Otherwise, firehose will reject them and treat that rejection as part of the data transformation failure.

- **Record ID**: Record ID is passed from the firehose to Lambda. The transformed record must have the same ID as the original record. Any mismatch between the ID of the original records and the ID of the transformed record is treated as the data transformation failure.
- **Result**: The status of the data transformation record and it contains the values that are "Ok," "Dropped," and "Processing Failed." "Ok" means the record is transformed successfully, "Dropped" means the record is dropped intentionally by processing logic that you have made, and "Processing Failed" means the record could not be transformed. If a record has s status of "Ok" and "Dropped," then firehose will consider it as successfully processed. Otherwise, firehose will consider it as unsuccessfully processed.
- **Data**: This is the transformed data payload after 64-bit encoding.

Failure Handling

If your Lambda function invocation is failed for some reasons, firehose retries the invocation for three times and then discard the batch of records if the retry is not succeeded. The retry delivery period is 24 hours. The escape records are treated as unsuccessfully processed records. Invocation errors and records that have the status of processing failed can be emitted to CloudWatch logs. If data transformation fails, the unsuccessfully processed records are sent to your S3 buckets in the processing failed folder.

Data Flow

For Amazon S3 destinations, streaming records are delivered on your S3 bucket. If data transformation is enabled, you could optionally back up supply data to any other Amazon S3 bucket.

For Amazon RedShift destinations, streaming records are brought in your S3 bucket first. To load data from your S3 bucket, the Kinesis Data Firehose issues an Amazon RedShift copy command in your Amazon RedShift cluster. If records transformation is enabled, you may optionally back up supply information to every other Amazon S3 bucket.

For Amazon ES destination, streaming statistics are delivered on your Amazon ES cluster, and it can optionally be backed up in your S3 bucket concurrently.

Data Delivery

Let's look at the frequency of Data Delivery. In S3, we had discussions on the buffer size (1MB to 128MB) and buffer interval (60-900 seconds). The frequency of data delivery is dependant upon the statistics. Firehose is capable of raising the buffer size dynamically to catch up on the issue where the data delivery to a specific application is falling behind. The frequency will depend on how fast the RedShift cluster finishes the COPY command. Firehose will issue a new COPY command automatically when the previous COPY command has completed running.

The frequency of data being sent to Elasticsearch from Firehose also depends on the buffer size (1MB to 100MB) and buffer interval (60-900 seconds). Similar to S3, firehose can raise the size of buffer dynamically, if the data delivery to Elasticsearch is falling behind.

In case, if you face any problem in the delivery of data to S3, firehose will retry delivery to your destination for up to 24 hours. The data is lost if delivery fails beyond this period. In RedShift, you can specify the retry duration from 0 (Zero) to 7200 seconds for the data that is being loaded from S3, and you can do this when you are creating a delivery stream.

With Elasticsearch, you can also specify the retry duration from zero to 7200 seconds, and if you have any issue with your Elasticsearch cluster, the firehose retries under specified conditions. It then skips the particular index request and skips the documents delivered to S3 bucket. You can then use the documents by using manual backfill, and the documents are in JSON format.

Amazon SQS

Amazon SQS is Simple Queue Service. It is reliable, scalable, hosted queues service for sending, storing and retrieving messages between servers. The SQS allows you to move data between distributed components of your application without losing messages or requiring each application component to be available all the time. Amazon simple queue service make it simple and profitable to decouple the items of a cloud application. You can use Amazon simple queue service to transfer any volume of data, at any level of throughput, without unsuccessful messages or requiring other services to be continuously available. SQS uses the buffer for storing and producing data. The SQS contains about 256 KB of messages in any format. The components of applications are stored in the queue and retrieved from the queue. Similarly, the message greater than 256 KB is managed

using the SQS extended library which uses S3. Any application can be stored or retrieved from the queue.

SQS ensures the delivery of messages at least once, and it supports multiple readers and writers which means many components can share a single queue. AWS supports FIFO (first in first out) queues, and with FIFO queues, the order in which messages are sent and received is preserved. The message delivered once, and it remains available until a consumer process deletes that message. Duplicates are not introduced into the queue.

A queue can be generated in any region and messages can be retained in the queue for up to 14 days. These messages can be sent and read simultaneously. SQS also provides an option called Long Polling which reduces frequent polling to help you in minimizing the cost while receiving new messages as quickly as possible. So, when the queue is empty, long poll request wait for up to 20 seconds for the next message to arrive.

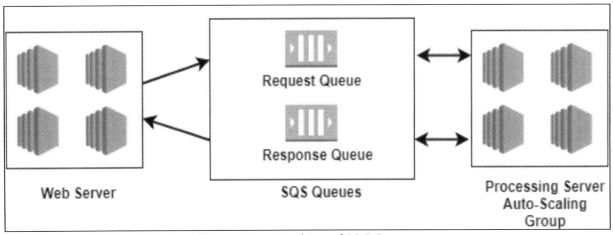

Figure 2-05: Working of SQS Queue

Let us say we have a web server auto-scaling group and it is a fleet of web servers taking orders to purchase the product. The web application places the order into an SQS request queue. These orders sit in the queue until they are picked up by one of the free processing servers. The server processes the order and sends the process order back to the response queue which is then sent to the customer. The advantage of using the SQS Queue is that the processing server auto-scaling group can be scaled back based on the items in the SQS queue. The working of SQS queue can be summarised as:

- The web server of the auto-scaling group requests an application through the SQS queue.
- The requests queue is forwarded to the processing group.
- The processing group reply back to the requests queue.

Queues can provide a convenient mechanism to determine the load on an application. You can use the length of the queue to determine the load, and CloudWatch integrates with SQS to collect, view, and analyze metrics, and you can make several different decisions based on the data.

Message Lifecycle

The diagram and process shown in the figure shows the life cycle of an Amazon simple queue service message, called Message A, from creation to cancelation. Assume that a queue already exists.

- Component one sends Message A to a queue, and the message is distributed redundantly across the Amazon SQS servers.
- When Component two is ready to develop a message, it recovers messages from the chain, and Message A is returned. While Message A is handled, it remains in the chain.
- Component two deletes Message A from the queue to prevent the message from being received and processed again after the visibility timeout expires.

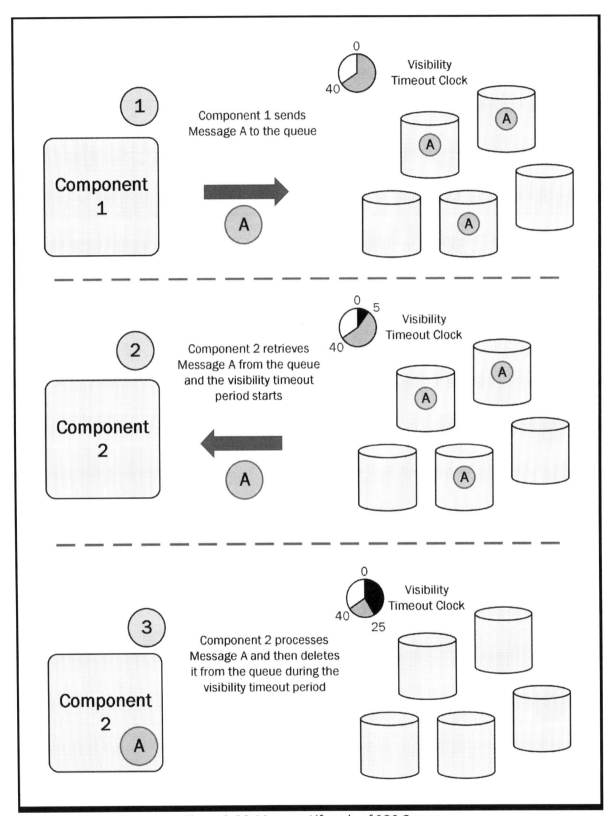

Figure 2-06: Message Lifecycle of SQS Queue

Amazon SQS Architecture

Priority Queue

Priority Queue follows a data structure that is designed to deliver messages at a different time. In this case, the messages delivered according to the priority assigned to them. Each message is assigned with a priority and messages are sent to their destination according to the priority assigned to them. For example, web server requests for an application which is assigned with a high priority and a low priority. The message with the high priority is processed first then the message with the low priority.

Fan Out Queue

The fan-out scenario involves SNS to send multiple topics using the SQS queue at the same time to decouple the processing further. It includes SNS messages which are sent to multiple topics, are replicated and pushed back in SQS queue to allow parallel processing. For example, you upload a picture on the web server which sends the message to SNS topic, the message is forwarded to multiple SQS queues subscribed to SNS topic. Fan-out Queue allows multiple parallel processing of data.

AWS IOT

Introduction

AWS IoT offers at ease, bi-directional communication among net-linked devices which include sensors, actuators, embedded micro-controllers, or smart home equipment and the AWS Cloud. This enables you to gather telemetry data from more than one device, and store and analyze the data. You could also create applications that permit your customers to govern these devices from their phones or tablets. The AWS IoT service is a managed cloud platform that connects devices easily and securely to interact with cloud applications and other devices. This service can support billions of devices and trillions of messages and process messages to other AWS services and other devices. IoT in general, and big data go together.

IoT and Big Data

IoT devices produce data, and in many cases, millions of devices produce a significantly large amount of data. Once you start collecting the data, you have to analyze the streaming data in real time. You then also need the services to process and store the large piles of data. You also do not need to worry about the capacity, scaling and administrative overhead for managing the infrastructure. This is where AWS IoT service comes to an end.

It is important to know to which service AWS IoT integrates with. Once a device or a client sends a message to the IoT service. The IoT service triggers the rule action to write data to Elasticsearch service domain, write data to Kinesis Firehose stream or a Kinesis stream, write data to a DynamoDB table or even send data to Amazon Machine Learning service to make the production based on machine learning model. So, that is the integration with big data services. The IoT service will action and allows you to change the CloudWatch alarm or capture CloudWatch metrics, write data to S3 bucket, write data to SQS queue, write data to SNS as PUSH notification and finally invoke a Lambda function.

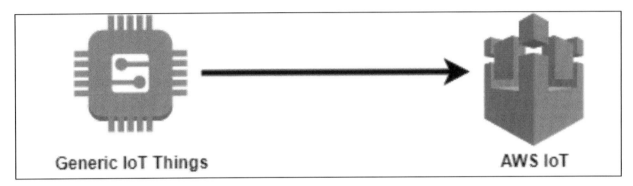

Figure 2-07: AWS IoT and Big Data

IoT Frame Work

AWS provides you with the SDK to help you in connecting your device or mobile application to connect, authenticate and exchange messages with the AWS IoT service using MATT, HTTP, or web sockets protocols. With AWS IoT, you can have mutual authentication and encryption at all point of the connection. The next component in AWS IoT is Device Gateway. The device gateway enables the device to securely and efficiently communicate with the AWS IoT services. Next, we have the Registry, and it establishes the identity for devices and tracks the metadata.

Device Shadow allows you to create a persistent shadow or virtual version of the state of the device. Then you have the Rules Engine which enables us to takes the messages, transform them based on specific rules and route the messages to AWS services.

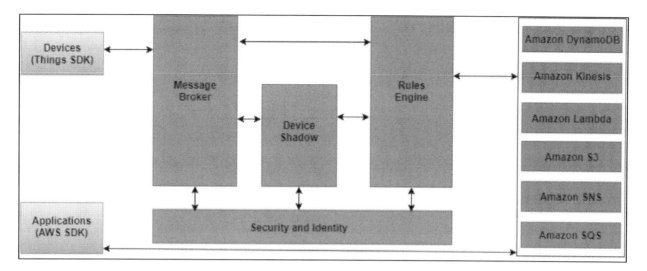

Figure 2-08: AWS IoT Framework

Let's get to know the details of the framework components:

Authentication

Communication exchange between a tool and AWS IoT is included via the use of X.509 certificates. AWS IoT is capable of generating a certificate for you, or you can use your very own. In both cases, the certificate should be registered and activated with AWS IoT, and then copied onto your device. When your device communicates with AWS IoT, it presents the certificate to AWS IoT as a credential. AWS IoT uses IAM policies for users, groups, and roles. For mobile application, you can use Amazon Cognito Identities to authenticate against AWS IoT. Cognito Identity can permit an individual mobile application user of your IoT application.

An Amazon Cognito Identity allows you to use your identity provider, or other popular identity providers such as login with Amazon, Facebook, Google, or Twitter. You can also use Open ID provider and SAML identity provider. You can also use Cognito identity User Pools that scale the users and allows you to create your directory.

When you log in to your identity provider, you receive access token back from the identity provider. The access token exchange with Cognito to get temporary credentials in return. The temporary credentials then grant access to AWS IoT.

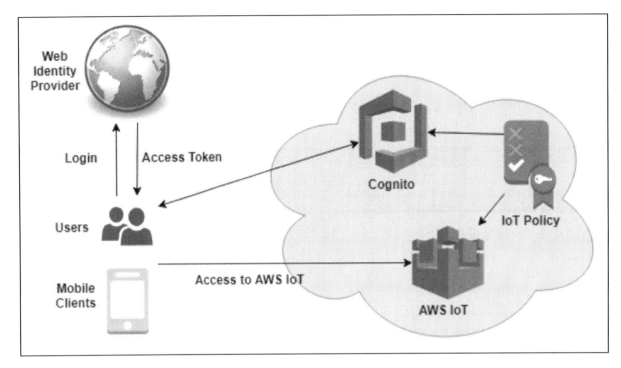

Figure 2-09: AWS IoT working with Cognito

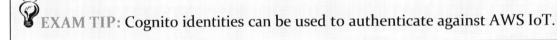

💡 **EXAM TIP:** Cognito identities can be used to authenticate against AWS IoT.

Authorization

With AWS IoT, two types of policies are attached to control the operations that an identity can perform, and these are AWS IoT policies and IAM policies. AWS IoT operations are split into two parts:

- The Control Plane API is used for an administrative task like creating certificates and creating rules.
- The Data Plane API is used for sending and receiving data from the AWS IoT service.

The policy that you will use will depend on the operation that you intend to perform.

Device Gateway (Message Broker)

It works to maintain the session and subscription for all the connected devices in an IOT service. It also allows one-to-one and one-to-many communication securely, that is why it is possible for a connected device to broadcast the data to multiple subscribers for a given topic. A topic is something which a device gateway uses to route messages from publishing clients to subscribing clients. The supported protocols are MQTT (Message Queue Telemetry Transport), Web sockets and HTTP. The Message broker implements

the MQTT protocol. The Message broker can scale to incorporate billions of responsive long-lived connections between things and your cloud packages. They could publish their state and may enroll in incoming messages. The post/subscribe model permits a single device to share its reputation correctly with any variety of different gadgets.

Device Registry

To start using AWS IoT services, let's first discuss Thing. A Thing represents a physical device or a logical entity which could be an application. The device registry is a central location used for storing attributes related to each thing. The device Registry does the task assigning and allocates a unique identity for every factor. It also helps within the monitoring of descriptive metadata like attributes and abilities for each issue.

The AWS IoT service also features the Device Shadow (Thing Shadow). The device shadow is the JSON document that is used to store and retrieve the current state for a thing. A device shadow is maintained for each thing connected to the AWS IoT service. It acts as a message channel to send commands reliably to a thing and stores the last known state in the AWS service.

Rules Engine

The Rule Engine collects the statistics dispatched to the IoT cloud and performs actions based totally on factors which might be a gathered data and routes them to AWS endpoints like Amazon DynamoDB, AWS Lambda, Amazon Simple Storage Service (S3), Amazon Simple Notification Service (SNS), and Amazon Kinesis. It offers message processing and integration with different AWS services. The movements have expressed the usage of an SQL-like syntax. You can use an SQL-based language to pick out data from message payloads, after which process and send the facts to other services, inclusive of Amazon S3, Amazon DynamoDB, and AWS Lambda. You can also use the message dealer to republish messages to other subscribers.

Context and contents of individual messages drive routing. For example, regular readings from a temperature sensor could be tracked in a DynamoDB table whereas a specific reading that exceeds a value stored in the thing shadow can trigger a Lambda function.

AWS Data Pipeline

Data Pipeline is a web provider that helps you in reliably processing and moving records between exceptional AWS compute and storage services as well as on-premises information sources at distinctive periods. With AWS Data Pipeline, you can regularly get access to your data wherein it is saved, remodel and process it at scale, and successfully switch the results to AWS services consisting of Amazon Simple Storage Service (S3),

Amazon RDS, Amazon DynamoDB, and Amazon EMR. Data Pipeline allows you to create an ETL workflow to automate the processing and movement of data at a scheduled interval, then terminate the resources after the ETL workflow has completed. AWS Data Pipeline enables you to create complex data processing workloads which are fault tolerant, repeatable, and relatively highly-available. You do not have to fear about resources availability, coping with inter-task dependencies, retrying temporary failures or timeouts in individual responsibilities, or developing a failure notification system. AWS data Pipeline also permits you to move and process data that changed into previously locked up in on-premises data silos. One of the features of the data pipeline is the ability to move data across the regions. You can copy an entire DynamoDB table to another region or an incremental copy of the table to another region. You can schedule the time and frequency of the copy table.

EXAM TIP: Data Pipeline is a web service that helps you reliably process and move data between different AWS compute and storage service.

Consider an example, in which you have a DynamoDB table in us-east-1 and a data pipeline is used to export the data out of the table into an S3 bucket which resides in us-west-2 region. We have another data pipeline in us-west-2 which imports that data into DynamoDB table from S3 bucket within the region. Behind the scene, the data pipeline is launching an EMR cluster to extract the data out of DynamoDB from us-east-1 and transfer it to S3 bucket in us-west-2. The data pipeline launches another EMR cluster to import the data into DynamoDB in the us-west-2 region.

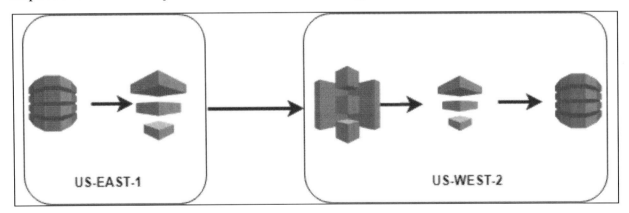

Figure 2-10: Example of a Data Pipeline

Key Concept

The pipeline is the name of the container that contains things like data nodes, activities, pre-conditions, etc. One of the most significant benefits of the pipeline is that they can be scheduled. All of the components work together to help you to move your data from one

location to another. Data Pipeline runs on an EC2 instance or an EMR cluster which are provisioned and terminated automatically.

The best feature of data pipeline is that it can run on-premises. It is feasible if you are running data pipelines on premise and you want to copy data to AWS on a scheduled basis. AWS provides you with a task runner package that can be installed on your on premise host. As soon as it is installed; the package polls the pipeline for work to carry out. While it is time to run a selected activity for your on premise resources, as an example, executing a DB stored process or a database dump, AWS Data Pipeline will issue an appropriate command to the task runner.

 EXAM TIP: Data Pipeline can be integrated with on-premises environments.

AWS Data Pipeline Components

Data Nodes

Data Node is the end destination for your data. In AWS Data Pipeline, a data node defines the location and type of data that a pipeline activity uses as input or output. Following data node types are supported by AWS Data Pipeline:

- DynamoDB Data Node: A DynamoDB table that contains data for Hive Activity or EMR Activity to use.
- SQL Data Node: An SQL table and database query that represent data for a pipeline activity to use.
- Redshift Data Node: An Amazon RedShift table that contains data for RedShift Copy Activity to use.
- S3DataNode: An Amazon S3 location that contains one or more files for a pipeline activity to use.

Activity

Activity is an action that the data pipeline initiates on your behalf as part of the data pipeline. In the AWS Data Pipeline, an activity is a pipeline factor that defines the work to perform. AWS Data Pipeline affords several pre-packaged activities that accommodate commonplace eventualities, together with moving statistics from one area to any other, running hive queries, and many more. Activities are extensible, so you can run your very own custom scripts to assist endless combinations.

AWS Data Pipeline supports the subsequent varieties of activities:

- Copy Activity: Copies the data from one location to another.

- EMR Activity: Runs an Amazon EMR Cluster.
- Hive Activity: Runs a hive query on the Amazon EMR cluster.
- Hive Copy Activity: Runs a Hive query on an Amazon EMR cluster with support for advanced data filtering and support for S3DataNode and DynamoDB Data Node.
- Pig Activity: Runs a pig script on the Amazon EMR cluster.
- Redshift Copy Activity: Copy data to and from the Amazon RedShift tables.
- Shell Command Activity: Run a custom Linux/ Unix command as an activity.
- SQL Activity: Run SQL query on database.

Pre-Condition

Pre-Condition is a readiness check that can be optionally associated with a data source or activity. If a data source has a pre-condition check, then that check must be completed successfully before any activities consuming the data sources are launched. This can be useful when you are running an activity which has expensive computation and should not be done until specific criteria are matched. If an activity has a pre-condition, then the pre-condition check must complete successfully before the activity runs. You can also specify custom pre-conditions. So, you can set the following pre-conditions:

- Does the data exist in the DynamoDB table?
- Does the DynamoDB table exist?
- Does the S3 path exist?
- Does the file exist within the S3 path?
- And you can set custom pre-conditions.

Schedule

The schedule defines when your pipeline activities run and the frequency at which the service expects your data to be available. It defines the timings of the scheduled events, such as when an activity runs.

 EXAM TIP: The Lambda function has removed a lot of Data Pipeline functionality.

Mind Map

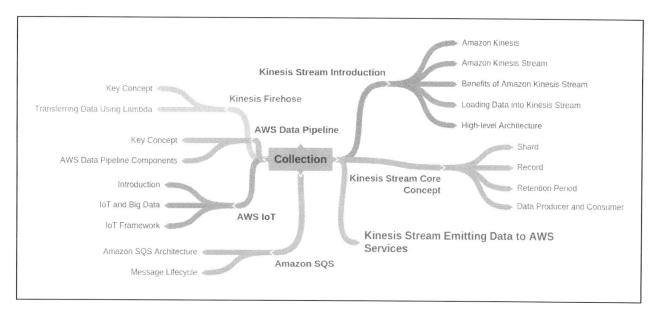

Figure 2-11: Chapter's Mind Map

Practice Questions

1. Which of the following enlisted below are classified as the uses of Kinesis Data Stream? (Choose 2)
   A. They can carry out real-time reporting and analysis of streamed data.
   B. They can provide long term storage of data.
   C. They can undertake the loading of streamed data directly into data stores.
   D. They can accept data as soon as it has been produced, without the need for batching.

2. In case of data delivery issue in Kinesis Firehose, what is the duration of retry delivery?
   A. 7 hours.
   B. 14 hours.
   C. 24 hours.
   D. 48 hours.

3. In which of the following services of AWS IoT, you cannot create the rule action? (Choose 2)
   A. Kinesis Firehose.
   B. Aurora.
   C. Redshift.
   D. DynamoDB.
   E. Cloud Watch.

4. _____ are uniquely identified group of data streams.
   A. Shard.
   B. Record.
   C. Retention Period.
   D. None of the Above.

5. _____ puts the data record to Kinesis Stream.
   A. Data Consumer.
   B. Data Producer.

C. Both of the Above.

D. None of the Above.

6. _____ gets data record from shards in the Kinesis Stream and processes the data.
A. Data Consumer.
B. Data Producer.
C. Both of the Above.
D. None of the Above.

7. Which library is used to emit data to certain services?
A. Kinesis Producer Library.
B. Kinesis Client Library.
C. Kinesis Connector Library.
D. None of the Above.

8. _____ is the standalone Java software application that allows you to collect and send data to firehose.
A. AWS SDK.
B. AWS IoT.
C. AWS Data Pipeline.
D. AWS Kinesis Agent.

9. Which one of the following features can specify a Lambda function that can perform transformation directly on the stream?
A. Firehose Data Transformation.
B. Transferring Data using Lambda.
C. Data Transformation Flow.
D. The parameter for Transformation.

10. Which parameters are used for transformation?
A. Record ID.
B. Result.
C. Data.
D. All of the Above.

11. Kinesis Stream is used for:
    A. To process and analyze a large stream of a data record in real time.
    B. To connect EC2 instances to cloud watch.
    C. To run standard SQL queries.
    D. To load streaming data from hundreds and thousands of sources into Amazon S3 and Amazon Redshift.

12. Three Amazon Kinesis services are:
    A. Kinesis Waterfall, Kinesis logs and Kinesis Fireman.
    B. Kinesis Waterfall, Kinesis Logs and Kinesis Firehose.
    C. Kinesis Streams, Kinesis Analytics and Kinesis Firehose.
    D. Kinesis Streams, Kinesis Analytics and Kinesis Fireman.

13. _____ provides secure, bi-directional communication between Internet-connected devices.
    A. AWS IoT.
    B. AWS SQS.
    C. AWS Data Pipeline.
    D. AWS Kinesis.

14. Which web service helps you to reliably process and move data between different AWS compute and store services as well as on-premise data sources at specified intervals?
    A. AWS IoT.
    B. AWS SQS.
    C. AWS Data Pipeline.
    D. AWS Kinesis.

15. Which of the following is AWS Data Pipeline Components?
    A. Data Node.
    B. Activity.
    C. Pre-Condition.
    D. All of the Above.

16. Which library allows and simplifies the creation of producer application?
    A. Kinesis Producer Library.
    B. Kinesis Client Library.
    C. Kinesis Connector Library.
    D. All of the Above.

17. The application that gets data from Kinesis Stream is called consumer application, and these consumer applications can be developed by using the library named as?
    A. Kinesis Producer Library.
    B. Kinesis Client Library.
    C. Kinesis Connector Library.
    D. All of the Above.

18. How can you create multiple shards in a stream?
    A. By using the Amazon Kinesis Stream.
    B. By using Amazon Kinesis Firehose.
    C. By using AWS Lambda.
    D. By using the AWS Data Pipeline.

19. A record consists of:
    A. Partition Key.
    B. Sequence Number.
    C. Data Blob.
    D. All of the Above.

20. Maximum duration after which the data added to the stream is expired is known as?
    A. Shard.
    B. Record.
    C. Retention Period.
    D. Data Producer and Consumer.

21. Which methods are used for loading the data into Kinesis Firehose Delivery Stream?
    A. AWS SDK.

B. Amazon Kinesis Agent.
C. Both A & B.
D. None of the Above.

22. How many operations are offered by firehose API for sending data to firehose delivery stream using AWS SDK?
A. One.
B. Two.
C. Three.
D. Four.

23. SQS contains _____ KB of messages in any format.
A. 100
B. 256
C. 1000
D. 64

24. In SQS, the long poll request has to wait for _____ seconds until the next message arrives.
A. 20
B. 30
C. 90
D. 50

25. The _____ gathers the data sent to the IoT cloud and performs activities based on factors that are present in the gathered data and routes them to AWS endpoints.
A. Device Gateway.
B. Device Registry
C. Rule Engine.
D. Message Broker

Chapter 03: Storage

Introduction

This chapter includes detailed information about Amazon Glacier, which is used for archival of data and DynamoDB, which is used for storage purpose. In DynamoDB, we will thoroughly discuss its Architecture, Partitions, Data Distribution, Streams, Replications, and Indexes.

Amazon Glacier

Amazon Glacieris an exceptionally low-cost service of AWS, which offers secure and substantial storage for data archiving and backup. To hold expenses low, Amazon Glacieris optimized for the data which is accessed infrequently, and for which retrieval time of numerous hours is appropriate. With Amazon Glacier, clients can reliably store huge or small amounts of data.

Companies generally over-pay for archival of data. They have to pay high price to achieve the facility for archiving of data. First, they are pressured to pay a high price for their archiving solutions (which, now does not include the ongoing value for operational costs which include power, facilities, staffing, and renovation). Secondly, the group should also know about the requirements and capabilities that are needed for data archival. They have to make sure that they get the sufficient ability for data redundancy and provision for an unexpected increase in rates — this set of circumstances effect in below-utilized ability and wasted cash. With Amazon Glacier, you only pay for the storage that you consume. Amazon Glacierchanges the game for archiving and backup of data as you do not pay anything upfront, pay a very low fee for storage and may scale your utilization up or down as needed, while AWS handles all the heavy operational lifting required to do records retention. It takes some clicks inside the AWS Management Console for configuration of Amazon Glacier, and then you can upload any amount of data.

Glacierand Big Data

Keep all your data that is needed to be archived at a lower cost, and if you have a significant amount of data operating at petabyte scale, then Glacierwill provide you a greater benefit in terms of objects and using object life cycle policy in S3 to automatically move data from S3 to Glacier. The nature of your business for compliance in regular reasons may require that you keep your data for a specific amount of time and during this time, the data could be read but not changed. This feature helps companies in the

financial service industries. And these companies are required by regulators to keep data for a specific period, but the data cannot be changed or deleted at any time.

The Vault Lock feature in Glacier helps in meeting the compliance requirements. It is used to deploy and enforce control for a vault with the Vault Lock policy. The policies can be locked from editing, and once the policy is locked, it cannot be changed. The policies are created by using IAM. The idea behind the Vault Lock feature is to enforce compliance control.

To lock a vault, you can use Console, API, and CLI. The first step in locking a vault is to initiate and execute the Vault Lock operation. This action attaches a Vault Lock policy to your vault. The lock is then sent to an InProgress state, and a lock ID is returned. You then have 24 hours to validate the lock. The lock expires after 24 hours if you do not validate it. To lock the vault, you initiate the complete Vault Lock operation. Once you initiate the request, the Vault Lock goes from the InProgress state to the Lock state. Once it is locked, it cannot be changed.

Vault Lock control includes the time-based retention control and the undelete-able control or sometimes both in the same policy.

 EXAM TIP: The Vault Policies are implemented by using IAM.

DynamoDB Introduction

DynamoDB is fast, flexible, and fully managed NoSQL database service for the applications that need consistent and scalable latency. DynamoDB supports both documents and key value data model. It is a flexible data model, which is reliable, and can be used in the number of cases. These use cases include mobile and web application, gaming, IoT, live online voting, session management, and storing S3 object metadata in the DynamoDB table.

As mentioned earlier, DynamoDB is fully managed, which means you do not have to manage any servers, you do not have to do patching, and you do not have to worry about any failure. DynamoDB provides predictable performance for seamless scalability. There are no servers to manage; the concept of underlying storage and compute engine is abstracted from the user. DynamoDB automatically allocates more storage as required. There is no practical limit on the storage size and no constraint on the number of items, or the number of bytes in the table.

DynamoDB runs on SSD, which helps in achieving single digit latency and scale them. DynamoDB is fully resilient, highly available, and fault tolerant. This is because the data

is being replicated across three geographically distinct data centers. The HTTPS endpoint accesses the data. That is why the hardware and data centers are transparent to your application and the performance scales in a linear way. DynamoDB is fully integrated with IAM, so it allows controlled granular access included with federated and web identity.

DynamoDB is the collection of tables in each region. As a resilient region service, the service namespace is at the regional level. Availability zones hold less importance in DynamoDB architecture. The tables are the highest-level structure in DynamoDB and performance is controlled and managed at table levels. Within DynamoDB, there is the concept of storage unit, and you specify the numbers of reads and writes per second to a database table.

- Write Capacity Units (WCU) is the number of writes of 1KB blocks per second to the table.
- Read Capacity Unit (RCU) is the number of read of 4KB blocks per second to the table.

DynamoDB supports eventually consistent reads. DynamoDB is the distributed system, when you write the data it means you are writing on multiple locations at a time. In DynamoDB, the data is replicated across three geographically distinct regions, so when you write data in DynamoDB, it is replicated to multiple locations at a time, but it is only acknowledged when at least two writes are confirmed. When performing a read operation, you can instruct the platform to perform eventually consistent and strongly consistent read. Strongly Consistent Reads use one read unit per 4KB block and eventually consistent read use half unit per 4 KB block. Billing in DynamoDB is done based on the number of write capacity unit and read capacity unit and the amount of data stored.

DynamoDB uses WCU and RCU values, and the amount of data stored in each table to manage the underlying performance. There is also a concept in DynamoDB called Partition (will be discussed in the next heading).

The Architecture of the DynamoDB Table

The table in the database is divided into rows. In DynamoDB terminology, each row is referred to as an Item. Each item contains some elements and each row can have a different number of elements or may be different elements. The individual elements are referred to as Attributes. Firstly, there are the tables Partitions Key, which is also referred to as a Hash Key. This attribute has to be specific in the region; it is used to uniquely identify an item and used when you want to retrieve data using the query operation. The Query operation is supplied with the Partition Key value and retrieves the item. The

second attribute is called the Sort Key also referred to as Range Key; it allows one-to-many relationships, and it can provide sorted items, for example, time and date. Query Operation can pull a range of values back by using the sort key. An item can have some different attributes or a different set of attributes.

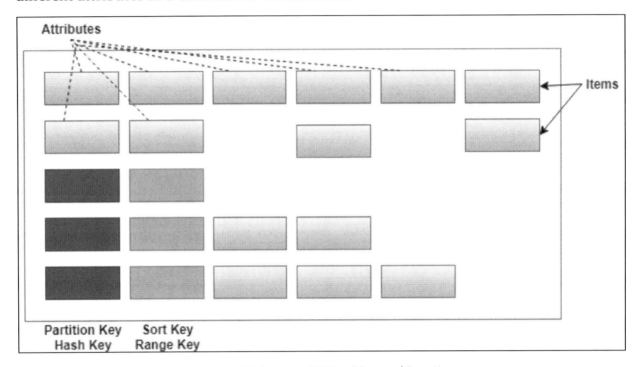

Figure 3-01: DynamoDB Partition and Sort Key

Attribute Types

At high- level, data is available in two groups:

- Scalar Data Types.
- DynamoDB Data Types.

DynamoDB holds the item such as strings, numbers (positive or negative integer), binary with base 64 encoding, Boolean values (true/ false), null, documents consist of lists and array maps, and allowing it to store complex JSON documents and set, which is an array data type allowing simple list storage.

DynamoDB in AWS Eco-System

Using the COPY Command in RedShift, you can copy data directly from DynamoDB to RedShift.

On EMR, DynamoDB is integrated with Apache Hive. Apache Hive is the data warehouse application built on top of Hadoop. By using Hive on EMR, you can read and write data in DynamoDB table. It allows you to query live DynamoDB data using a SQL type language.

You can copy data from DynamoDB table to a bucket in S3 and vice versa. You can export DynamoDB data to S3, and you can import data from S3 into DynamoDB, this is done using a data pipeline. When you want to export data from DynamoDB, Data Pipeline launches an EMR cluster. EMR reads from the DynamoDB table and writes it to your S3 bucket. If you want to import data from S3 into DynamoDB, again Data Pipeline launches an EMR cluster to read from your S3 bucket and write to the DynamoDB table.

You can copy data from DynamoDB table into Hadoop Distributed File System (HDFS) and vice versa. Using EC2 instances and DynamoDB API you can create an application, which writes and reads data from DynamoDB. DynamoDB is also integrated with Lambda so that you can create triggers that automatically respond in DynamoDB streams. With triggers, you can build an application that reacts to data modification in DynamoDB tables. Using the Kinesis Client Library (KCL) and the Kinesis Connector Library consumer applications can consume data from Kinesis Streams and emit that data to DynamoDB. It is a high-level look at how DynamoDB interacts with other AWS services in the AWS Eco System.

DynamoDB Partitions

Partitions are the underlying storage and processing nodes of DynamoDB. When you create a table with the default settings, DynamoDB allocates your table to one underlying node. By default, until things change all storage and any computation like insert, delete, and that one partition handles update operation. The key element of DynamoDB is that you do not need to control the number of partitions directly, but they can be influenced. A Partition can store 10GB of data maximum, and it can handle 3000 RCU and 1000 WCU. There is a direct relationship between the amount of data stored in the table, the performance requirement and the number of partitions allocated. You need to design applications and tables so that the read and write activity spreads evenly across all the items in your table and avoid I/O hotspot or hotkeys that can degrade the performance.

When you go beyond 10GB or 3000RCU or 1000WCU, an extra partition is added, and the data is spread between the partitions for your table.

Data Distribution

When multiple Partitions exist, the partition for a particular item is selected based on the Partition Key for each unique value. The item is assigned to a particular partition. Let's have an example of a table called test. It stores information related to student test results for a particular test. Each test has a unique ID. If the test is repeated, each test gets a new ID, and you store the result for each of those tests. Initially, one partition may be enough because there are few tests and students or the performance requirement is low.

However, if the application that uses the table is needed to display the national result for every school, millions of tests, millions of students, then you will either have the 10GB limit of data or hit the performance limit. This is where partitions start being used to improve performance. For our test example, the system allocates each test ID or rather the Hash of the value to a particular partition.

A Partition may host multiple partition values. Within each Partition Key, there may be many students taking the test; in this case, a student ID is the ID of sort key value. It will allow many items per Partition Key. By this, we can store the one to many test student relationships and also allow the sorting of test results by student ID or the selection of test result through a group of students.

By adding partitions and moving data between them, you can scale almost infinitely, based on size and performance requirement of your data but there are some limitations. DynamoDB manages the number of partitions, and partitions will grow automatically to accommodate performance and capacity requirement. While this is true for increases, there is no automatic decrease in partition during capacity and performance reduction. The allocated WCU and RCU is split between partition means if you allocated 30,000RCU to your table, DynamoDB would create ten partitions, each having 3000RCU. This exposes some key performance and capacity characteristics of DynamoDB. One partition can hold many Partition Keys, but the Partition Key can only be held to one partition. Which means that each single Partition Key value is limited to 10GB of data because each Partition Key is limited to one partition, which provides 3000RCU and 1000WCU. Be careful while increasing the WCU and RCU values as an additional partition is created but in case of decrement of WCU and RCU, the additional partition is not removed.

Key Concepts

If the table contains a composite primary key (partition and sort key), DynamoDB calculates the hash value of the Partition Key within the identical manner as defined in data distribution, but it contains all of the items with the same Partition Key value physically near collectively, ordered with the aid of sort key value.

To write down an item to the table, DynamoDB calculates the hash value of the Partition Key to determine which partition should include the item. In that partition, there might be several items with the equal Partition Key value, so DynamoDB stores the item with many of the others through the identical Partition Key, in ascending order via sort key.

To examine an item from the table, you need to specify its Partition Key and sort key value. DynamoDB calculates the hash value from Partition Key, yielding the partition in which the object may be observed.

You could study more than one items from the table in a single operation (query), supplied that the item you need has the identical Partition Key value. DynamoDB returns all the items with that Partition Key value. Optionally, you may observe a condition on the sort key so that it returns handiest items within a sure variety of values.

There are a few key concepts which you need to remember:

- Having an awareness of the underlying partition concept is critical.
- Be aware of the elements which influence the needs and number of partitions.
- Additional partition is added when capacity is increased to 10GB.
- The partitions can be increased but cannot be decreased.
- Performance reservation applied at the table level is equally split between the partitions.
- True performance is based on performance allocated, key structure and time and key distributions of reads and writes.

DynamoDB GSI/ LSI

DynamoDB offers two main data retrieval operations, Scan and Query. The scan is a very inefficient operation because scans go through the table, returning all the attributes for all items in the given table or index. The query can be used to select a single item by specifying one Partition Key value or a partition and sort key value if the table uses partition and sort keys. Additionally, by using a single Partition Key and a range of sort value multiple items can be returned in a very data efficient way. Without indexes, the query operation is limited in what can be retrieved. In indexes, your query has to base on single Partition Key value or a partition and sort combination. Indexes allow secondary representation of the data using alternative sort key attribute or even alternative partition and sort key attributes. Indexes come in two forms, Global Secondary, and Local Secondary Indexes.

Local Secondary Index (LSI)

Let's assume you have a table which is recording the weather data for a fleet of weather stations. In this data model, the Partition Key is the weather station ID, and the sort key is the date, time value of the specific incoming measurement. One attribute is tracking any movement or intrusion event which can impact the accuracy of the readings. The other attribute represents a single value temperature or rainfall. With such a model for a table, it is easy to call data for a particular weather station and easy to poll specific time and date ranges. It is inefficient to get access to data when the movement or intrusion value is true. The only way is to either scan the entire table and pull all values into

replication then compare it with the values of the intrusion table. The scan is an inefficient model and to avoid this inefficiency you can create a Local Secondary Index.

Creating a Local Secondary Index

The LSI can only be created at the time of table creation. Creating a Local Secondary Index allows us to maintain a secondary data set showing the Partition Key which is the weather station ID and also uses an alternative sort key. In this case true or false is based on intrusion.

Local Secondary Index by default contains the Partition Key, the original sort key, and the new sort key. Any other attributes can be added as the projected value. Therefore, projected values are a non-key attribute that are stored in the table if additional lookups are required. As per our example, this might be the actual reading from the weather station, which is neither a Partition Key nor a sort key. The information written to an LSI is copied asynchronously from the main table. Keep this in mind when designing an application, anything using Local Secondary Indexes, should assume an element of eventual consistency as the data is copied between the table and indexes. Writing and reading to an index consumes read capacity units and write capacity units of the main table.

Local Secondary Indexes are known as the sparse indexes. Only table item with an attribute matching the new sort key on the index will have an index item. Our table contains four items, but LSI contains only two because only two have the attribute which is the sort key in the index. This is known as the sparse index, and it allows very efficient data lookup when you are actively looking for the data based on the presence of a certain attribute.

Querying a Local Secondary Index

By default, any non-key value is not stored in a Local Secondary Index. If you retrieve an item which is projected, then you are charged accordingly just for the item being retrieved. The projections are attributes other than the Partition Key and sort key that are copied from the main table into the index. If you query an attribute which is not projected, then you are charged for the entire item cost from pulling it from the main table. If an attribute is not stored in the LSI and you perform a query that involves this attribute, then you have two penalties. The first one is that you have additional query latency while the item is being retrieved from the main table and secondly, the DynamoDB will have to check the item from the main table in addition to the index. Let's take the ongoing example of the weather station. So, we have a set of weather stations. Each producing data such as temperature, sunlight hours and UV strength and we have a

Partition Key highlighted in blue containing the weather station ID and a sort key of date and time value highlighted in orange. You have noticed a set of temperature anomalies and increasing the ambient temperature with body heat. The current model is very inefficient with cooling back data only where intrusions are detected as this is not the key value. The practical solution is to create a Local Secondary Index when the table is created.

Now, let's assume that you created a Local Secondary Index when the table was created while having the same Partition Key. The sort key of this index is the intrusion detection field highlighted in green. This allows you to pull back only records for a given weather station when an intrusion value is true. And during your design, you have the foresight to project one of the attributes into the index highlighted in grey. In this case, it could be a temperature value. You perform the query across the Local Secondary Index and select a single Partition Key and the sort key with the value of true so that it will be intrusion detection. The query returns four rows each of two hundred bytes. All the item size is combined including headings, and the query is rounded up to 4K from the throughput perspective. This is an efficient and good usage of Local Secondary Indexes.

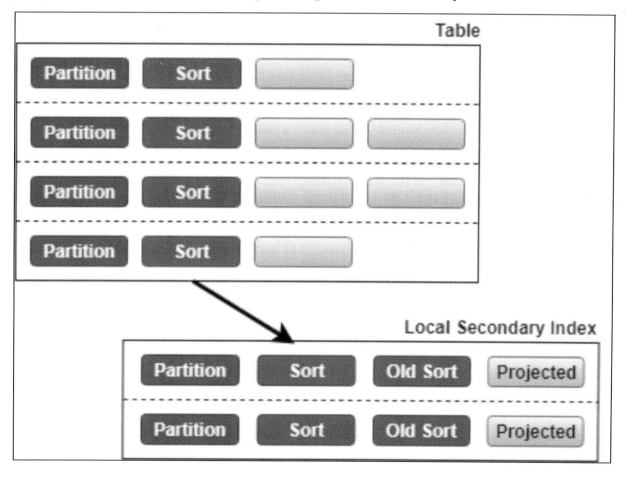

Figure 3-02: Example of LSI.

Now, let's assume that you began to inspect the intrusion acting your sunlight sensor indicating in red in Figure 3-02. Now, when you create the LSI, you did not project the value into the LSI. The query will complete but at some cost from a financial and performance perspective. DynamoDB will initially query the LSI in the same way as the query with the non-projected value, but then it will query the main table to retrieve the non-projected value. The first issue is that there will be an additional query latency generated by the table query and the second issue is that you will be built for the retrieval of the whole item from the main table for each row that returned from LSI query.

A Local Secondary Index maintains a sort key alternatively for a given Partition Key value. An LSI also includes a duplicate of a few or all of the attributes from its base table. You specify the attributes which are projected into the Local Secondary Index while you create the table. The information in a Local Secondary Index is prepared through the identical Partition Key as the base table, but with a specific sort key. It lets you get access to the data items effectively throughout the different dimensions. For more question or test flexibility, you could create as much as five local secondary indexes in line with the main table.

Item Writes and Local Secondary Indexes

DynamoDB automatically maintains all local secondary indexes synchronized with their respective base tables. Applications by no means write directly to an index. But, it is important to know how DynamoDB keeps these indexes.

While you create a local secondary index, you specify an attribute to function the sort key for the index. You can also specify a data type for that attribute. Which means every time you write an object to the base table if the item defines an index key characteristic, its type needs to match the index key schema's records type. There is no need for a direct relationship among the items in a base table and the objects in a local secondary index; in reality, this conduct can be advantageous for plenty of packages.

A table with multiple local secondary indexes will incur a higher cost for write activity than tables with fewer indexes.

Storage Considerations for Local Secondary Indexes

While an application writes an object to a table, DynamoDB mechanically copies the appropriate subset of attributes to any local secondary indexes wherein the ones attributes should appear. Your AWS account is charged for an item of the object within the main table and additionally for storage of attributes in any local secondary indexes on that table.

The quantity of space utilized by an index object is the sum of the following:

- The scale in bytes of the base table primary key (Partition Key and sort key).
- The scale in bytes of the index key attribute.
- The dimensions in bytes of the projected attributes (if any).
- A hundred bytes of overhead consistent with an index object.

To estimate the storage necessities for a Local Secondary Index, you could estimate the common size of an item within the index and then multiply through the variety of items within the base table.

If a table carries an object where a selected characteristic is not described, that attribute is defined as an index sort key, then DynamoDB does not write any statistics for that item to the index.

You need to be aware of the item Collections. Item Collection is any collection of items that have the common Partition Key value within the table, and all of its LSI. Item collection only applies to the tables with a Local Secondary Index. Item collection limits the dimensions of information storable as much as 10GB in step with Partition Key value. They limit the range of sort key values for a given Partition Key.

Global Secondary Index (GSI)

The Global Secondary Indexes can be created at any time, and unlike the Local Secondary Index, it allows the use of an alternative Partition Key and Sort key. With GSI you have the number of options for attribute projection.

- KEYS_ONLY: This includes the new partition and sort key value, and the old Partition Key and the old sort key.
- INCLUDE: This allows you to specify custom projection values.
- ALL: This allows you to project all attributes into the GSI.

Unlike the Local Secondary Indexes where the performance is shared with the table based on the common set of RCU and WCU, the GSI can have a separate set of reserved performance by its RCU and WCU. As with LSI, changes are written to the table are asynchronously copied to GSI means it is eventually consistent. Your application needs to be able to correlate with the eventual consistency since the GSI only support eventual consistent reads.

Attribute Projection in GSI

When you select the attributes to project into a GSI, you must consider the relation between provisioned throughput costs and storage costs:

- In case you want to get access to only a few attributes with the lowest possible latency, do not forget projecting most effective the one's attributes right into a

global secondary index. The smaller the index, the much less that it is going to pay to store it, and the much less your write charges will be.

- If your software frequently accesses a few non-key attributes, you need to recollect projecting the one's attributes into a global secondary index. The additional storage fees for the global secondary index will offset the fee of performing frequent table scans.

- In case you want to access the maximum of the non-key attributes frequently, you can project these attributes or maybe the whole base table right into a global secondary index. This will provide you with the most flexibility; but your storage value might increase, or maybe doubled.

- In case your utility desires to query a table infrequently but should carry out many writes or updates against the information in the table, keep in mind the projecting KEYS_ONLY. The global secondary index could be of minimal length, but could nevertheless be available when wanted for query interest.

Querying a Global Secondary Index

The query operation is used to access one or extra items in a global secondary index. The query has to specify the name of the base table and the name of the index that you want to apply, the attributes to be returned in the query outcomes, and any query situations which you want to use. DynamoDB can go back to the outcomes in ascending or descending order.

Scanning a Global Secondary Index

You may use the scan operation to retrieve all of the records from a global secondary index. You need to offer the base table name and the index call in the request. With a scan, DynamoDB reads all the information within the index and returns it to the application. You may additionally request that just a few of the records return and that the remaining records get discarded.

Data Synchronization Between Tables and GSI

DynamoDB synchronizes its base table with Global Secondary Index. An application writes or deletes items in a table. The global secondary indexes on that table are updated asynchronously, using an eventually consistent model. Applications by no means write at once up to date on the index. But, it is far critical that you understand the implications of ways DynamoDB maintains those indexes. While you create a global secondary index, and you specify one or extra index key attributes and their data types. This means that whenever you write an object up to the main table, the data type for the ones attributes up-to-date to match the index key schema's records types. While you place or delete items in a table, the global secondary indexes on that table are up-to-date in an ultimately

regular fashion. Changes up to the table data are propagated; update the global secondary indexes inside a fraction of a second, below regular conditions. However, in some not going failure scenarios, longer propagation delays would possibly arise.

If you write an object to the main table, you do not need to specify the attributes for any global secondary index sort key.

DynamoDB Stream & Replication

DynamoDB Stream

DynamoDB Stream is an ordered record of updates to a DynamoDB table. You enable stream on a particular table, and it records all changes in the table and stores these values for 24 hours. Entries over 24 hours are expired, and other entries can be referred. A stream can be enabled on the table from the console or API but it can only be processed through the stream endpoints and API requests.

AWS guarantees that each change to a table occurs in the stream once and all changes to the table occur in the stream in near real-time. DynamoDB Streams give a time-ordered series of item changes in any DynamoDB table. The changes are duplicated and stored for 24 hours. This functionality enables you to increase the power of DynamoDB with cross-area replication, continuous analytics with RedShift integration, alternate notifications, and plenty of different scenarios.

Changes recorded in the stream has some limitations. When a DynamoDB table records a change in the table, you initially do not know the nature of operation on the Partition Key. To overcome these core limitations, streams are configured with four possible views.

- KEYS_ONLY: In this method, the key attributes are written to the stream when an item is updated. It applies some limits which impact the functionality of stream.
- NEW_IMAGE: This stores the entire item to the stream. The entire item post update is written to the stream — means you can create code which reacts on changes and performs an action.
- OLD_IMAGE: The entire item, as it appeared before it was modified. The entire item is written to the stream pre-update.
- NEW_AND_OLD_IMAGES: The pre and post operation state of the item is written to the stream allowing more complex comparison operations to be performed.

Use Cases

Many programs can enjoy the potential to capture modifications to items stored in a DynamoDB table, on the point in time when such adjustments occur. Below are a few example use cases:

- An application in one AWS location modifies the data in a DynamoDB table. The 2nd application in another AWS area reads these records modifications and writes the data to any other table, creating a duplicate that stays in sync with the unique table.
- A mobile application modifies the data in a DynamoDB table, at the charge of thousands of updates consistent with second. Another software captures and stores statistics about these updates, supplying near actual-time usage metrics for the mobile application.
- A worldwide multi-participant recreation has a multi-master topology, storing information in multiple AWS areas. Each master stays in sync via consuming and replaying the adjustments that occur in the remote regions.
- A software routinely sends notifications to the cellular devices of all friends in a group as soon as one friend uploads a new photo.
- A brand new client adds information to a DynamoDB table. This occasion invokes every other utility that sends a welcome email to the new purchaser.

There are some categories currently, which uses DynamoDB Stream:

- Replication
- Trigger
- A database table in one AWS region, replicating to another AWS region for DR failover.
- A Lambda function triggered when items are added to a DynamoDB stream, performing analytics on data or a Lambda function triggered when a new user or new data added on the application and data is entered to the user table.
- A large distributed application with worldwide users. The application may frame using a multi-master database model. You might have two or three master database models in different regions. Users in Europe and the USA need to be able to have access to the same data. In this case, you can use the stream to keep the tables in sync with changes from other regions.

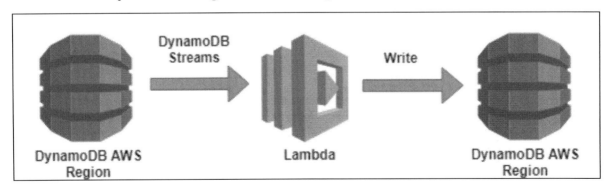

Figure 3-03: Lambda Function triggering DynamoDB

Cross-Region Replication

You could create tables which might be mechanically replicated across or over AWS regions, with complete aid for multi-master writes. This offers you the capability to build rapid, vastly scaled applications for a global consumer base without having to control the replication procedure. To create a Replication Model, you have to follow some steps:

- The first step is to create a source table.
- Download the replication template and apply the template into CloudFormation and wait for completion.
- After a brief period of completion, the stack will be shifted to complete and you Login to the replication console and create a replication group identity. You will need to provide the source and destination region in tables.
- Wait until the process completes. In the background, additional tables will be created for check-pointing.
- The whole process takes 1 and 30 minutes of duration to shift the status to "Active." The replication will occur automatically. At this point, you now have synchronization between regions.

EXAM TIP: DynamoDB Stream is combined with Lambda to allow traditional database triggers.

DynamoDB Performance Deep Dive

In DynamoDB, performance is all about Partitions. They are the key performance building blocks in DynamoDB. Partitions are like a unit of storage and performance which underpins the reads and writes between DynamoDB and the underlying storage infrastructure. To build an effective high-performance database you need to understand Partitions.

First, let's discuss how can you determine the approximate number of partitions that DynamoDB will create. There are two formulas to determine the number of partitions created. One is based on Performance while the other is based on Capacity.

In terms of Performance, the number of partitions is equal to desired read capacity units (RCU) divided by 3000 RCU added with desired write capacity unit divided by 1000 WCU. The number should be rounded up to the largest number, and that will provide the number of partitions needed.

Partition (Performance) = (Desired RCU ÷ 3000 RCU) + (Desired WCU ÷ 1000 WCU)

Now, let's look at the formula which is based on the size of the data stored within the table. So, partitions must base on the size equal to the actual size of your data divided by 10GB.

> Partition (Size) = Data Size in GB ÷ 10GB

One partition can cope with 10GB of data, 3000 RCU, and 1,000 WCU, indicating a right away relationship among the quantity of data stored in a table and performance requirements. A new partition may be added while more than 10 GB of data is saved in a table, or WCUs are greater than 1,000, or RCUs are greater than 3,000. Then, the records get unfolded throughout those partitions.

Partition Key Selection

For a low volume, table either reads and writes, the key selection is less important. Anything below 3000RCU or 1000WCU is achievable even with the badly selected key. When you need to provide high-performance, there is a criterion which assists DynamoDB with scaling performance. The first key criteria for an effective Partition Key is that you pick something with an attribute having many distinct values. For example, student ID, or candidate ID. There is a direct relationship between the performance and the number of distinct Partition Key. The second criteria is that the attribute should have a uniform white pattern across all Partition Key values. The attribute should have a uniform temporal write pattern across time that is written, and reads should ideally occur across the key value in a uniform way across time.

If any of the above is not possible with the existing data set, then you can consider a synthetic or hybrid value. At last, you should not mix hot and cold key values within a table.

Let's study an example that makes use of the 2016 US Elections to highlight everything we've simply mentioned. Especially, when we need to store a file of all the votes for all the applicants.

Every political party may have many applicants competing for the celebration's electoral nomination. You may have everywhere from 1 to 10 candidates. The hassle is that the votes between candidates will no longer be dispersed uniformly — there could be one or more applicants so that it will get a hold of most of the people of the votes.

For the sake of this example, allow the count on which we anticipate 10,000 WCU worth of votes to be received. Say that, in the first example, we create a table and naively pick the candidate ID as the Partition Key and range key as date and time.

DynamoDB will create ten partitions for this example (ten partitions are needed to guide 10,000 WCU). This version is essentially flawed. First, we're prescribing the performance

for a candidate for a value much lesser than 10,000 WCU. As we mentioned above, actual-international candidate vote casting might be heavily weighted closer to one or two popular candidates.

Even supposing balloting is uniformly weighted among candidates, their citizens can be located in distinct time zones and can vote at some particular time. Consequently, there might be spikes of votes for sure applicants at unique instances as compared to others. In spite of carefully designing the Partition Keys, you may run into time-based problems.

Let's think about a scenario when there are handiest applicants within the countrywide election. To enhance overall performance potential, 100,000 WCUs are assigned, and DynamoDB creates a hundred partitions to aid this. But, if the candidate id is chosen as the Partition Key, every candidate record will be confined to one partition — even though there are ninety-eight unused partitions. Consequently, you'll hit the storage restriction quickly, inflicting the application to fail and forestall recording also votes.

This issue is resolved by using a key-sharing plan. This means for every candidate — i.e. for each partition — the partition secret is prefixed with a fee of 1-10 or 1-1,000 (depending on the size of your data set). This offers us a far wider range of Partition Keys. That means DynamoDB will distribute this information across more than one partitions frivolously.

Global Secondary Index (GSI)

GSI has their performance reservation. RCU and WCU are defined separately then the main table and the indexes can also have an alternate partition and sort key than the main table. An index with a sort key and Partition Key that can be specified from those on the base table. A global secondary index is taken into consideration "global" because queries on the index can span all the records in the base table, across all partitions. A global secondary index has no length obstacles and has its very own provisioned throughput settings for read and write activity that is independent of those of the table.

> **EXAM TIP:** Each table in DynamoDB is limited to 20 global secondary indexes (default limit) and five local secondary indexes.

Writes in DynamoDB

Let's consider the example of a weather station. A table contains the data from the fleet of the national weather station. The Partition Key of the table is the weather station ID; the sort key is date and time. Additionally, the table stores the number of attributes such as temperature, rainfall, UV level, wind speed, and specific attribute, which identifies any intrusion alarms with the true or false value. Writes on the table are well distributed from a Partition Key perspective and a good time and critical distribution of writes to the

database. We create a GSI which has a Partition Key of intrusion and a sort key of station ID. It also contains the original sort key of date and time and attributes that we have decided to project. This means you create a GSI based on intrusion equals to true, filter and sort based on the station ID, and get values which can be viewed as suspect.

There are two issues which could impact this design. We allocate 12000WCU to the main table, DynamoDB allocates 12 partitions on this level of load. The writes from the main table will start copying asynchronously to the Global Secondary Index (GSI). The writes will begin to be throttled at GSI or also at the main table. We have 12000WCU at the main table and 12000WCU at GSI. The performance reservation is independent of each other, but the data structure of GSI is a problem. Its Partition Key is intrusion, which has two possible values, true or false which means we have a maximum of two Partition Keys because we have two Partition Key values. This produces throttling at the index and the main table.

Let's say you have a small data collection application that has some data centers with a fair number of reads and writes over time. The application receives the data at the starting of the time. Now, with this type of the situation, you may set the WCU and RCU value which covers the majority of settings without your hourly connection window. So, you expect to be throttled by DynamoDB which could lead to application errors and missed data points. To overcome this, you have three options. Firstly, you can rely on burst; you get 300 seconds of your RCU and WCU in a pool which can cope with the short burst. The other option you have is that you could change your application code to provide built-in leveling by buffering data and spreading excess writes over time. In the last option, you could use SQS as a managed write buffer where your application writes burst traffic into an SQS queue which is then passed by a separate application or a Lambda function, then reads items from the SQS queue and store them into the database in a sufficient way.

Reads in DynamoDB

DynamoDB supports eventually consistent and Strongly Consistent Reads.

In eventually consistent reads, when you examine records from a DynamoDB table, the reaction might not replicate the effects of a recently finished write operation. The response may encompass a few stale statistics. If you repeat your examine request after a short time, the up-to-date reaction returns the latest data.

In Strongly Consistent Reads, DynamoDB returns a reaction with the maximum facts, reflecting the updates from all prior write operations that had been successful. A strongly consistent read may not be available or updated if there is a network postpone or outage. Consistent reads are not supported in GSI.

Let's take the scenario of an online store containing seven products. Generally, the products are all fairly popular with an average of 200 or 300 reads per second and a very small number of writes. Let's say the store is having a sale and the prices of product 1 and product 2 are reduced. Now, the products will be ordered more because of the cost reduction and also every visit to the front page of the site will pull in data from the products as well as a burst from the large increase in passive views caused by simple page looks. For this problem, you do not need to increase the read capacity for the nominal load because this will cause an increase in the partition. So, the increase in RCU is dangerous. Also, burst capacity, in this case, won't work. We can use static HTML replacing the front page, but it would diminish the user experience because the dynamic site nature would be removed.

Now, you could use Caching. By using this architecture, the request for the product will be read into the in-memory caching engine. Demand from the web server will be delivered from the in-memory caching engine rather than using read capacity data units. You can avoid out of date caching entries by using DynamoDB streaming feature.

Mind Map

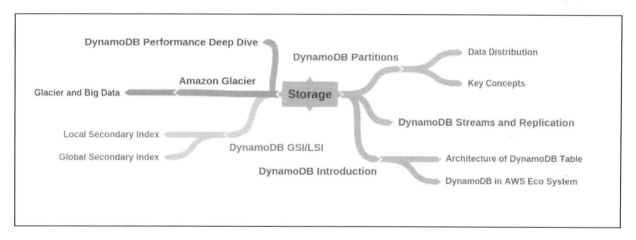

Figure 3-04: Chapter's Mind Map

Practice Questions

1. _____ is an exceptionally low-cost service provider that offers secure and sturdy storage for information archiving and backup.
   A. Amazon Glacier.
   B. AWS DynamoDB.
   C. AWS S3.
   D. None of the Above.

2. Which of the following feature in Glacier helps in meeting the compliance requirements?
   A. AWS SDKs.
   B. API Reference.
   C. Vault Lock.
   D. Archives.

3. After how many hours the lock validation is expired in Amazon Glacier?
   A. 12.
   B. 24.
   C. 48.
   D. 6.

4. To lock a vault, which of the following can you use?
   A. Console.
   B. API.
   C. CLI.
   D. All of the Above.

5. In DynamoDB architecture, at high-level data is available in _____ groups?
   A. Two.
   B. Three.
   C. Five.
   D. Four.

6. _____ are the underlying storage and processing nodes of DynamoDB.
   A. Write Capacity Unit.
   B. Read Capacity Unit.
   C. Partitions.

D. Attributes.

7. To examine an item from the table in DynamoDB, what do you need to specify?
   A. Partition Key Value.
   B. Sort Key Value.
   C. Both A and B.
   D. None of the Above.

8. How many data retrieval options are offered by DynamoDB?
   A. Two.
   B. Three
   C. Four.
   D. Five.

9. _____ allows the use of an alternative partition and sort key.
   A. LSI.
   B. GSI.
   C. None of the Above.
   D. DynamoDB.

10. How many attribute projections are offered by GSI?
    A. One.
    B. Two.
    C. Three.
    D. Four.

11. Which option is used to access one or more extra item from GSI?
    A. Query.
    B. Scan.
    C. Reading of Data.
    D. Writing of Data.

12. Which operation is used to retrieve all the records from the global secondary index?
    A. Query.
    B. Scan.
    C. Reading of Data.
    D. Writing of Data.

13. In which method, the key attributes are written to the stream when an item is updated?
    A. KEYS_ONLY.
    B. NEW_IMAGE.
    C. OLD_IMAGE.
    D. NEW_AND_OLD_IMAGES.

14. Which method is used to write the POST-item updates to the stream?
    A. KEYS_ONLY.
    B. NEW_IMAGE.
    C. OLD_IMAGE.
    D. NEW_AND_OLD_IMAGES.

15. Which method is used to write the PRE-item update to the stream?
    A. KEYS_ONLY.
    B. NEW_IMAGE.
    C. OLD_IMAGE.
    D. NEW_AND_OLD_IMAGES.

16. Which method is used to write the PRE and POST state of the operations to the stream?
    A. KEYS_ONLY.
    B. NEW_IMAGE.
    C. OLD_IMAGE.
    D. NEW_AND_OLD_IMAGES.

17. DynamoDB stream combines with Lambda to perform which of the following function?
    A. Scan.
    B. Query.
    C. Replication.
    D. Trigger.

18. One Partition can cope with _____ GB of data,
    A. 10GB.
    B. 100GB.
    C. 1000GB.
    D. 500GB.

19. What is the maximum read and write capacity unit in DynamoDB?
    A. 1000RCU and 3000WCU.
    B. 3000RCU and 1000WCU.
    C. 3000RCU and 3000WCU.
    D. 1000RCU and 1000WCU.

20. What are the maximum deliverables from one DynamoDB Partition?
    A. 3000WCU, 1000RCU, 10GB Data Volume.
    B. 1000WCU, 3000RCU, 10GB of Data Volume.
    C. No maximums.
    D. 4000WCU, 1000RCU, and 20GB of Data Volume.

21. Which operation or feature will you use to locate all items in a table with a particular Sort key value? (Choose 2)
    A. Query with GSI.
    B. Query with LSI.
    C. Scan against the table with filters.
    D. Item Collection.

22. Which of the following attribute data types can be considered as item keys? (Choose 3)
    A. String.
    B. Number.
    C. Binary.
    D. Blob.

23. After the creation of the table, you can add a Local Secondary Index to DynamoDB.
    A. True.
    B. False.

24. Write Capacity Units (WCU) is the number of writes of _____ blocks per second to the table.
    A. 1KB.
    B. 4KB.
    C. 16KB.
    D. 48KB.

25. Read Capacity Unit (RCU) is the number of read of _____ blocks per seconds to the table.
    A. 1KB.
    B. 4KB.
    C. 16KB.
    D. 48KB.

Chapter 04: Processing

Introduction

In this chapter, we will discuss AWS technology Elastic MapReduce (EMR) in detail. We will discuss basic knowledge of EMR, its architecture, EMR cluster operations, EMR in AWS EcoSystem, programming of Frameworks and Project and Hue (Hadoop User Experience). All the provided information in this chapter will be enough for passing the AWS Big Data Speciality exam.

Amazon Elastic MapReduce (EMR)

EMR is a managed service of AWS which is a clustered platform and allows to process and analyze the large datasets. Because processing of large datasets is a problem, so using Hadoop Cluster in EMR, can help you mitigate the processing issue. In EMR, the data is split into small jobs which are then distributed among multiple compute nodes. All this working in EMR is performed by Big Data Frameworks and Open-source projects.

Big Data Frameworks include Apache Hadoop, Apache Spark, Presto, and Apache HBase. While some open source projects are Zeppelin, Pig, Hive, Sqoop, Hue, etc.

As we discuss few Big Data Frameworks and projects from exam perspective, but you have more options on both. Consider a Big Data Framework like Presto which is a query engine. You may see in previous releases they use impala, but in the recent release, they use Presto. Presto performs analytics queries on large data sets.

Use Cases

Amazon EMR is suitable for a variety of cases like:

- Log processing generated by the application and convert unstructured data into structured data.
- It can be used to understand user desires and partition the user with the help of analyzing clickstream data. You can also deliver impressive ads through this.
- EMR can also process a large amount of genomics data and scientific data quickly in an efficient way.
- It can be used in ETL (Extract, Transform and Load). Loading of data is on Redshift and then analyzing query is applied on that.
- For machine learning via the use of Spark Machine Learning.

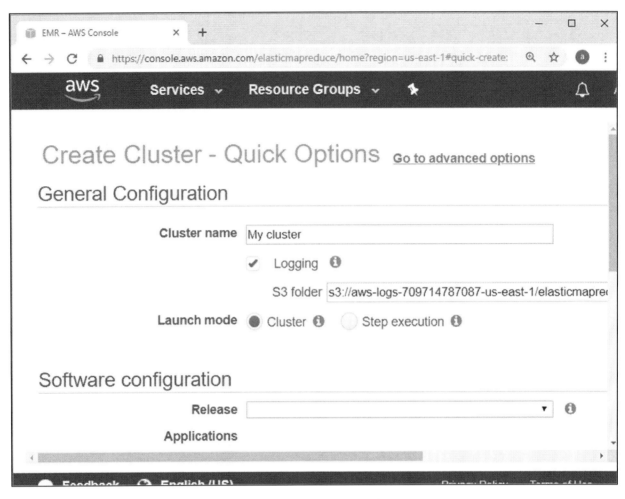

Figure 4-02: EMR Console

Apache Hadoop

Before understanding the Hadoop in EMR, you need to know the basics of Apache Hadoop. As we have discussed above that EMR use Hadoop architecture, so the basic structure of Hadoop is same.

What is Hadoop? Hadoop is a software library, like Frameworks, which allows distributed processing of a large data set over the cluster of compute resources using simple programming tools. Hadoop allows you to scale up from a single server to thousands of resources with their individual storage and local compute. In EMR, S3 is used as storage. Hadoop libraries are much efficient, so they identify the fault and handle it at the application level.

Architecture Modules

Hadoop architecture is composed of 4 modules.

- Hadoop Common
- HDFS
- Hadoop YARN
- Hadoop MapReduce

Hadoop Common

It is also known as Hadoop core as it provides important services and basic processes like an abstraction of the necessary OS and its Filesystem. It also contains the libraries and utilities that are required by other Hadoop modules. In this, JAR files and scripts are defined to start the Hadoop.

HDFS (Hadoop Distributed File System)

HDFS is the primary storage of Hadoop. It is a file system in which all replicated data is present to fortify the durability. It is fault tolerant as it detects the failure and performs recovery quickly. In this, large files are reliably stored across the cluster. Each file is stored in the sequence of blocks and block size is the same for the entire file except the last block. It also provides high throughput.

Hadoop YARN

In this module, YARN stands for Yet Another Resource Negotiator. The main task for this module is to schedule the job and cluster resource management.

Hadoop MapReduce

This module is for processing of large datasets with the parallel distributed algorithm on a cluster. The processing can be done on the file system or in a data set. It also performs processing on the basis of data location, so that transfer distance is reduced.

MapReduce has 2 tasks; Map and Reduce

- Map performs the splitting of large data sets into small pieces and processes them in parallel.
- Reduces creation of output by taking the output of the map as its input and then produce output with reduced data chunks.

Architecture

In the basic Architecture of Hadoop, there is a master and slave node concept. Master node manages the resources for the cluster and then schedule the jobs to multiple slave nodes using HDFS. Slave node can communicate to the master node or to other slave nodes.

As you know about Hadoop YARN, it has some main components in architecture.

- There is resource manager in the master node which is generally a scheduler that allocates the resources in a cluster among the computing application like if you have two applications, then resource manager is responsible for providing their respective resources.
- On the slave node, there is a node manager which takes direction from the resource manager and manages the resources in the slave node.
- Application master is also in slave node which is assigned with the task of negotiator of resources for RM and works with node manager to execute the container and its monitoring as well.

In actual, data processing is at container which is executed by the application master. It has an appropriate right to the application as if an application needs a specific command of memory and storage on the specific slave node.

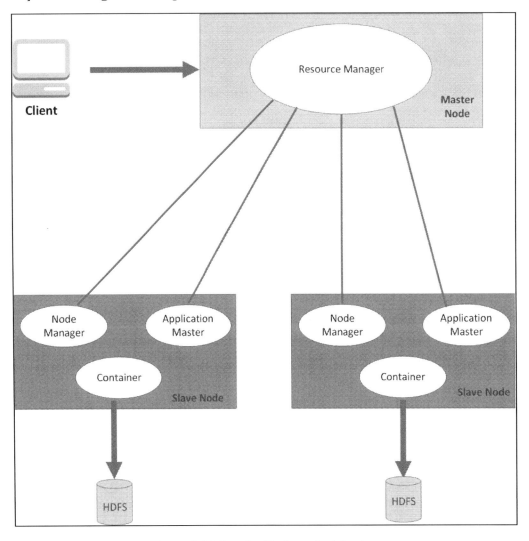

Figure 4-03:Apache Hadoop Architecture

We have also discussed Hadoop MapReduce that it has 2 tasks which are further divided into more detail like input, split, Map, shuffle, reduce and result.

Let's discuss an example, if you have unstructured data as input then MapReduce application reads and processes records into input split. Each record is understood by MapReduce to be key-value pair. Now resource manager assigns Map phase appropriate resource to start parallel processing. In this way, the intermediate key-value pair is generated.

In the shuffle phase, key-value pairs are moved to reducers then individual key pair sorted by key to data list and data list equivalent key together. Now it is easy to evaluate these key-value pairs in reduce phase. In the end, reduce phase takes these key-value pairs and run reducer function, so the data is filtered and aggregated and the result is provided.

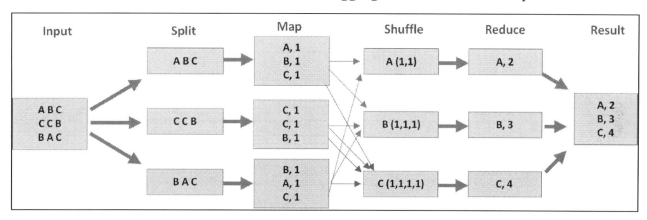

Figure 4-03: Working of Hadoop

EMR Architecture

As we know that EMR architecture is almost similar to Hadoop architecture. In this architecture, there is the master node, Core node as a slave node and task node also as a slave node. We will also discuss the storage option for EMR and single AZ concept of EMR.

In EMR architecture, node is categorized by instance group. So we have three instance groups. Instance group is a collection of instances to organize them. In EMR cluster, you can have up to 50 instance groups.

- Master instance group has only one instance
- Core instance group can have 1 or more core nodes
- Task instance group can have up to 48 instance groups.

Task instance group comes up when you do not have the instance type available for Spark instance then you can create task instance group with a type which has the capacity of Spark instance. Now we will discuss each node type in detail.

Master Node

It is the same as the master node in Hadoop architecture. It has a single master node, so failure chances are more, so we store its metadata in the data store. If a failure occurs, then using this metadata create a new master node in the new cluster. The master node is for managing the resources like tracking and directing against HDFS. It also coordinates the distribution and parallel execution of MapReduce executable. It also monitors the health of core and task nodes. The master node contains metadata which provides information about directories and files in a cluster.

Core Node

It is the same as slave node in Hadoop Architecture. It stores data as part of HDFS and EMRFS. On the core node, there is a data node which manages the data blocks, read, write access on the core node. It also has a node manager and application master which is already discussed above. In this core node, there is shrink operation which we will discuss later in this chapter.

Task Node

It is also a slave node but optional. It has no HDFS, and you can add and remove them from a running cluster. They have enough capacity to manage a high amount of load.

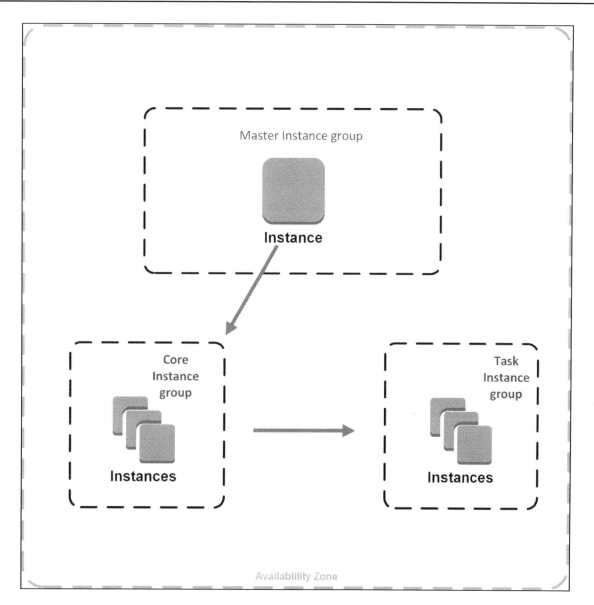

Figure 4-04: EMR architecture

HDFS (Hadoop Distributed File System)

To learn about HDFS, you need to know what a distributed file system is. It is a system that allows simultaneous access of data and files from multiple clients to the set of distributed machines. But this file system does not work well with EMR, so we use HDFS in MapReduce. HDFS holds Terabyte or petabyte of data and it is designed for higher throughput for accessing data.

HDFS in a cluster provides single Global Name Space for the entire cluster and is maintained by the master node. Name Space provides a consolidated view of all files in the cluster because managing a large number of files is difficult. HDFS is a block file system in which individual files break into an equal block size of the block. These blocks

are stored in the slave node of the cluster randomly means all blocks are not stored in the same slave node. But there is the point of failure, means if any of the slave nodes that have any block of the file goes down then file become unavailable. So in HDFS, there is replication property through which the block is replicated across the number of the slave nodes. By default, replication factor is 3; meaning that initially 3 copies are replicated across the 3 slave nodes.

HDFS block size

The block size and files in HDFS tend to be large in size because HDFS holds a large amount of data. The default block size is 64 MB, but you can put block size as much large as you want generally range from 64 MB to 256 MB.

The block size is depending on input data if you have large input files then select 256 MB for maximum throughput and if you have small input files, then you can select 64 MB. The key point that needs to be remembered is block size, access pattern, and master & slave size.

In HDFS, large block size is used to minimize the random disk seeks and latency. Disk seeks means the time which disk drive took to locate the file which needs to be read.

In HDFS, the location of the file is sequentially on disk. Block size is set per file, and when the client writes a file into a disk, they can send the block size of own choice at creation time. The replication factor in HDFS is set on the hdfs-site.xml file. By changing in the file, you can change the replication factor.

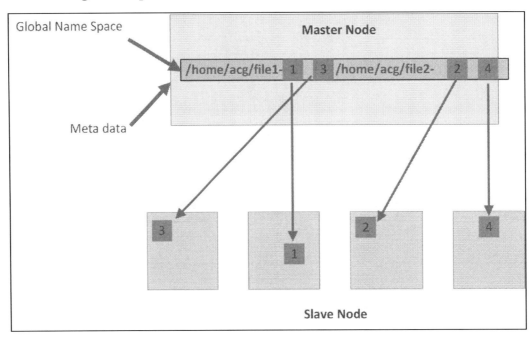

Figure 4-05: HDFS

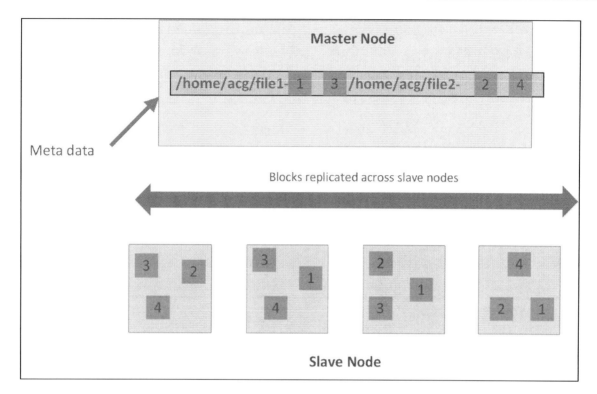

Figure 4-06: HDFS with Replication

Storage Options

There are three storage options in EMR architecture which are discussed below.

Instance store

Amazon EC2 Instance Storage is generally ephemeral drives that give temporary block-level storage for various Amazon EC2 Instance types. Amazon EC2 Instance storage is dedicated to a single EC2 instance. Data on instance storage persists only during the life of the associated Amazon EC2 instance. When an instance is stopped, terminated, re-started and failed, all data on the instance storage is lost. It provides high I/O performance and high IOPS at low cost.

EBS

It provides persistent block storage volumes to use with Amazon EC2 instances in the AWS Cloud. EBS enables you to create storage volumes and attach those to Amazon EC2 instances in the same Availability Zone.

But when using EBS with EMR, then data is lost on termination of the cluster.

EMRFS (EMR file system)

EMRFS is a type of Hadoop file system, which stores cluster directly into the Amazon S3. EMRFS helps you to store data for a prolonged period in Amazon S3 for further use with

Hadoop. EMRFS helps to protect the stored data in Amazon S3 at a low cost in case of a cluster failure. EMRFS stores data into S3 directly without ingesting into HDFS. As S3 provides reliable, durable, and scalable storage, so does EMRFS provides these properties. You can also point multiple clusters to same S3 files.

You can use HDFS and EMRFS together by copying data from S3 to HDFS by using S3DistCp. DistCp is an open source tool for copying a large amount of data. So we use S3DistCp as we want to work with S3. For processing the same data set frequently, you use EMRFS and HDFS. EMRFS has high I/O throughput.

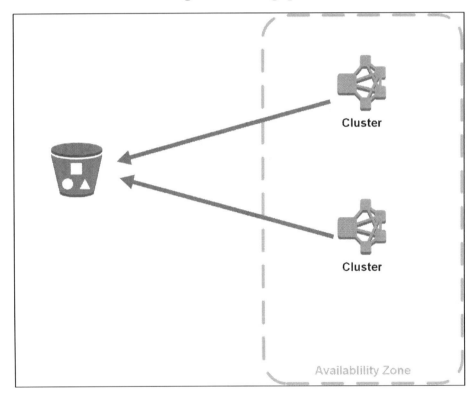

Figure 4-07: EMRFS

EMRFS and Consistency View

As in S3, we have two consistency modes: Read after Write consistency for new PUTS (immediately propagate) and Eventual Consistency for overwrite PUTS and DELETES (can take some time to propagate). So, if we do listing after quick write may be incomplete means if you add any object then immediately list that object in consequent operation, list of object and set of object that is incomplete. This is an issue mostly in ETL pipeline where the input is taken from multiple steps for any future step.

So EMR consistence view is a feature which checks the list and read after write consistency of S3 for new objects written by or sync with EMRFS. Consistency view puts object metadata into the DynamoDB to track consistency of S3 object. If Consistent view

detects any inconsistency during file put request operation, then it retries the operation according to the rule which you define.

Single-AZ Concept

As in EMRFS, there is block replication with low latency in single AZ while replication in other AZ. The communication between master, core, and task node within the same AZ is efficient. If the core node in another AZ is trying to access metadata in the master node is not efficient. In the EMR cluster, there is a single master node, so there is no concept of a secondary master node. You can launch a replacement cluster easily without losing data if using EMRFS. So, there is no need to run EMR cluster in Multi-AZ.

EMR Operations

EMR Releases

To understand the EMR operation, you need to know about EMR Releases. Releases are a set of software applications and components which can be installed on the EMR cluster. AWS provides two Hadoop distributions: MapR and Amazon.

In EMR, there is open source project and frameworks which are considered as an application, and related components for each application are installed and configured depending on the application. The components are divided into 3 main categories.

1. Open Source Community like Hadoop and Spark.
2. Open Source Community that Amazon modifies to work with EMR.
3. Only the component that is provided just to use with EMR.

Launching a Cluster

Launching of the cluster can use pre-built scripts and applications of different programming languages like Java, .NET and Python, etc. This script can be used to launch and process cluster. You also have an option to launch the code directly from S3 or by using interactive mode in which login to master node and execute the script on the master node.

Quick and Advanced Setting Option

When you launch a cluster in EMR via console, then you have the default option of quick setting. The quick option is faster than the advanced option, but it has some restrictions which are as follows:

- No debugging option
- VPC of your own choice not allowed
- Defined 4 packages that are available for software application

- In its hardware configuration, you have the option to define instance type that is the same for both master and core node.
- No option for tasks node.
- The only new version of releases is available.

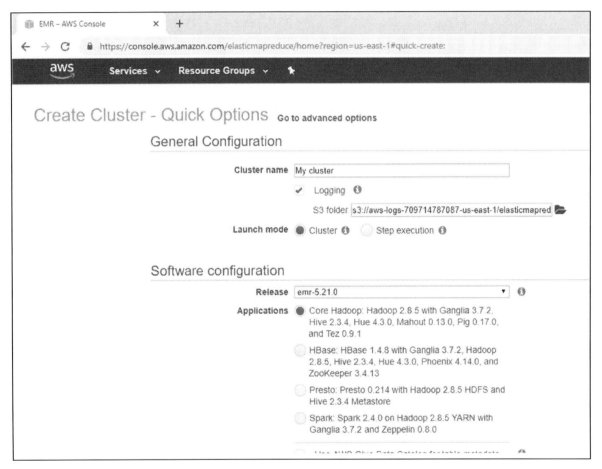

Figure 4-08: Quick Option Window

Security and access section is already there so you do not necessarily need to define custom Security Group. But you have an option to create a custom Security group, but the default Security group is also available with EMR. You can make changes while the cluster that has been launched.

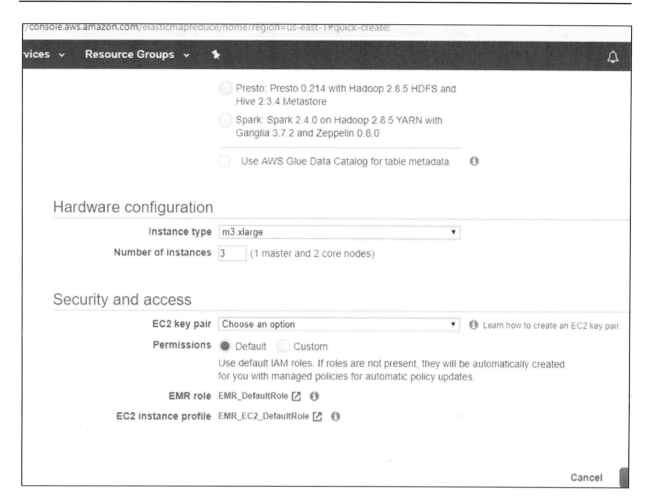

Figure 4-09: Quick Security option

In advanced setting option, you have an available older version of releases. In that, there are no application packages, you can choose the application of your requirement for installation in the launchi of the cluster. You have an option to set software configuration setting like changing the size of core node etc.

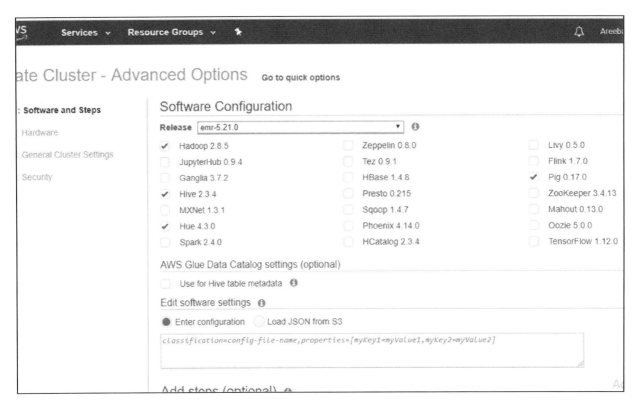

Figure 4-10: Advanced Options Window

In advanced setting, you have "add step" option in which you define the way of cluster working in the form of script which is executed after cluster launching. In Quick Option, you also have added steps option.

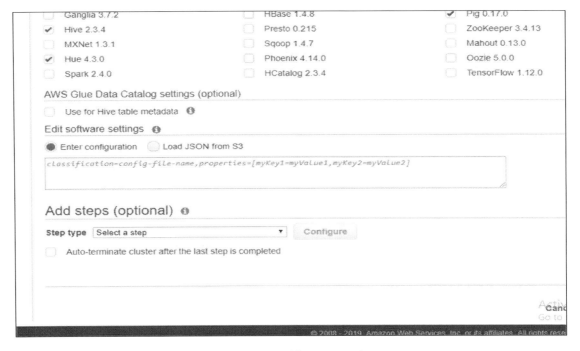

Figure 4-11: Add Steps Option

After defining the step, you can select an option of terminating the cluster after execution of the last step. You can also select VPC of your choice and subnet as well. EMR is generally launched in public subnet as it wants to interact with public services or if EMR is launched in private, subnet then you need to use endpoint for accessing the public services.

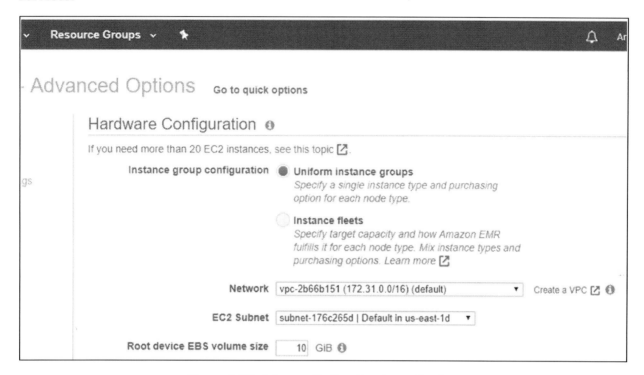

Figure 4-12: Advance Option Hardware Setting

You can also choose different instance type for master, core and task node. It is your choice to mix and match the instance type for all the nodes. You can also change the instance storage for node or request for a spot with a bid. By defining an auto scaling group, you can resize the cluster. Tags can also be defined but it can be done via EMR console, CLI and API as EMR does not understand the tags defined by EC2 console. EMRFS consistence view option is also available.

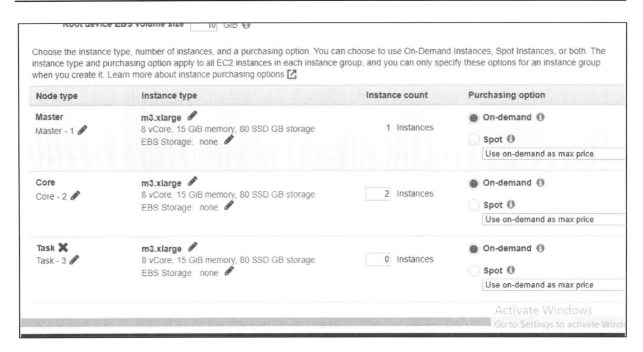

Figure 4-13: Instance selection

Bootstrap script option can also be defined to execute the script before setting up Hadoop setup on every cluster node. Bootstrap can also be used to define the installing of additional software.

Security option has two options, either to proceed without a key pair or by using a key pair. Proceed without key pair is used for the transient cluster which has no requirement of connecting to the master node while the key pair is used for long run cluster and they need to connect to the master node.

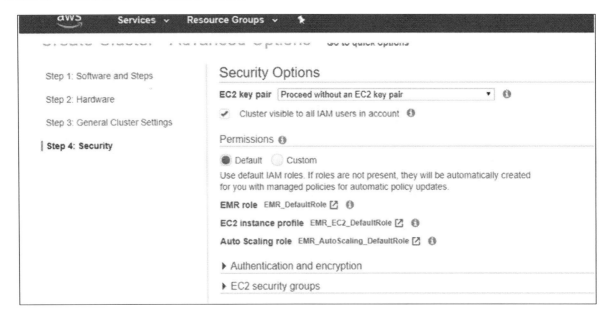

Figure 4-14: Security Option in Advance Configure Setting

It has default or custom permission setting with encryption setting. In encryption, you define either encryption at rest required or at transit.

When the EMR cluster is created, two default surety groups are created. One for master and other for core and task nodes. An option of adding additional security group is also available as you do not want to perform changes in the default security group.

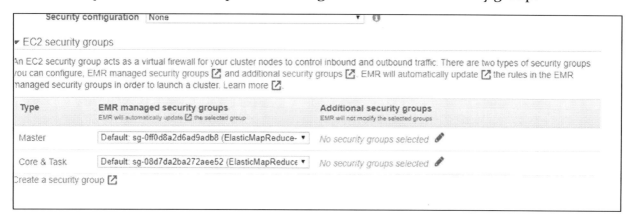

Figure 4-15: Security Group Option

Long-running Cluster

While launching a long-running cluster and load data into it. Cluster stay up and running for queries against the storage like HBase. It is for the use case where jobs on a cluster running frequently and datasets may be too large so loading of data in the new cluster each time may be inefficient.

In a long-running cluster, you have a feature of HDFS data on core nodes. Auto termination is kept disabled which is by default and termination protection is enabled against the accidental termination of the cluster.

Transient Cluster

It is a temporary cluster which terminates after processing. Its ideal use case is a batch job. By using this type of cluster, you can reduce the cost as you only need to pay when the cluster is running. Its input, output, and code data is stored in S3, so, new cluster will start easily.

If a failure occurs before termination, there is an easy recovery option, but Hive metastore which is stored in MySQL DB is not available, so we overwrite the path into MySQL RDS DB. In this way, your metastore are accessible for next time.

Choosing Instance Type

As per your requirement, you can choose an appropriate instance type.

- MapReduce - these jobs are batch-oriented as jobs are running against a large amount of data, so it takes a long time. So, in this case, use general purpose instance M3 and M4. As load increases the potential for job increases and in order to pass job in expected time, you need to scale the cluster horizontally.
- Machine Learning - it is compute intensive so use P2, C3 or C4 instance type.
- Spark - it is in-memory caching which is helpful for fast performance then use R3 or R4.
- If you need large instance stored based HDFS for MapReduce jobs that need high I/O performance and high IOPS at low cost or using large Hbase cluster then use I2 and D3.

Number of instances

For efficient processing of data in the cluster you need to choose instance type and number of instances for the handling of data. But rather than thinking on these factors, AWS gives you flexibility by allowing the addition of node as per requirement. So you need to think intelligently because if the cluster size is very large, then you need to pay extra cost or if size is small, then it works slow.

Consider a master node which requires less computation because it performs coordination rather than processing. For this, AWS offers you to use m3.xlarge or m4.xlarge for 50 or less than nodes while for more than 50 use m3.2xlarge or m4.2xlarge.

If we consider core node sizing, then this node run task and processing of data as per direction from the master node. Core node stores data in HDFS but you have EMRFS option as well. In EMRFS we have replication factor on which sizing depends. Like if you are using a cluster of 10 or more nodes then replication factor is 3, if 4-9 nodes then 2, and for 3 or less nodes it is 1. But you have an option to overwrite it by going into the specific file as we discussed earlier.

In AWS, you have a guideline to calculate the capacity of HDFS and EMRFS as well. When using HDFS, you can use EBS or instance store which is for high I/O.

Let's consider an example, you want high I/O and your data set size in HDFS is 3TB so if we select 10 core nodes of a specific type with EBS size of 800GiB. Then 10*800=8 TB, so HDFS capacity is 8/3 as its replication factor is 3. Now the capacity is 2.6TB, and we required 3TB, so we need to change the size of EBS, instance type or by changing instance number. In this way, you can check or test your requirement.

Best preference is to use a small cluster with larger nodes as you have a few large nodes, so the management cost reduces, and also failure possibilities reduce.

Monitoring

The monitoring of EMR can be done via CloudWatch, via web interfaces and some open tools. CloudWatch monitoring is done via Events and metrics. Just overview of the event, it is a response to a change in state of a resource. Once it responds to the event then it is sent to the event stream. From CloudWatch console you need to select the service, which monitoring you need with different details, such as what type of monitoring, which specific of that attribute. While in target you need to define which function is used for monitoring like Lambda and SNS topic.

CloudWatch metric is another service which is by default provided with EMR, so no extra charges will be incurred. CloudWatch metric updates after every 5 minutes and are not configurable. These metrics are archived for two weeks, and after that, these will be removed. Metrics are provided for all clusters in EMR. To search a specific cluster, you can use cluster ID.

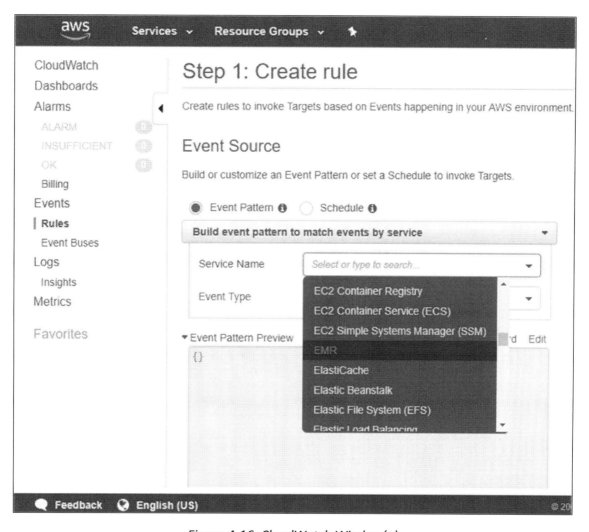

Figure 4-16: CloudWatch Window(a)

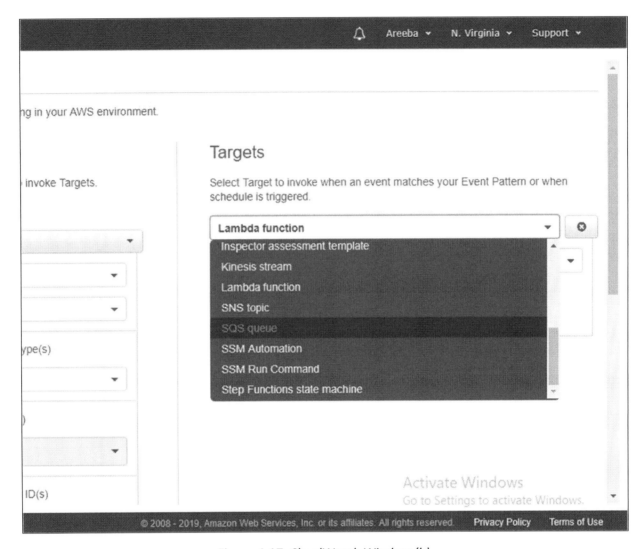

Figure 4-17: CloudWatch Window (b)

As we know that web interfaces are also available for monitoring. There is a list of web interfaces.

Name of interface	URI
YARN Resource Manager	http://master-public-dns-name:8088/
YARN Node Manager	http://coretask-public-dns-name:8042/
Hadoop HDFS Name Node	http://master-public-dns-name:50070/
Hadoop HDFS DataNode	http://coretask-public-dns-name:50075/
Spark History Server	http://master-public-dns-name:18080/
Zeppelin	http://master-public-dns-name:8890/

Hue	http://master-public-dns-name:8888/
Ganglia	http://master-public-dns-name/ganglia/
HBase	http://master-public-dns-name:16010/
Jupyter Hub	http://master-public-dns-name:9443/

Table 4-01: Interface with URI

From these web service some use for master node and some for slave nodes like core and task node. As some interfaces are not available for master node then the easiest way to connect to the master node is to use SSH. Either SSH tunnel with local forwarding and SSH tunnel with Dynamic port forwarding with SOCKS proxy. Once the SSH tunnel is established, then the interfaces are accessible over the console.

Ganglia is another open source monitoring tool. With this, you can generate the report and view performance of cluster as a whole. Monitoring can also be done at the individual level.

Resizing of Cluster

With EMR, cluster resizing is done manually or by use of auto-scaling. For manual resizing, you can use Console, API, and CLI. In console, click on the resize button, now the number of running instances is shown in a window where you can change the number of nodes as per demand but only for core and task node. When scaling down a cluster, you get a warning about the reduction in size of the cluster. The scale down process of both task and core node is known as a graceful shrink. Always remember one thing i.e. when you resize the core node, that the number of core nodes is not less than the replication factor.

For resizing of the cluster using auto-scaling feature is invented on Nov 16. As we know that in the EMR cluster there is only one master node so its auto-scaling feature is not available but for core and task node this feature is valid. In security option, while creating cluster you need to define the role; if you do not define the role then you are not allowed to use auto-scaling. By default, the IAM role for autoscaling group is automatically selected with EMR. In custom security option, you need to define the role for auto scaling group because after the cluster is created, you cannot add a role for auto scaling group.

Using Hue with EMR

The Hue is "Hadoop User Experience" which is an open source web interface for Apache Hadoop and other non-Hadoop applications. It brings a group of different Hadoop ecosystem projects into a configurable interface. It is a browser-based way to run and

create a script on Hadoop cluster, manage jobs, view HDFS and manage metastore, etc. by using hue, managing of EMR cluster becomes very easy.

Figure 4-18: Hue Window

By default, hue is installed at the creation of a cluster, but in advance option, you can choose not to install hue at the creation of the cluster. Once cluster is created with a hue, you connect to hue interface. In the beginning, it asks the user name and password before displaying the hue browser. Via hue browser, you can view S3 browser that is for EMR cluster and also HDFS browser is available to access HDFS files. Although by default S3 browser is not configured, so we need to configure that. In hue, Pig and Hive editor is available which is easier to use rather than CLI as in CLI you need to login to the cluster to run a script. You can also run a query on that script and save it for future purpose.

In hue browser, you have an option to manage the metastore through which you can access the metastore in master node or in RDS DB. In that, you can view all information of metastore like owner, creation time of metastore, table type, etc. job browser is also available to view the job status. The server log is also available to view or for download.

In hue, you have oozie editor option which is workflow scheduler system to manage Hadoop jobs. With oozie, you can schedule sqoop jobs that are batch data migration tool for transferring data between relational DB and Hadoop. In hue, you have multiple

authentication providers, so you do not need to manage individual user in Hue. The authentication providers are LDAP, PAM, SPNEGO, OAuth, etc.

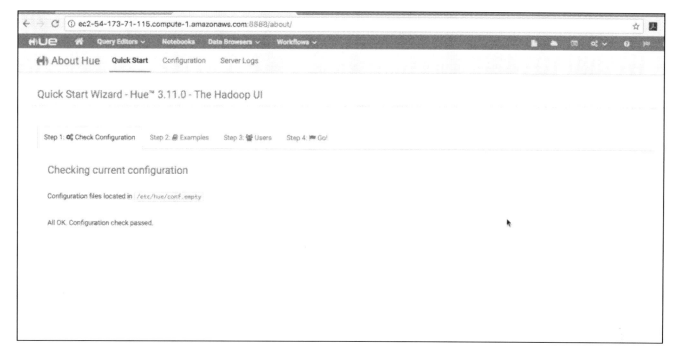

Figure 4-19: Hue Window (a)

Setup hue for LDAP

1. Go to hue browser and go to the configuration tab.
2. In the config section go to the desktop.
3. Now login to the cluster via CLI and go to cd /etc/hue/conf
4. In this directory, you have ini format file.
5. View the file "vi hue.ini."
6. LDAP settings are defined here.
7. Now put these LDAP setting configuration file in JSON format into the s3 bucket as it is the best place to put configuration for security purpose.
8. Now at creation time of cluster configure software configuration as "use load json from S3" where you specify that JSON file.
9. Now hue is configured with LDAP.

Hive on EMR

Hive is a data warehouse infrastructure built on top of Hadoop. It is used to summarize query and analyze the large data sets. All these things are done via an SQL-like interface (Hive-QL). Hive is useful for non-java programmers. Hadoop implemented in Java, so

Hive provides you SQL abstraction to integrate Hive QL queries into Java API without writing the java program.

Hive is a high-level programming language, which is easy to read, write and maintain, but it needs an interpreter as its functions and commands are not directly implemented on server or processor.

Use Cases

- It is used in the processing of logs and performs analytics on these processed logs
- For joining large tables
- Batch job
- As-hoc interactive queries against the data in HDFS and S3

Architecture

Hive QL queries issues via hive CLI or hue, but you can use JDBC and ODBC along with third-party rules to issue queries. Then for programmatically accessing Hive by applications created using Ruby, PHP, Python, etc. need Thrift server service. Once application sends query reuqest then driver receives Hive QL statement and compiles, and executes Hive QL. In Hive, metastore is also present which is for more information about data.

Now query converts into MapReduce code and executed by YARN which allocates the resources among the cluster. You also have Tez option which is for improving the performance for batch and interactive queries then after that it coordinates with YARN for resource allocation. For tez query is converted in tez.

In the newer versions of EMR, there is by default Tez for execution engine rather than MapReduce. After that, query runs against the data in HDFS and S3. Data stored in both is of different format.

The Hive with EMR is directly integrated with S3 and DynamoDB. EMR also has a connector for Kinesis stream if you want to use Hive for data in Kinesis.

Let's discuss S3 in EMR, EMR can read and write to and from the S3. EMRFS extended Hadoop to access S3 data as a file system. In a Hive, partitioning is also supported so if using Hive with EMR, partitioning is supported for S3. Partitioning is done in two ways: time based and source based. As we know, DynamoDB is also highly integrated with EMR where you are joining Hive and DyanmoDB tables using Hive QL. You can also query data in DyanmoDB via Hive QL. There are other multiple works that can be done via DyanmoDB connector.

- Copy data from DyanmoDB to HDFS or vice versa

- Copy data from DyanmoDB to S3
- Copy Data from S3 to DyanmoDB

In Hive, Serialize and De-serialize (SerDe) concept which allows Hive to read and write to HDFS or EMRFS in any format or vice versa. In SerDe to read log file "RegEx SerDe" is used while for writing in SerDe you can use any format file like JSON SerDe.

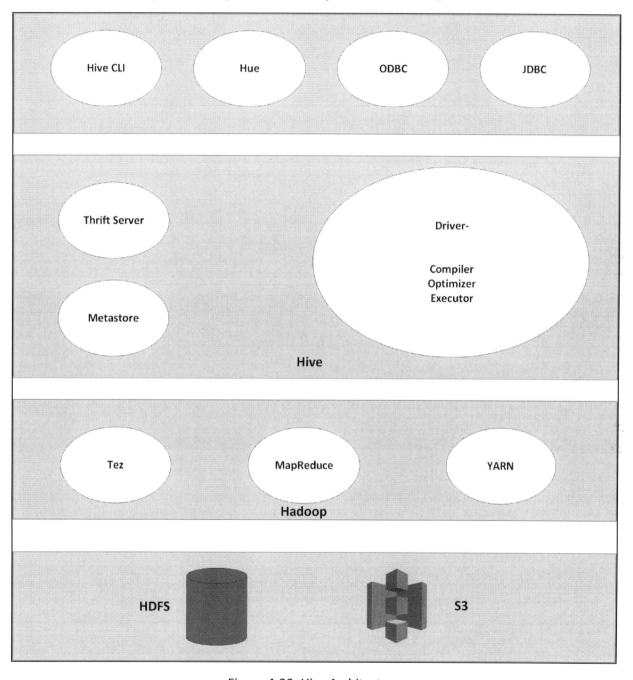

Figure 4-20: Hive Architecture

HBase with EMR

HBase is massively scalable, distributed big data store in the Apache Hadoop ecosystem. It is an open source on a relational, versioned database which runs on top of Amazon S3 (using EMRFS) or HDFS. It is built for random, strictly consistent real-time access for tables with billions of rows and millions of columns.

Apache HBase integrates with Apache Hadoop, Apache Hive, Apache phoenix so in this way, you can combine massively parallel analytics with fast data access.

Use Cases

- For Ad-tech companies where clickstream is analyzing is needed.
- Content (Facebook/Spotify)
- Financial Data

Where to use HBase

- If you have a large amount of data like 100s of GB to PB then via HBase, you can put them in a distributed environment.
- For high throughput and update rates
- For NoSQL, flexible schema
- For fast access to data, randomly and real-time
- Fault tolerance in a non-relational environment

Where not to use HBase

- Transactional application
- Relational database type feature
- A small amount of data

HBase v/s DynamoDB

1. HBase database model is a wide column while DynamoDB model is key-value store
2. In size restriction, HBase has no restriction while DynamoDB has an item size restriction
3. Hbase is a flexible row key data type while DynamoDB has a scalar type.
4. In HBase index created manually while DynamoDB it is much easier

HBase v/s Redshift

1. In terms of storage both are column oriented.
2. HBase is used where high write throughput and updates perform well while in Redshift Batch Write means copy command used and updates are slow.

3. HBase is used for real-time lookup and Redshift used for OLAP (joins, queries, aggregation)

HBase Architecture

In HBase architecture, there is zookeeper which is used to maintain the service state in the cluster. It provides which service is available and alive and sends server failure notification. In HBase tables are split into the region and serve by region servers.

Hmaster is a service in architecture that distributes service to different regions and also assign region to a region server. Hbase has a built-in type of HDFS for storing and retrieving data.

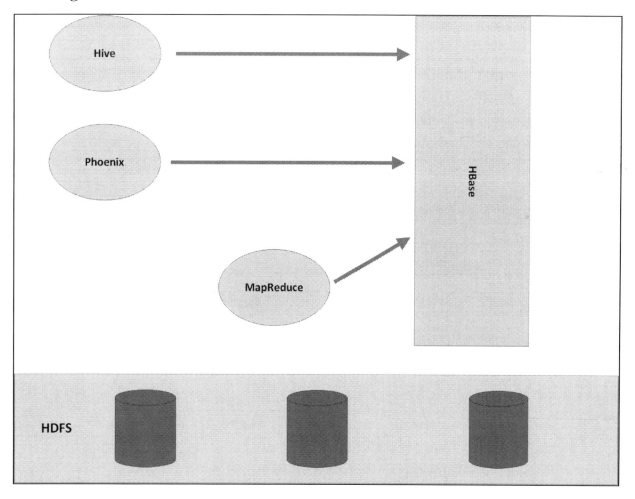

Figure 4-21: HBase Architecture

HBase and EMRFS

When HBase and EMR are running, then Zookeeper runs on EMR cluster. Core node and task node are regional servers. If you use HDFS then chose HDFS on the core node, but if you use EMRFS, then you get some benefits like direct access to S3.

HBase integration

It integrates with Hadoop, so the tables in Hbase are concerned as input and output for MapReduce job run in Hadoop. To access the HBase table, you can use Hive or Apache Phoenix. Or, if you want direct access to the HBase table without using Hive and Phoenix then use Hbase shell.

Presto with EMR

Presto is an Open Source in-memory fast distributed SQL Query engine. It is used to run interactive analytics queries against a variety of data source with size ranging from GBs to PBs. It is significantly faster than Hive.

Advantages of Presto

1. You can use Presto for querying different types of data source from Relational DB, NoSQL DB, and frameworks like Hive to stream processing platform like Kafka. In Presto, you have a connector that is used to access data from data sources. When use connector with cluster you need to define JSON format file.
2. It has high concurrency like it runs thousands of queries per day
3. In-memory processing, it helps you to avoid necessary I/O, lead to low latency.
4. Presto runs directly on resto engine, so there is no need to use an interpreter.

Not To use Presto

1. It is not a typical database and not designed for OLTP
2. Joining very large tables then optimization required so better to use Hive.
3. Batch Processing

Presto Architecture

- Queries from the client via CLI and sends to the coordinator.
- Coordinator process, analyze and plan the execution.
- Coordinator use connector for specific data source you are connecting to in order to get metadata from resource and build query plan.
- After query is planned, executor in coordinator perform execution.
- Now coordinator assigns processing to the workers.
- Workers process rows from HDFS and S3.
- The result will besent to the client.

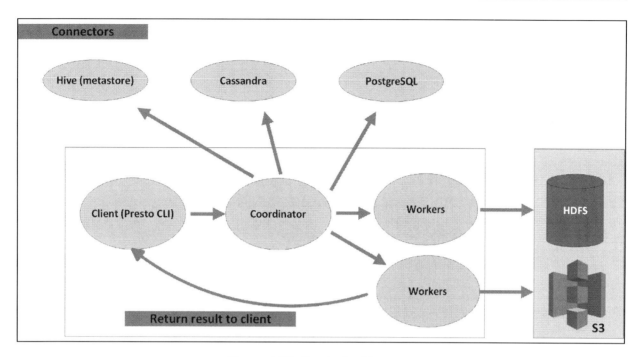

Figure 4-22: Presto Architecture

Spark with EMR

Spark is the fast engine for processing a large amount of data. It can run in-memory 100 times faster than MapReduce. Spark can also run on disk, and it runs 10 times faster than MapReduce. In Big Data, Spark is one of the important tools that are used for processing.

Use Cases

1. Interactive Analysis –it runs query faster than a Hive, also it has flexibility in term of languages. Also, it queries live data (spark 2.0). The feature of live data query is known as structured streaming.

2. Stream processing- in this, it takes data from disparate data sources and data is small in size.

3. Machine Learning- as it uses Machine learning algorithm so if we have repeated queries against the dataset gets then it will be helpful. Machine Learning has MLlib which is used for a recommendation engine, fraud detection, and customer segmentation and security.

4. It is also used in data integration like ETL, so cost and time both reduces.

Not to use Spark

1. It is not a typical database and not designed for OLTP
2. Batch Processing

3. Avoid using it for multi-user reporting environment with high concurrency, but if you have this case, then you can use ETL in Spark to copy data to a typical reporting database.

Spark Components

In Spark stack, there is Spark core which consists of four modules which are referred to as libraries. These modules are Spark SQL, Spark Streaming, MLlib, and Graph-X. Spark stack runs on top of cluster managers like Standalone scheduler, YARN, and Mesos. As you know that in this architecture there are a lot of features, so in this way, we do not need any additional things like if we want query streaming data, then we do not need to install its respective tool, so it reduces cost as well as management.

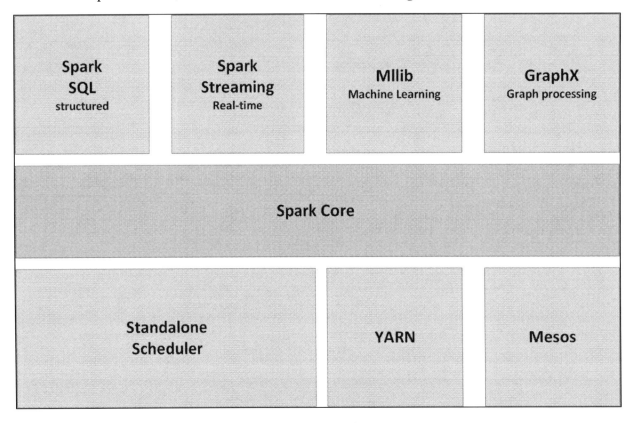

Figure 4-23: Spark Architecture

Spark Core

It is a general execution that has all functionality built. This functionality includes dispatching and scheduling of task along with memory management. Both functionalities expose to API for Scala, Python, Java, R, and SQL. The Spark core supports following API to access the data.

1. Resilient and Distributed Data sets (RDDs)- they are a logical collection of data partitioned across machines.
2. Data set- it is the distributed collection of data
3. Data-frame- it is data set organized into columns.

Spark SQL

It allows you to run low latency, interactive SQL queries against structured data (like from log file or web application). You can use RDDs and Data frame API to access data from a different data source using Scala, Python, R, etc. the format of data is Avro, Parquet, ORC, and JSON. With Spark SQL you can join across data sources. Spark SQL also support query Hive table by using HiveQL. You can also use JDBC and ODBC in Spark SQL to query and copy the data on existing databases.

Spark Streaming

It is an extension core, Spark API in which processing of live data stream is enabled with scalability, high throughput, and fault tolerance. In Spark streaming, data is inserted from HDFS/S3, Kafka then processes the data and sends output to the HDFS, database, and dashboard. Further detail about spark streaming is that it takes input data first and divide into batches then Spark engine processes the batches and sends output also in batches.

MLlib

It is the Spark's scalable machine learning library which gives a lot of out of box scalability and distributed Machine Learning Algorithm. Data read into MLlib is done via HDFS, HBase, or any Hadoop data source. You can also write MLlib application using Scala, Python, etc.

Graph X

It is Spark API for graph and graph-parallel computation that allow to build and transform graph-structured data at scale interactively. It supports a number of graph algorithm.

Cluster Manager

As we know about Spark component, so Spark application runs as an independent set of process on the cluster which is referred to as a driver program. Driver program connects to cluster manager. There is cluster manager that can be used to allocate the resources to the application, once it is connected to the cluster. After that, Spark acquires executers on nodes in the cluster. The driver process is responsible for converting user application into small executer called task. Once the executer acquires by spark on nodes for processes,

they run computation and store data for application. Spark sends application code to the executors and driver program sends the task to the executor to run it.

Spark does not need Hadoop as it runs standalone scheduler as long as file system stored. You can run spark on EMR with standalone scheduler but EMR by default using YARN. By using YARN, you can get the benefit of Kerberos authentication, dynamic allocation, Dynamic sharing, and central configuration of the resource.

You can also use mesos which allow storing resource between Hadoop and Spark, Kafka and Elasticsearch. Mesos do this for API in resource management and scheduling across the data center and cloud environment.

Spark Integration With EMR

When spark run on EMR, then its processing engine is deployed on each node of the cluster. The spark framework replaces MapReduce Framework, but sparks SQL still be able to interact with HDFS or S3 also available. You can integrate spark with multiple AWS service like DynamoDB, Redshift, Kinesis, Elasticsearch, RDS.

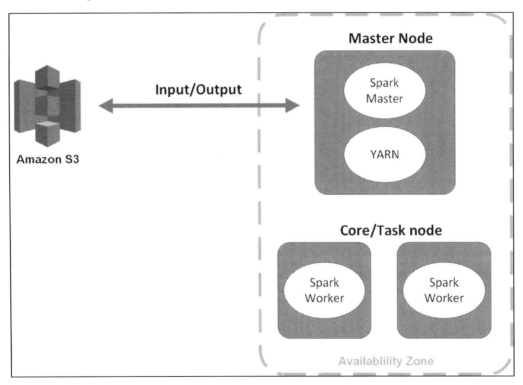

Figure 4-24: Spark Integration with EMR

Let's discuss Spark integration with DynamoDB and Kinesis Stream from exam perspective.

Spark Streaming and Stream

As we know basic Spark working so for streaming input data Spark streaming has a high-level abstraction called Dstream (Discretised Stream) which is for continuous streaming of data. Dstream created to form the Input data stream via data source likeKinesis stream. It is basically the collection of RDDs and transformation applied to RDDs and then results are sent to the destination like HDFS, Database, and dashboard.

Now discuss spark stream with Kinesis stream. There is Kinesis producer that is developed from Kinesis producer library for Spark. Now from the producers, data is sent to Kinesis stream where the shards present that take data. In the last, there is a connection between the Kinesis stream and Spark stream. Spark stream uses the Kinesis client library to consume the data from Kinesis stream. This Kinesis library handles complex things like a Load balancer, failure recovery, and checks priority. To build consumer application as we discussed above, we use the Kinesis Client library for Spark, and this library is provided by Amazon in the software license. Consumer application instantiates the worker with configuration information then use the record processor to process the data received from shards in Kinesis stream. And after processing the output is sent to Redshift and S3.

Spark streaming with Redshift

Spark can be used for extraction, transformation, and loading (ETL) of a large amount of data. This can be done by Hive table in HDFS or S3, text file, parquet, etc. when you use Spark with ETL, then it is a benefit in performance. After the ETL process, you can shift data to Redshift for analysis. For integration of Spark with Redshift, you need a library which is provided by databricks. This library reads data from Redshift and writes back into the Redshift by loading data into Spark SQL data frames. To do all these, you need following steps; first in Redshift execute Redshift UNLOAD command to copy data to S3. The files in S3 are read and Spark SQL DataFrames are generated. After generation these data frames they registered as a temporary table, and SQL query can be executed directly against it. You can use Spark Redshift library with various sources like S3, Hive tables, text files on HDFS.

Spark with DynamoDB

You can also use DyanmoDB with Spark for storage of data from Spark ETL processing, but for that, you need to use DyanmoDB connector which is already installed in an EMR cluster. DynamoDB connector has Hadoop library in it to interact with Spark.

EMR File Storage and Compression

In this, we will discuss HDFS v/s S3. If you are using HDFS, then your data is by default split into chunks by Hadoop automatically. If your data is stored in S3 then Hadoop will split data on S3 by reading files in multiple HTTP range requests.

Using compression algorithm that allows splitting which is one of the important factors when using HDFS and S3 because if compression algorithm does not allow splitting then, Hadoop does not split the data file and use single map task to process that compresses the file.

If compressed file allows the splitting, then Hadoop splits the compressed file into chunks and process chunks in parallel.

Algorithm	Splitable	Compression Ratio	Compress-Decompress speed
GZIP	No	High	Medium
Bzip2	Yes	Very high	Slow
LZO	Yes	Low	Fast
Snappy	No	Low	Very fast

Table 4-02: Compression Algorithm

Hadoop checks the extension of the file to detect compressed files, so from exam point of view you need to remember this table.

Compression

Compression is one of the useful facts for a number of reasons. Performance is the primary benefit or reason for using compression. With this, you get better processing performance when less data is transferred between S3, mapper, and reducers. When you use compression, then you have less network traffic between S3 and EMR. The cost also reduces for storage.

Supported File Format

- Text (CSV and fav)
- Parquet (Columnar oriented file format)
- Sequence (Flat files consisting of binary key/value pair)

- ORC (Optimized Row Columnar file format one of the best and efficient places to store Hive data)
- Avro (Data serialization framework which uses JSON for primary data type and protocol. The serialize data is in compact binary format)

File Size

- As we know that GZIP file is not split-able, so keep its file size between 1-2 GB range.
- Avoid using small files (100MB or less). Plan to use a few large files
- You can use S3DistCp to combine small files into large files. S3DistCp is an extension of DistCp which allows copying data between cluster or within the cluster. As we use S3DistCp to copy between S3 to HDFS, S3 buckets or HDFS to S3. S3DistCp can also define in step if you want to copy the file as a part of the cluster.

Lab 4.1: EMR

Scenario:

An organization needs a tool for big data analytics for analyzing its large data set. They also want to check query from different querying tools, for all this, first they need to identify which querying tool perform query fast.

Solution:

For the requirement, they use Elastic MapReduce tool for analyzing the process and in that use Hive and Spark for querying.

1. First, create a Security group with appropriate SSH rule for EMR master node.

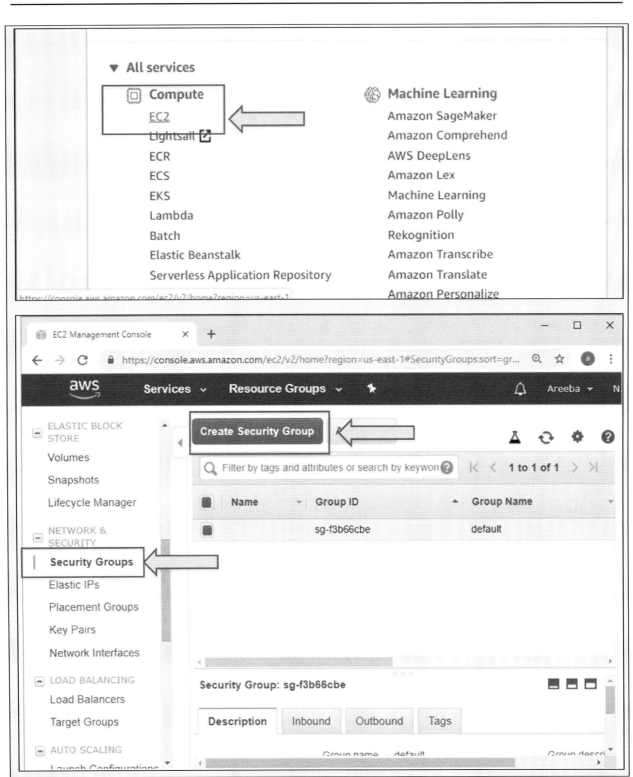

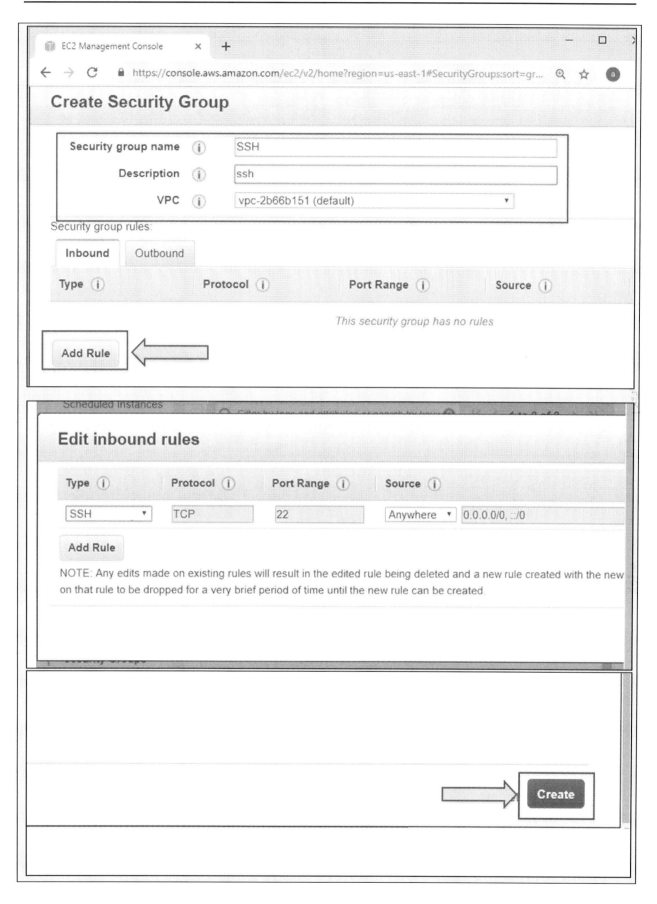

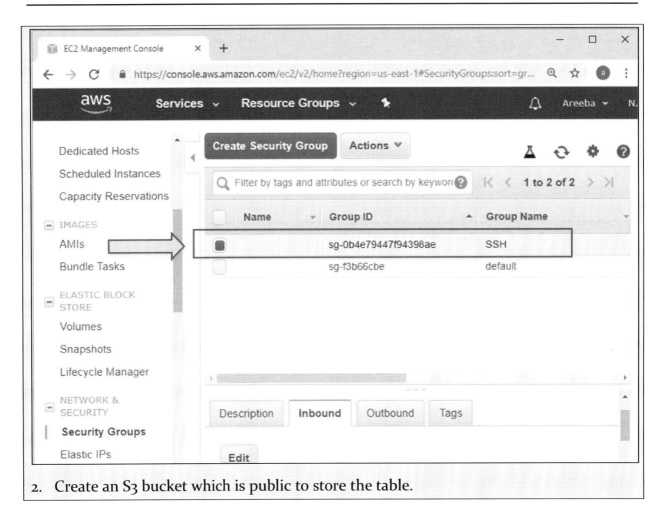

2. Create an S3 bucket which is public to store the table.

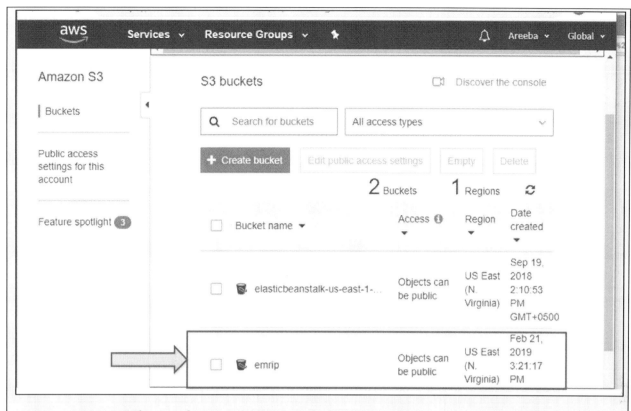

3. Go to EMR under Analytics on AWS Console

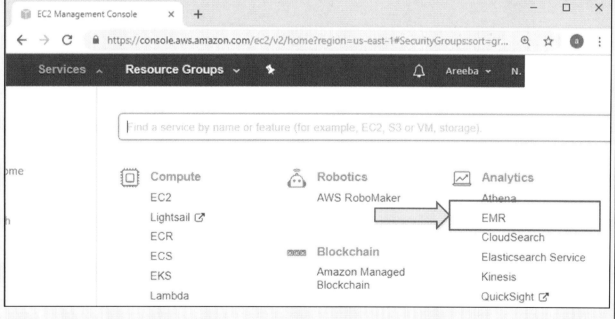

4. Click on Create Cluster and go to advanced options.

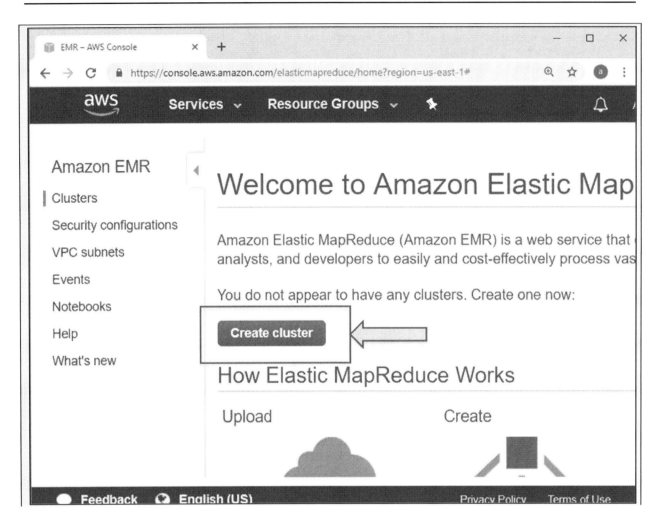

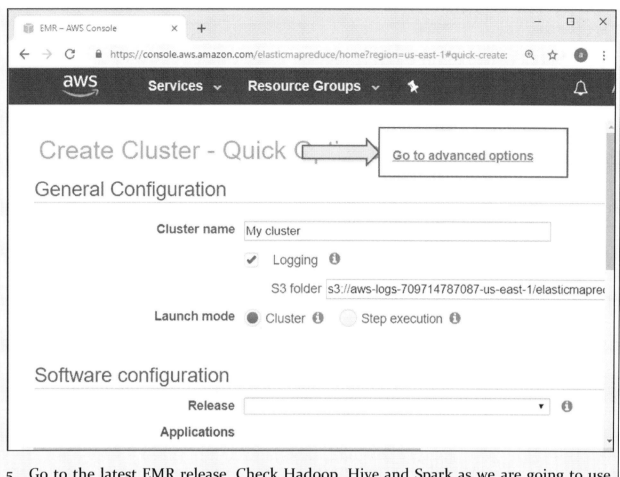

5. Go to the latest EMR release. Check Hadoop, Hive and Spark as we are going to use these tools. Click Next.

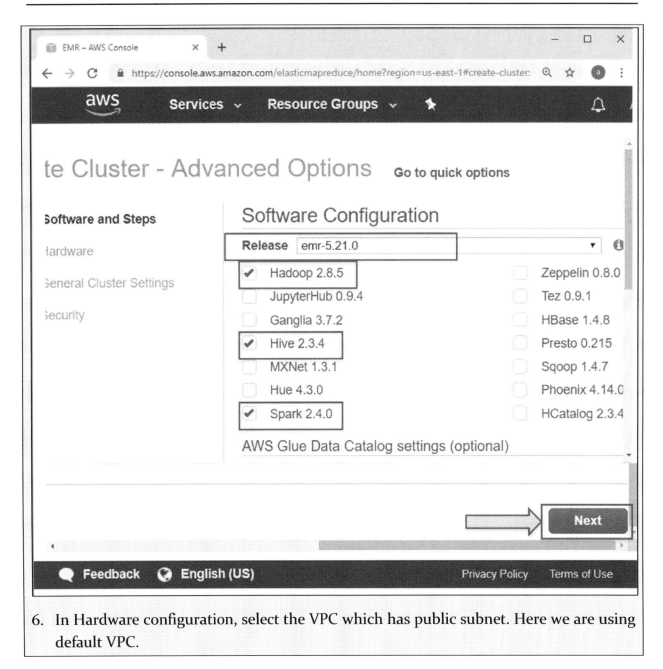

6. In Hardware configuration, select the VPC which has public subnet. Here we are using default VPC.

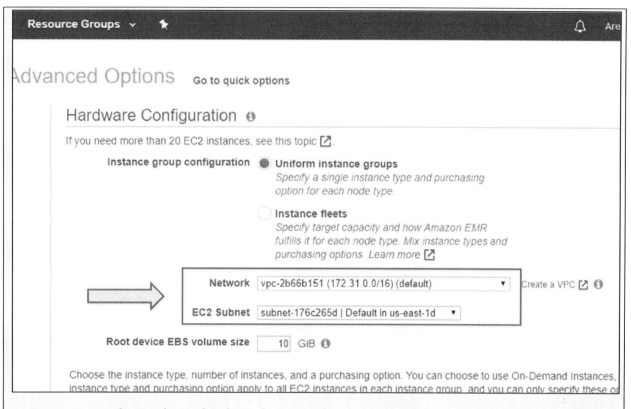

7. Now go to the node and select the type for master node and its purchasing option. There is no need for a core node and task node.

Node type	Instance type	Instance count	Purchasing option
Master Master - 1 ✎	m3.xlarge ✎ 8 vCore, 15 GiB memory, 80 SSD GB storage EBS Storage: none ✎	1 Instances	● On-demand ❶ ○ Spot ❶ Use on-demand as max price
Core Core - 2 ✎	m3.xlarge ✎ 8 vCore, 15 GiB memory, 80 SSD GB storage EBS Storage: none ✎	0 Instances	● On-demand ❶ ○ Spot ❶ Use on-demand as max price
Task ✖ Task - 3 ✎	m3.xlarge ✎ 8 vCore, 15 GiB memory, 80 SSD GB storage EBS Storage: none ✎	0 Instances	● On-demand ❶ ○ Spot ❶ Use on-demand as max price

8. Click Next

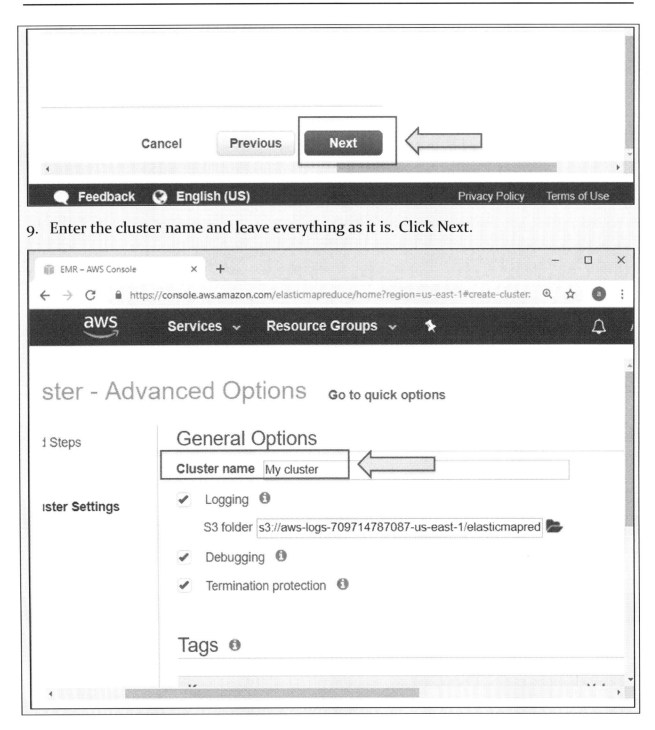

9. Enter the cluster name and leave everything as it is. Click Next.

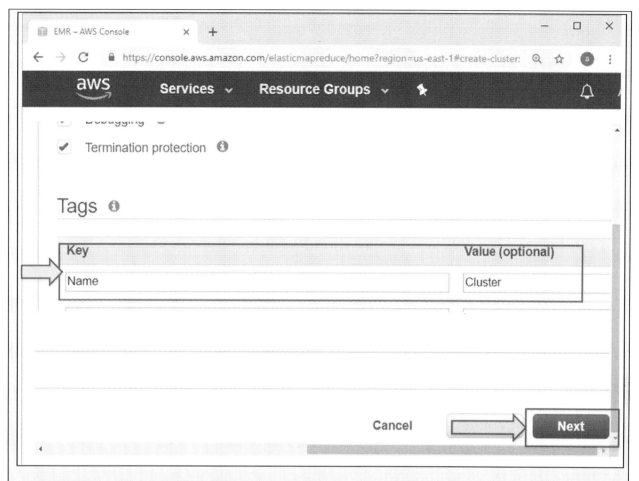

10. In security option, select EC2 key pair as we want that to SSH the master node. Here we have used the key which already created in EC2 service.

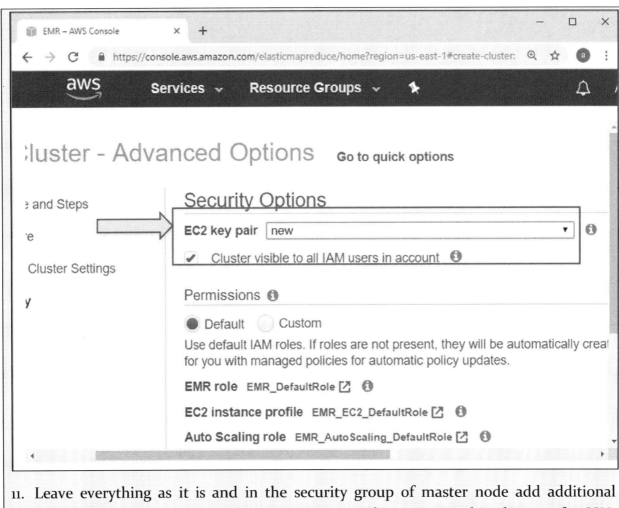

11. Leave everything as it is and in the security group of master node add additional security group. Here we add that Security group that we created in the start for SSH. Click on Assign Security group.

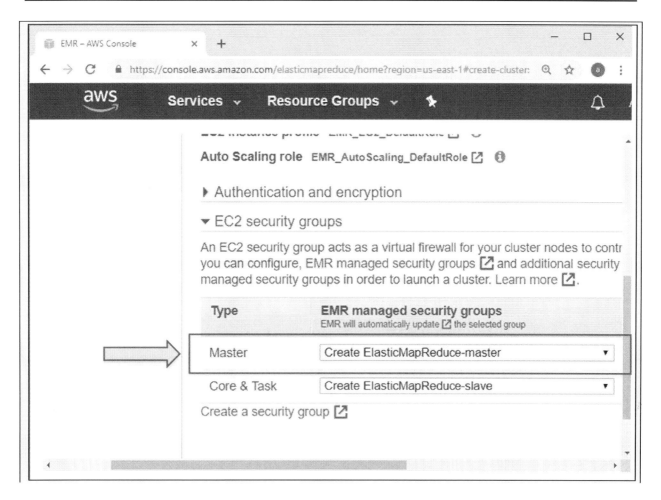

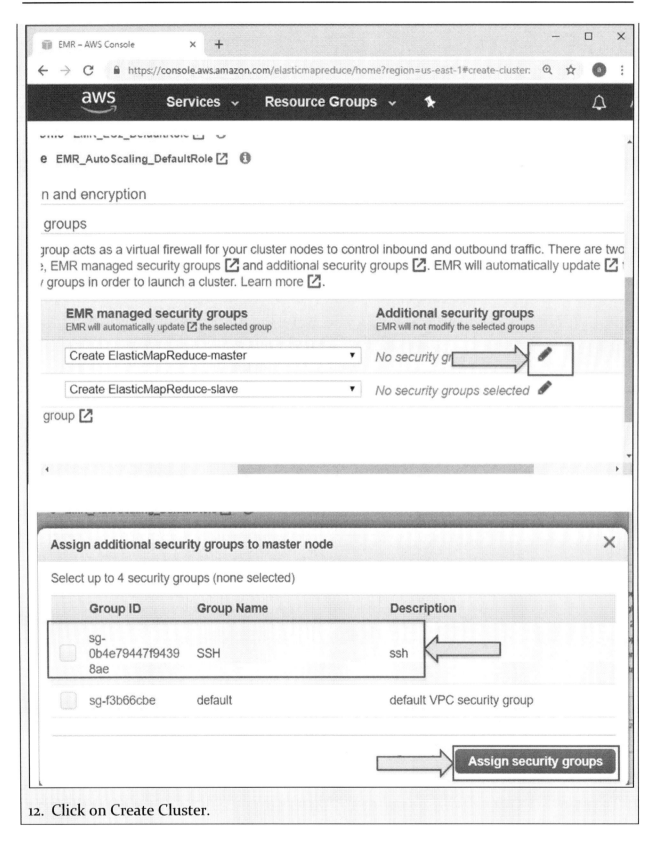

12. Click on Create Cluster.

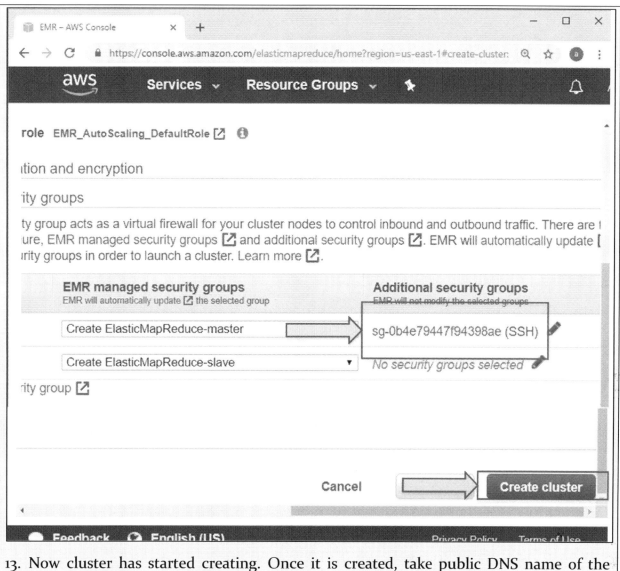

13. Now cluster has started creating. Once it is created, take public DNS name of the cluster for SSH.

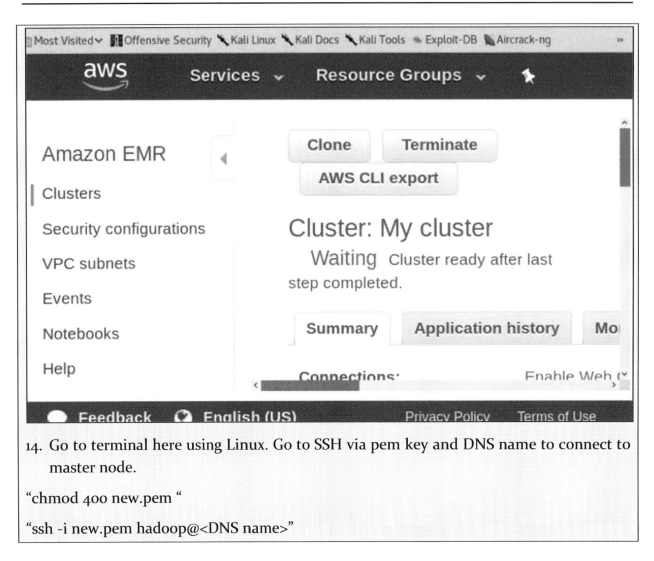

14. Go to terminal here using Linux. Go to SSH via pem key and DNS name to connect to master node.

"chmod 400 new.pem "

"ssh -i new.pem hadoop@<DNS name>"

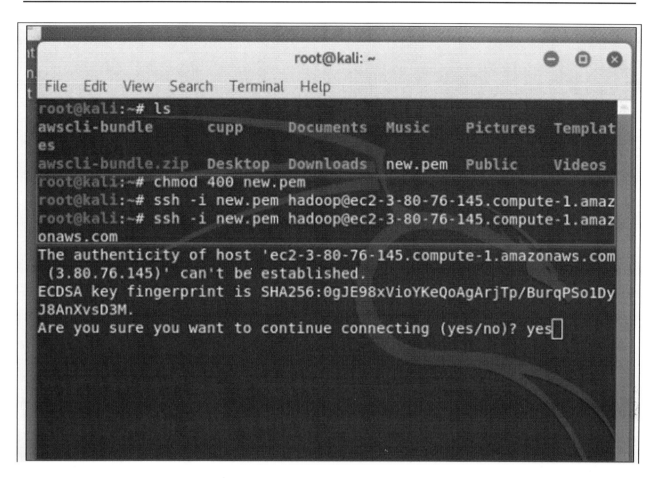

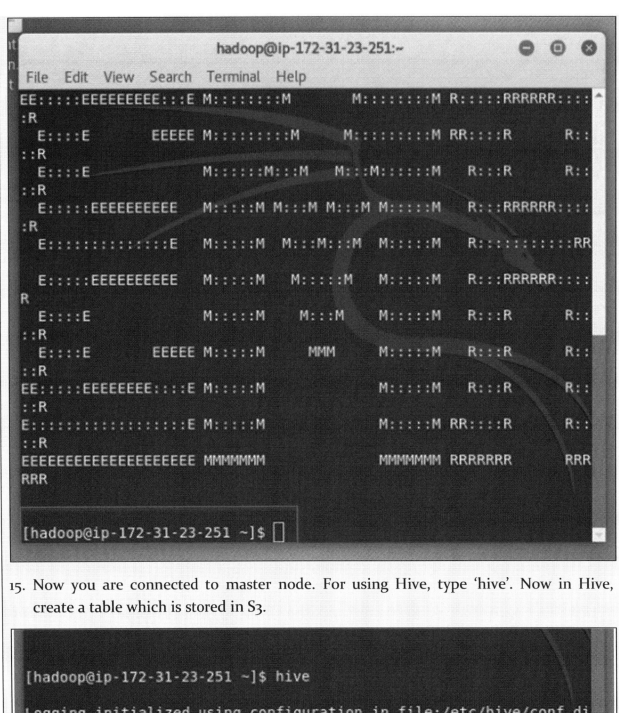

15. Now you are connected to master node. For using Hive, type 'hive'. Now in Hive, create a table which is stored in S3.

create external table <tablename1>

(O_ORDERKEY INT,

O_CUSTKEY INT,

O_ORDERSTATUS STRING,

O_TOTALPRICE DOUBLE,

O_ORDERDATE STRING,

O_ORDERPRIORITY STRING,

O_CLERK STRING,

O_SHIPPRIORITY INT,

O_COMMENT STRING)

ROW FORMAT DELIMITED FIELDS TERMINATED BY '|'

LOCATION 's3://<bucket name>/<foldername>/';

insert   into   <table   name1>   values('001','123','Complete','15000','15-01-02','high','Data','1','Ordertable')

```
hive> create external table ips-table    TERMINATED BY '|'
    > (O_ORDERKEY INT,                    data/';
    > O_CUSTKEY INT,
    > O_ORDERSTATUS STRING,
    > O_TOTALPRICE DOUBLE,
    > O_ORDERDATE STRING,
    > O_ORDERPRIORITY STRING,
    > O_CLERK STRING,
    > O_SHIPPRIORITY INT,
    > O_COMMENT STRING)                   ','0.15','0.13','none','inpr
    > ROW FORMAT DELIMITED FIELDS TERMINATED BY '|','HIP',d
    > LOCATION 's3://databaseip/emr1/';
OK
Time taken: 1.013 seconds                 ging);
```

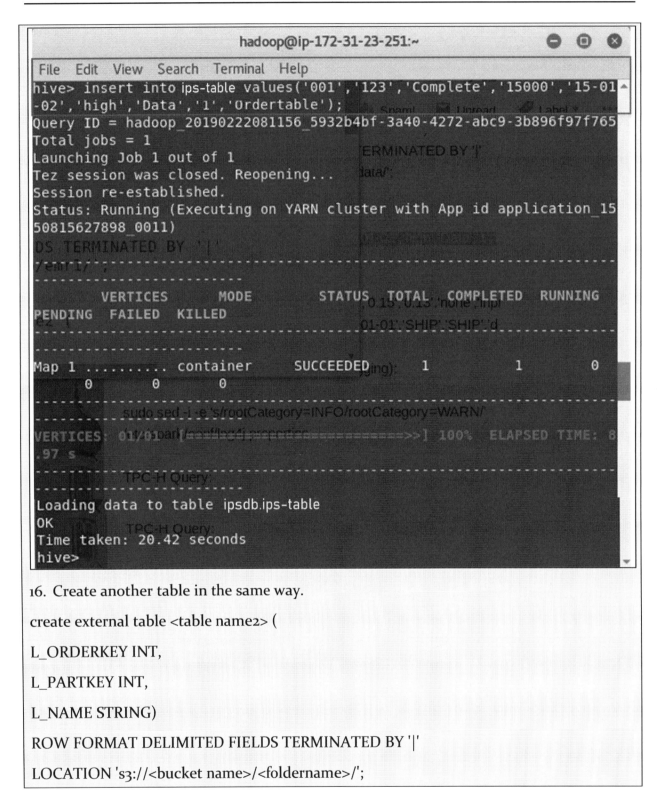

16. Create another table in the same way.

create external table <table name2> (

L_ORDERKEY INT,

L_PARTKEY INT,

L_NAME STRING)

ROW FORMAT DELIMITED FIELDS TERMINATED BY '|'

LOCATION 's3://<bucket name>/<foldername>/';

```
insert    into    <table    name2>    values(001,    123,    complete)
     > ;
hive> create external table line2 (
     > L_ORDERKEY INT,
     > L_PARTKEY INT,
     > L_NAME STRING)
     > ROW FORMAT DELIMITED FIELDS TERMINATED BY '|'
     > LOCATION 's3://databaseip/emr1/';
OK
Time taken: 0.163 seconds
hive> insert into line2 values('001','123','Complete');
Query ID = hadoop_20190222081332_48b32b3e-8f1f-4ae4-98dd-230ed0392fc0
Total jobs = 1
Launching Job 1 out of 1
Status: Running (Executing on YARN cluster with App id application_15
50815627898_0011)

--------------------------------------------------------------------
--------------------------------------------------------------------
        VERTICES      MODE        STATUS  TOTAL  COMPLETED  RUNNING
PENDING  FAILED  KILLED
--------------------------------------------------------------------
```

```
                        hadoop@ip-172-31-23-251:~                    ⊖  ⊡  ⊗
File  Edit  View  Search  Terminal  Help
Time taken: 0.163 seconds
hive> insert into line2 values('001','123','Complete');
Query ID = hadoop_20190222081332_48b32b3e-8f1f-4ae4-98dd-230ed0392fc0
Total jobs = 1
Launching Job 1 out of 1
Status: Running (Executing on YARN cluster with App id application_15
50815627898_0011)

----------------------------------------------------------------------
        VERTICES       MODE      STATUS  TOTAL  COMPLETED  RUNNING
PENDING  FAILED  KILLED
----------------------------------------------------------------------
Map 1 ........... container    SUCCEEDED      1       1         0
        0       0       0
----------------------------------------------------------------------
VERTICES: 01/01 [==========================>>] 100%  ELAPSED TIME: 8
.22 s
----------------------------------------------------------------------

Loading data to table ipsdb.line2
OK
Time taken: 11.446 seconds
```

17. Now both tables have been created. Run query on tables

"select * from <table name1> where O_SHIPPRIORITY = '1'; "

```
hive> select * from ips-table where O_SHIPPRIORITY = '1';
OK
1       123     Complete        15000.0 15-01-02        high    Data
      1       Ordertable
Time taken: 0.507 seconds, Fetched: 1 row(s)
hive> ▯
```

Now you will get the output with the time it takes to run the query.

18. Now turn off verbose logging for Spark SQL query.

"sudo   sed   -i   -e   's/rootCategory=INFO/rootCategory=WARN/'
/etc/spark/conf/log4j.properties"

For Spark SQL type "spark-sql".

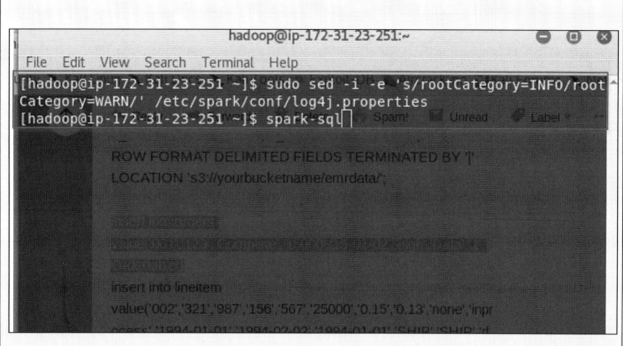

19. Cache the table from Hive via "cache table <table name1>" and "cache table <table name2>".

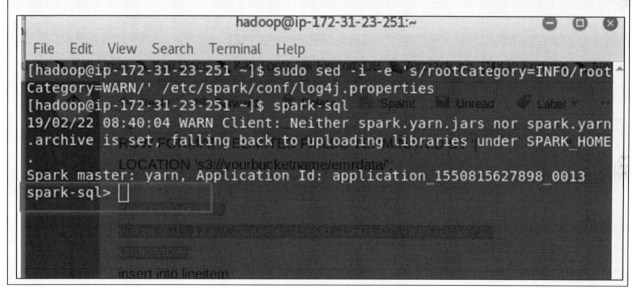

```
                    hadoop@ip-172-31-23-251:~
 File  Edit  View  Search  Terminal  Help
[hadoop@ip-172-31-23-251 ~]$ sudo sed -i -e 's/rootCategory=INFO/root
Category=WARN/' /etc/spark/conf/log4j.properties
[hadoop@ip-172-31-23-251~]$ spark-sql
19/02/22 08:40:04 WARN Client: Neither spark.yarn.jars nor spark.yarn
.archive is set, falling back to uploading libraries under SPARK_HOME
.
Spark master: yarn, Application Id: application_1550815627898_0013
spark-sql> cache table ips-table
```

20. After caching both tables into Spark memory, you have to run the query so remember that Spark query is compatible with the Hive metastore so you do not need to create the table again in Spark.

```
                    hadoop@ip-172-31-23-251:~
 File  Edit  View  Search  Terminal  Help
hadoop@ip-172-31-23-251 ~]$ sudo sed -i -e 's/rootCategory=INFO/root
ategory=WARN/' /etc/spark/conf/log4j.properties
hadoop@ip-172-31-23-251~]$ spark-sql
9/02/22 08:40:04 WARN Client: Neither spark.yarn.jars nor spark.yarn
archive is set, falling back to uploading libraries under SPARK_HOME
park master: yarn, Application Id: application_1550815627898_0013
park-sql> cache table ips-table;
ime taken: 20.138 seconds
park-sql> cache table line2;
ime taken: 0.362 seconds
park-sql> select * from ips-table where O_SHIPPRIORITY = '1';       <===
```

21. Now copy the same query "select * from <table name1> where O_SHIPPRIORITY = '1'; and you observe that the time taken in Spark for the query is less than the Hive.

```
spark-sql> cache table line2;
Time taken: 0.68 seconds
spark-sql> select * from ips-table where O_SHIPPRIORITY = '1';
1       123       Complete       15000.0 15-01-02       high      Data1
Ordertable
Time taken: 0.215 seconds, Fetched 1 row(s)
spark-sql>
```

AWS Lambda in AWS BigData Ecosystem

To understand this, you need to know about AWS Lambda. You might know AWS Lambda in detail, not as a refresher, we will discuss basic details about Lambda.

Lambda is Function as a Service (FaaS) product which means you have function provided with code and AWS execute that code. In this, unlikely of traditional Compute, you are only billed for amount of milliseconds in which your code run. Lambda runs the code in an isolated environment and also it is stateless, but you are responsible for persistence as the environment where Lambda runs have default access to no information except incoming payload. Lambda does not maintain any result of data after termination of a function, so it is your responsibility to put the result in a secure place.

Lambda functions can be triggered by events enabling you to build event-driven reactive systems. Lambda can be used in various scenarios such as: A Lambda function can be triggered when there are changes occurring in your data, let us say, in an AWS DynamoDB table, or in your S3 bucket. Or, it can be used in response to HTTP requests by using the Amazon API Gateway. So we can say that you can integrate Lambda with other AWS services.

When there are multiple events to respond to, Lambda runs copies of your function in parallel to provide scaling by the size of the workload. Architects use the Lambda function to reduce wasted capacity. You can run Lambda functions for any application; it will scale your code with high availability.

Portions of each Lambda functions are; codes that you want to execute, the configuration which defines how the code will execute, and event sources which detect the events and invoke your function.

It works in such a way that when an event happens, event data with its format is sent to Lambda function. The function then accesses data and performs computation and optionally generate a result. As a result, it does not generate anything, but it may interact with AWS service or make internet HTTP calls. Lambda function can also generate a result in the destination or generate an event in which it needs to interact with AWS service or invoke other Lambda function.

Lambda with S3 is a common pattern like when files arrive at S3 bucket then Lambda function invokes the trigger and performs work as defined after the trigger. It means whenever the operation occurs on S3 it invokes Lambda function.

Lambda is also configurable with DynamoDB. When data is changed in the table, database trigger the style functionality that allows real-time event-driven data processing and summarization.

You can also use Lambda to read records of Kinesis stream and process them if records are detected in the stream. Lambda can also use with Redshift database loader to get the data file in Redshift. Files first pushed in S3 and then automatically loaded into Redshift Cluster.

Lambda can be integrated with IoT. So whenever device sends message or data to IoT service then IoT trigger rule action to invoke Lambda function. Kinesis Firehose also invokes Lambda function to transform incoming source data and then deliver this transform data to S3, Redshift or ElasticSearch.

ElasticSearch can also be integrated with Lambda and S3 to log data into the service. When any new data triggers Lambda, the function runs the processing of data. After that it puts that data into stream data in Elasticsearch domain. For activating the Pipeline when any object sends in S3, you can use Lambda function. By using S3 and Lambda, you can create a serverless architecture to run MapReduce jobs.

 EXAM TIP: Lambda can triggered by the following AWS Services:

Amazon S3, Amazon DynamoDB, Amazon Kinesis Data Streams, Amazon Simple Notification Service, Amazon Simple Email Service, Amazon Simple Queue Service, Amazon Cognito, AWS CloudFormation, Amazon CloudWatch Logs, Amazon CloudWatch Events, AWS CodeCommit, Scheduled Events (powered by Amazon CloudWatch Events), AWS Config, Amazon Alexa, Amazon Lex, Amazon API Gateway, AWS IoT Button, Amazon CloudFront, Amazon Kinesis Data Firehose

Let's discuss an overview of the input after the Lambda function is invoked by an event. There are two input, context object and event object. Context object contains the method and attributes that are used to allow the function to get some information about invocation. You can query the context object to identify a function name or any other information. In general, context object allows the function to see metadata related to its invocation and run time environment. The event object is different based on what event is that like a single data structure (cron).

Limitations of Lambda

There are some limitations of Lambda that are defined below:

- Local temporary disk space within the function for runtime environment is 512 MB.
- Limit of 1024 number of processing and threads
- Maximum execution time is 300 seconds

Lambda and Kinesis Stream

As we know, Lambda automatically reads records of Kinesis stream and processes them if any record is detected in the stream. Lambda polls the stream every second for new records. When Lambda is invoked, it assumes an execution role which is assumed by Lambda automatically to access other AWS services. For picking up the records, AWS Lambda needs permission from Kinesis.

Lambda and Redshift

As we know that Redshift database loader is Lambda-based and used to load files in Redshift. When file sent to S3, Lambda function maintain the list of files to be loaded in Redshift cluster from S3. In DynamoDB table there is a list to manage that data loaded only once. It also shows when the file is uploaded and in which Redshift Table. Lambda function support csv or JSON files. So by using the Lambda, you can increase the scalability, high availability and also the CloudWatch logging. Lambda can also use SNS to send notification about load status.

HCatalog

It is a tool that allows you to access metastore of the table in Hive with other data processing tools like Pig, Spark SQL, and Custom MapReduce Application.

Lab 4.2: HCatalog

Scenario:

An organization needs a tool for big data analytics for analyzing its large data set. They need to access the metastore of the table of Hive.

Solution:

By using HCatalog, you can access the metastore from a different processing tool.

1. Continue the same steps as we did but during cluster creation, select Pig tool as we use this tool for accessing the metastore.
2. Login to SSH connection to master node and go to Hive. Create the table in the same way and insert values in it. Here we use the following table.

create external table student

(STUDENT STRING,

STUDENT_ID INT)

ROW FORMAT DELIMITED FIELDS TERMINATED BY '|';

insert into student values('ipspecialist','001');

```
                        hadoop@ip-172-31-23-251:~
File  Edit  View  Search  Terminal  Help
[hadoop@ip-172-31-23-251 ~]$ hive

Logging initialized using configuration in file:/etc/hive/conf.dist/h
ive-log4j2.properties Async: true
hive> create external table student
    > (STUDENT STRING,
    > STUDENT_ID INT)
    > ROW FORMAT DELIMITED FIELDS TERMINATED BY '|';
OK
Time taken: 1.366 seconds
hive> insert into student values('ipspecialist','001');
Query ID = hadoop_20190222085108_f4ae1f37-39c6-4bcd-9032-ced98b494e65
Total jobs = 1
Launching Job 1 out of 1
Status: Running (Executing on YARN cluster with App id application_15
50815627898_0014)

Map 1: 0/1
Map 1: 0/1
Map 1: 0(+1)/1
Map 1: 1/1
Loading data to table default.student
OK
Time taken: 9.653 seconds
hive> exit:
```

3. Now exit Hive and copy "pig –useHCatalog" command.

```
  'exit'
hive> exit;
[hadoop@ip-172-31-23-251 ~]$ pig -useHCatalog
```

4. You are now in pig tool copy the following command to load the table into a pig.

```
                    hadoop@ip-172-31-23-251:~                    ─ ▢ ✖
 File   Edit   View   Search   Terminal   Help
60     [main] INFO   org.apache.pig.Main   - Logging error messages to: /
mnt/var/log/pig/pig_1550825617393.log
19/02/22 08:53:37 INFO pig.Main: Logging error messages to: /mnt/var/
log/pig/pig_1550825617393.log
84     [main] INFO   org.apache.pig.impl.util.Utils   - Default bootup fi
le /home/hadoop/.pigbootup not found
19/02/22 08:53:37 INFO util.Utils: Default bootup file /home/hadoop/.
pigbootup not found
19/02/22 08:53:38 INFO Configuration.deprecation: mapred.job.tracker
is deprecated. Instead, use mapreduce.jobtracker.address
808    [main] INFO   org.apache.pig.backend.hadoop.executionengine.HExec
utionEngine   - Connecting to hadoop file system at: hdfs://ip-172-31-
23-251.ec2.internal:8020
19/02/22 08:53:38 INFO executionengine.HExecutionEngine: Connecting t
o hadoop file system at: hdfs://ip-172-31-23-251.ec2.internal:8020
1922 [main] INFO   org.apache.pig.PigServer   - Pig Script ID for the s
ession: PIG-default-54512623-e765-4361-bb10-a16f3fc54a7e
19/02/22 08:53:39 INFO pig.PigServer: Pig Script ID for the session:
PIG-default-54512623-e765-4361-bb10-a16f3fc54a7e
19/02/22 08:53:39 INFO impl.TimelineClientImpl: Timeline service addr
ess: http://ip-172-31-23-251.ec2.internal:8188/ws/v1/timeline/
2598 [main] INFO   org.apache.pig.backend.hadoop.PigATSClient   - Creat
ed ATS Hook
19/02/22 08:53:39 INFO hadoop.PigATSClient: Created ATS Hook
grunt> ▯
```

"B = LOAD 'student' USING org.apache.hive.hcatalog.pig.HCatLoader();"

```
19/02/22 08:53:38 INFO executionengine.HExecutionEngine: Connecting t
o hadoop file system at: hdfs://ip-172-31-23-251.ec2.internal:8020
1922 [main] INFO   org.apache.pig.PigServer   - Pig Script ID for the s
ession: PIG-default-54512623-e765-4361-bb10-a16f3fc54a7e
19/02/22 08:53:39 INFO pig.PigServer: Pig Script ID for the session:
PIG-default-54512623-e765-4361-bb10-a16f3fc54a7e
19/02/22 08:53:39 INFO impl.TimelineClientImpl: Timeline service addr
ess: http://ip-172-31-23-251.ec2.internal:8188/ws/v1/timeline/
2598 [main] INFO   org.apache.pig.backend.hadoop.PigATSClient   - Creat
ed ATS Hook
19/02/22 08:53:39 INFO hadoop.PigATSClient: Created ATS Hook
grunt> B = LOAD 'student' USING org.apache.hive.hcatalog.pig.HCatLoad
er();
```

5. Now use Dump operator to get the result "dump B;"

```
File  Edit  View  Search  Terminal  Help
utionEngine  - Connecting to hadoop file system at: hdfs://ip-172-31-
23-251.ec2.internal:8020
19/02/22 08:53:38 INFO executionengine.HExecutionEngine: Connecting t
o hadoop file system at: hdfs://ip-172-31-23-251.ec2.internal:8020
1922 [main] INFO  org.apache.pig.PigServer  - Pig Script ID for the s
ession: PIG-default-54512623-e765-4361-bb10-a16f3fc54a7e
19/02/22 08:53:39 INFO pig.PigServer: Pig Script ID for the session:
PIG-default-54512623-e765-4361-bb10-a16f3fc54a7e
19/02/22 08:53:39 INFO impl.TimelineClientImpl: Timeline service addr
ess: http://ip-172-31-23-251.ec2.internal:8188/ws/v1/timeline/
2598 [main] INFO  org.apache.pig.backend.hadoop.PigATSClient  - Creat
ed ATS Hook
19/02/22 08:53:39 INFO hadoop.PigATSClient: Created ATS Hook
grunt> B = LOAD 'student' USING org.apache.hive.hcatalog.pig.HCatLoad
er();
19/02/22 08:54:36 INFO conf.HiveConf: Found configuration file file:/
etc/hive/conf.dist/hive-site.xml
19/02/22 08:54:36 INFO common.HiveClientCache: Initializing cache: ev
iction-timeout=120 initial-capacity=50 maximum-capacity=50
19/02/22 08:54:36 INFO hive.metastore: Trying to connect to metastore
 with URI thrift://ip-172-31-23-251.ec2.internal:9083
19/02/22 08:54:36 INFO hive.metastore: Opened a connection to metasto
re, current connections: 1
19/02/22 08:54:36 INFO hive.metastore: Connected to metastore.
grunt> dump B;
```

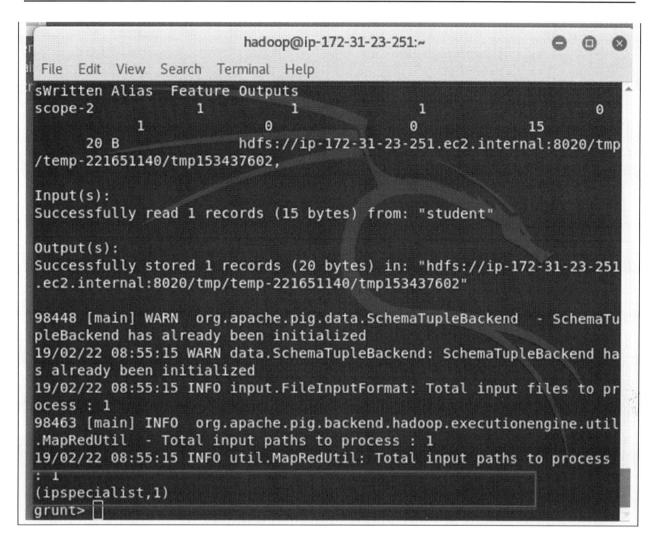

MindMap

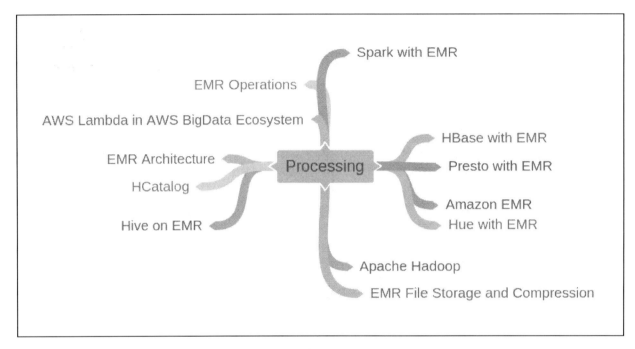

Figure 4-25: Chapter Mind Map

Practice Question

1. How many modules does Spark have?
   A. 1
   B. 2
   C. 4
   D. 3

2. From the following, what are the Spark modules (Select 4)?
   A. Apache Mesos
   B. Spark SQL
   C. Graph X
   D. YARN
   E. MLlib
   F. Spark Streaming

3. From the following options, which compression algorithm is used for the highest compression ratio to maximize the performance of S3?
   A. Bzip2
   B. Snappy
   C. GZIP
   D. LZO

4. An organization has a huge amount of data in different data sources, and its employees need to query the data. The queries are processed in-memory, and avoid high I/O and latency. Which open source its employees used as they do not know about the language for multiple data sources?
   A. Hive
   B. Spark SQL
   C. Big Data Query Engine
   D. Presto

5. Is Presto a Database engine?
   A. True
   B. False

6. Which storage option does EMR cluster use for high I/O performance at low cost?
   A. EMRFS

B. Instance Store

C. EBS volume with IOPS

D. EMRFS with consistency view

7. For consuming data from Kinesis stream, Spark streaming use?

A. Kinesis Connector Library

B. Kinesis Client Library

C. Kinesis Consumer Library

D. Kinesis Producer Library

8. When you use EBS with EMR, then it will persist even after the cluster terminated?

A. False

B. True

9. In which case would you prefer not to use Spark?

A. Interactive analyzing

B. Batch processing

C. Machine Learning

D. ETL workloads

10. Which open source tool can you use to manage the metastore, run queries and view server logs?

A. Ganglia

B. Zeppelin

C. YARN

D. Hue

11. From the following options, which slave node does not have HDFS?

A. Task

B. Master

C. Core

D. None of the above

12. How many components does apache Hadoop have?

A. 1

B. 4

C. 6

D. 8

13. From the Hadoop architecture which module is for processing of large datasets with the parallel distributed algorithm on a cluster?

A. YARN

B. HDFS

C. Hadoop common

D. Hadoop MapReduce

14. Resource manager resides in _____

A. Master node

B. Task node

C. Core node

D. None of the above

15. In master instance group you have _____ instance/s

A. 2

B. 1

C. 3

D. 4

16. The default replication factor in HDFS is _____

A. 2

B. 5

C. 3

D. 6

17. Which file system stores cluster data directly into the Amazon S3?

A. HDFS

B. EMRFS

C. Both

D. None of these have the capability to do this

18. In which case would you prefer to use Hive?
A. Interactive analyzing
B. Batch processing
C. Machine Learning
D. ETL workload

19. In which case, would you prefer not to use HBase?
A. For ad-tech companies where clickstream is analyzing is needed.
B. Content (Facebook/Spotify)
C. Financial Data
D. Relational database type feature

20. HBase is used for real-time lookup
A. True
B. False

Chapter 05: Analysis

Introduction

This chapter is related to the analysis of Big data by using various Amazon services such as RedShift, SageMaker, Elasticsearch, RStudio, and Athena.

RedShift

RedShift is an enterprise-class relational database query and management system provided by AWS, which is a fully managed warehouse service for data. Its storage scale is up to petabytes or more. This service was first introduced in November 2012, and it is one of the fastest growing services of AWS. This service is dedicated to the Online Analytic Processing (OLAP) and Business Intelligence (BI) Applications. It is not recommended to use RedShift for Online Transaction Processing (OLTP) because OLTP stores data in rows whereas RedShift stores data in columns. RedShift is ANSI SQL compatible service.

Why learn RedShift?

- It is a cost-effective solution to provision multi-terabyte clusters in minutes.
- It is the easiest way to store and manage a large amount of data.
- The data should be stored and managed properly, as RedShift receives data from different types of applications.
- RedShift can be used with other AWS services to offer practical solutions.
- RedShift can be added to an existing skill set for earning potential.

Used cases of RedShift

- Traditional Data Warehousing: RedShift provides data warehousing in 20 times the lower cost.
- Log Analysis: RedShift makes it possible to store raw data.
  Mission-critical workloads Business applications.

RedShift Architecture

Cluster

A set of nodes is known as RedShift cluster. All the nodes of cluster are in a single Availability zone selected by the user.

Leader Node

Leader node assists the communication between the SQL clients or BI tools and Compute nodes. Some of the SQL functions can only be applied through the leader node; you cannot use a compute node for them. There is a SQL endpoint in each leader node.

The Function of the Leader Node

- Leader node coordinate the parallel query execution. When a query is received by SQL client to a leader node, the leader node develops an execution plan based on the client in which it compiles a code of C++ and then delivers it to compute node. Then this query is executed by compute nodes and data is sent back to the leader node. The output results are displayed in the SQL client.
- Leader node is also responsible for storing metadata. The metadata is provided by compute nodes. The compute nodes have log files, which are sent to the leader node. Leader node stores them in system tables.

Compute Node

- Parallel query execution takes place in multiple compute nodes. When the leader node compiles the code and sends it to compute nodes, all compute nodes execute this code and then send the result back to the leader node, which is then delivered to the SQL client.
- Compute nodes have Memory, CPU and local storage.
- Compute node scaling is possible, i.e., they can be scaled: in/out or up/down.
- For the backup purpose, compute nodes use S3. This backup process takes place in parallel.
- Each compute nodes consist of slices. They are the portions of disk or memory. Data is loaded in parallel. The total number of slices are dependent on the type of compute node.

High-speed network

RedShift operates on 10Gbit Ethernet mesh network for maximizing throughputs between the nodes.

Types of Nodes:

There are two types of generation, i.e. Current generation and Previous generation.

Current generation Node

Dense Compute Nodes

Supports high-performance databases. It provides fast CPUs, high RAM, and SSD.

Dense Storage Nodes

Supports large data warehouses and provides hard disk drives.

	vCPU	ECU	Memory (GiB)	Storage	I/O	Price/hr
Dense Compute						
dc2.large	2	7	15	0.16 TB SSD	0.6 GB/sec	$ 0.25
dc2.8xlarge	32	99	244	2.56 TB SSD	7.5 GB/sec	$ 4.80
Dense Storage						
ds2.xlarge	4	14	31	2TB HDD	0.4 GB/sec	$ 0.85
ds2.8xlarge	36	116	244	16TB HDD	3.3 GB/sec	$ 6.80

Table 5-01: Current Generation Nodes Price

Previous Generation Compute Nodes

They can be used, but concerning price and specification, the current generation is better.

MPP Database

RedShift is a Massive Parallel Processing Database (MPP). Where data is stored in multiple nodes having dedicated CPU, Memory and Local storage. Nodes are self-sufficient and independent, i.e., disk sharing is not required. This is one of the reasons why RedShift can deal with a large number of data sets.

RedShift in the AWS Ecosystem

AWS provides some services that can integrate directly with RedShift. Some of the services help in data migration to RedShift, and some can be used as a part of RedShift cluster.

Amazon S3

It is the most important service used with RedShift. S3 may act as the main source of loading data into RedShift. Data can be unloaded from RedShift into S3. Copy command and unload commands are used to integrate with RedShift.

IAM role for security is used as credentials.

Amazon DynamoDB

DynamoDB is the AWS fully managed SQL Database service. For transferring data from DynamoDB table to RedShift, the copy command is used.

Amazon EMR

Data can be loaded to RedShift from Amazon EMR, using copy command which is done by SSH.

Amazon EC2

Data can be loaded to RedShift from Amazon EC2 Instance, using copy command which is done by SSH.

AWS Data Pipeline

For moving and processing data in and out of Amazon RedShift, AWS Data Pipeline is used.

The recurring job can also be processed, for example, if you have a job where you want to copy data to RedShift from DynamoDB or S3. Similarly, if you want to unload data out of RedShift, then Data pipeline can be used.

AWS Lambda

AWS Lambda is a serverless event-driven computing platform provided by AWS. Combination of Amazon Lambda with RedShift enables you to automatically drop down the data into S3 or copy it from S3. Instead of managing any script by cron job on an EC2 instance, Lambda can be used for snapshots.

Amazon QuickSight

QuickSight is the Business Intelligence service that can be used with RedShift for BI tools.

AWS Database Migration Service

This service is used for migrating data from an existing database on AWS or any on-premises database.

Amazon Kinesis

For Real-time data stream, you can use Amazon Kinesis with RedShift. To analyze or process streaming data from various sources (IT Logs, Financial transactions, Social media feeds, and IoT devices), custom applications can be created by using Amazon Kinesis streams. Amazon Kinesis Firehose made a large amount of data ingestion easier. Amazon Kinesis Analytics is used for analyzing data using SQL.

Amazon Machine Learning

When data related to Machine learning is necessary to be analyzed, then the data from RedShift can be unloaded into S3 and then analyzed by using Amazon Machine Learning.

Columnar Databases

RedShift is a service that stores data in columns; therefore, it is based on columnar databases. Columnar databases directly write and read data to and from disk storage for the fast returning results of the query. Columnar databases contain compressions and algorithms that are responsible for reducing the stored amount of data on the disk; therefore, when this data is needed, it requires less number of I/O requests because of the small data size. Columnar Databases avoid scanning and discarding unwanted rows, as the entire data is saved in columns only, the query performance is increased.

Columnar vs. Row-based Databases

Both have the same logical structure, but they differ with each other in physical structure. In Row, store data is stored row by row on the disk while in column; the store data is stored on disk in a columnar structure.

Advantages of Columnar Databases

For understanding the benefit of columnar databases, consider the following example:

Product order tables are stored in the columnar database having a number of columns, and these tables contain thousands of rows. Let us say, an organization wants to know all of the customers that have ordered their products. Therefore, the database query for such records would require only a couple of columns; skipping all the irrelevant data in the database. This will assist in avoiding wastage reads, thus enhancing query performance.

Columnar databases are helpful in the data aggregation process, i.e., collecting data from various sources and compiling a summary for data analysis.

The data stored on the disk via columnar databases will compress the size of data therefore, whenever the data is read; less number of disk I/O is required, thus improving the query performance.

The total cost of ownership is less, as you can store a large amount of data in a compressed form.

Where not to use Columnar Databases

- If the user wants to query a specific value from a large database, do not use a columnar database.
- Use a row-based database whenever the size of data is small.

- It is not the ideal application for large binary objects.
- It is not recommended to use in Online Transaction Processing because in actual, each column is mapped to a file so when performing transactions; the data will be inserted in multiple files which will slow down the transaction process.

For example, if you have 51 single line statements and you execute them in RedShift, it would take approximately 4 seconds, whereas when the same amount of rows is executed in RedShift using copy command, it will take less than half a second which shows that single line execution will take more time.

RedShift Table Design - Introduction

Table design has a great impact on the level of performance.

Pre-Design Consideration

- You should know your data.
- You should know the relationships between your data.
- For column-oriented databases, you should think differently.

Table design and RedShift Architecture

The designing approach in columnar databases is different from Row-based databases.

- In a row-based database, linking tables and maintaining Referential Integrity is required by using primary keys and foreign keys. In RedShift, primary keys and foreign keys are available for query planning and grab performance.
- Row-based databases use indexes for a table while RedShift uses sort keys, which are different from indexes, but the concept is same.

You have to learn the table design of RedShift before using this service.

Data Model

Star schema is used to develop data warehouses and dimensional data marts, which consists of multiple fact tables referencing any number of Dimension tables. Fact tables are the part of data warehouse, which include facts, metrics or measurements of Business process. For answering the business related questions, facts and measurements are further categorized in Dimension tables.

RedShift Table Design - Distribution Styles

There are three types of distribution styles for Table in RedShift:

- Even
- Key
- ALL

Even Distribution

In this style, regardless of values in a particular column, the rows are distributed in slices. It is the default distribution style.

Consider a scenario, where you have two compute nodes, i.e., Compute node 1 and Compute node 2, and there is a column providing supplier id. In total, there are four node slices (Node slice 1, Node slice 2, Node slice 3 and Node slice 4) then the all supplier ids are evenly distributed across each slice, i.e., 2 supplier ids on each slice. Id at each slice is not in order as it was in supplier id column.

Key Distribution

Key distribution style is implemented where joining tables are required. This distribution divides data evenly across the slices, and matching rows can be collocated on the same slice.

Let us consider a case where there are two tables, i.e., product shipping and product orders. Analyst of that company runs large queries on each table that add values of both tables and want to join order numbers, so it should be noted that the value of ordered numbers is matched, therefore, it should be mapped on the same slices. For this process, if the key distribution style is not used then the matching order numbers of both tables are not on the same slice. Let's say, a query is generated for joining product shipping and product order table, and want the order number 10001-10005 then it leads to trans node traffic which results in slower performance.

ALL Distribution

In this distribution, a copy of the table is distributed across each node, which means that each node contains the same table, which increases memory requirement.

Guidelines for using Distribution

Let us see how to accordingly use the type of distribution style

Key Distribution

- Use key distribution whenever tables used in joins are provided.
- For large fact tables in a star schema.
- It will distribute data evenly across slices.
- Matching rows are collocated on the same slice.

Even Distribution

- It is used where no joins are required
- Where Reduced parallelism can be tolerated

- Where Key and ALL distribution is not applicable
- The distribution of rows across the slices are independent on the value of the particular column.
- It is a default distribution style that is, if no distribution is mentioned in the table statement then it will follow even distribution style.

<u>ALL Distribution</u>

- This distribution is used where there is no frequent modification of data in tables.
- When the size of the table is reasonable (few million rows).
- If there is no common distribution key, then you can use ALL distribution style.

RedShift Table Design - Sort Keys

Data is stored in the disk by sort keys. Sort order is used by Amazon RedShift query optimizer for determining optimal query plans. Sort keys are important; therefore, skipping them, or incorrect selection can result in poor performance. If the dimension table is very small, then there is no need for sort keys.

Block size of typical databases is less than 32 kB whereas of RedShift, it is 1 MB. By default, the block size is set, so there is no need to change it while launching any RedShift cluster. Large block size minimizes the I/O requests.

Zone Map

RedShift uses zone maps to track minimum and maximum values. If the data is in sort order (according to the defined sort keys), zone map can find out the maximum and minimum value. For example, if you execute the query: SELECT ORDER_NUMBER, CUSTOMER_ID, TOTAL_PRICE FROM ORDER_DATE WHERE ORDER_DATE='02/05/2015'; if the data is in sorted order, zone map will locate the minimum and maximum value of block which will help in avoiding irrelevant block to be read. By executing this command, the data of February is extracted from which the 02/05/2015 data can be easily extracted.

Sort Order

For example, in a data, the sort key is order_date and data is loaded by copy command without order, i.e., first March data is loaded, then April, February, and January. All blocks are read when the query is executed to find the data of "02/05/2015", so the reads are wasted as the data is not loaded in sort order even when we have the sort key available. Whenever the data is not loaded in sort order, vacuum command needs to be executed.

Types of Sort Keys

- Compound
- Interleaved

Compound Sort keys

This sort key includes all the columns listed in the sort key definition. The given figure shows the table with a compound sort key. At the end, in sort key there are two columns listed that are the part of sort key.

```
CREATE TABLE public.lineitemcompound
(
    l_orderkey BIGINT NOT NULL ENCODE mostly32 DISTKEY,
    l_partkey BIGINT NOT NULL ENCODE mostly32,
    l_suppkey INTEGER NOT NULL,
    l_linenumber INTEGER NOT NULL ENCODE delta,
    l_quantity NUMERIC(12, 2) NOT NULL ENCODE bytedict,
    l_extendedprice NUMERIC(12, 2) NOT NULL ENCODE mostly32,
    l_discount NUMERIC(12, 2) NOT NULL ENCODE delta,
    l_tax NUMERIC(12, 2) NOT NULL ENCODE delta,
    l_returnflag CHAR(1) NOT NULL,
    l_linestatus CHAR(1) NOT NULL ENCODE runlength,
    l_shipdate DATE NOT NULL ENCODE delta,
    l_commitdate DATE NOT NULL ENCODE delta,
    l_receiptdate DATE NOT NULL ENCODE delta,
    l_shipinstruct CHAR(25) NOT NULL ENCODE bytedict,
    l_shipmode CHAR(10) NOT NULL ENCODE bytedict,
    l_comment VARCHAR(44) NOT NULL ENCODE text255
)
SORTKEY
(
    l_shipdate,
    l_orderkey
);
```

Figure 5-01: Compound Sort Keys (Multiple)

Single sort key can also be included

```
Tab 5   x    Tab 7   x   New
    CREATE TABLE public.lineitem
    (
        l_orderkey BIGINT NOT NULL ENCODE mostly32 DISTKEY,
        l_partkey BIGINT NOT NULL ENCODE mostly32,
        l_suppkey INTEGER NOT NULL,
        l_linenumber INTEGER NOT NULL ENCODE delta,
        l_quantity NUMERIC(12, 2) NOT NULL ENCODE bytedict,
        l_extendedprice NUMERIC(12, 2) NOT NULL ENCODE mostly32,
        l_discount NUMERIC(12, 2) NOT NULL ENCODE delta,
        l_tax NUMERIC(12, 2) NOT NULL ENCODE delta,
        l_returnflag CHAR(1) NOT NULL ENCODE lzo,
        l_linestatus CHAR(1) NOT NULL ENCODE lzo,
        l_shipdate DATE NOT NULL ENCODE delta,
        l_commitdate DATE NOT NULL ENCODE delta,
        l_receiptdate DATE NOT NULL ENCODE delta,
        l_shipinstruct CHAR(25) NOT NULL ENCODE bytedict,
        l_shipmode CHAR(10) NOT NULL ENCODE bytedict,
        l_comment VARCHAR(44) NOT NULL ENCODE text255
    )
SORTKEY
(
    l_shipdate
);
```

Figure 5-02: Compound Sort Key (Single)

The compound sort key is the default type, it can be used with JOINS, ORDER BY and GROUP BY operations. It can also be used with PARTITION BY and ORDER BY windows function.

When a large amount of data is added using compound sort keys, a large portion of data is left unsorted for which then vacuum operation has to be executed on disk and after that analyze operation has to be run. Analyze operation is the way to update the statistics.

If the query does not include a primary sort key column, it will lead to poor performance. In Figure 5-03, l_partkey is the primary sort key column, and l_shipdate is the secondary sort key column. So if the query only contains l_shipdate and does not include l_partkey, then the benefits of compound sort key are not realized.

```
Tab 5   ×   Tab 7   ×   Tab 9   ×   Tab 11   ×   New

CREATE TABLE public.lineitemcompoundpart
(
    l_orderkey BIGINT NOT NULL ENCODE mostly32 DISTKEY,
    l_partkey BIGINT NOT NULL ENCODE mostly32,
    l_suppkey INTEGER NOT NULL,
    l_linenumber INTEGER NOT NULL ENCODE delta,
    l_quantity NUMERIC(12, 2) NOT NULL ENCODE bytedict,
    l_extendedprice NUMERIC(12, 2) NOT NULL ENCODE mostly32,
    l_discount NUMERIC(12, 2) NOT NULL ENCODE delta,
    l_tax NUMERIC(12, 2) NOT NULL ENCODE delta,
    l_returnflag CHAR(1) NOT NULL,
    l_linestatus CHAR(1) NOT NULL ENCODE runlength,
    l_shipdate DATE NOT NULL ENCODE delta,
    l_commitdate DATE NOT NULL ENCODE delta,
    l_receiptdate DATE NOT NULL ENCODE delta,
    l_shipinstruct CHAR(25) NOT NULL ENCODE bytedict,
    l_shipmode CHAR(10) NOT NULL ENCODE bytedict,
    l_comment VARCHAR(44) NOT NULL ENCODE text255
)
SORTKEY
(
    l_partkey,
    l_shipdate

);
```

Figure 5-03: Compound Sort Key (Primary and Secondary Sort Key)

Interleaved sort key

Interleaved sort key provides equal weight to each column in the sort key. Whereas, in compound type sort key, the primary columns are given more weight than the secondary columns. They are useful with multiple queries containing different filters that are run by BI analyst.

```
Tab 1   ×   Tab 2   ×   Tab 3   ×   Tab 4   ×   New

CREATE TABLE public.ordersinterleaved
(
    o_orderkey BIGINT NOT NULL ENCODE mostly32 DISTKEY,
    o_custkey BIGINT NOT NULL ENCODE mostly32,
    o_orderstatus CHAR(1) NOT NULL ENCODE lzo,
    o_totalprice NUMERIC(12, 2) NOT NULL ENCODE mostly32,
    o_orderdate DATE NOT NULL ENCODE delta,
    o_orderpriority CHAR(15) NOT NULL ENCODE bytedict,
    o_clerk CHAR(15) NOT NULL ENCODE lzo,
    o_shippriority INTEGER NOT NULL ENCODE runlength,
    o_comment VARCHAR(79) NOT NULL ENCODE text255
)
INTERLEAVED SORTKEY
(
    o_orderkey,
    o_custkey,
    o_orderdate
);
```

Figure 5-04: Interleaved Sort Key

They are useful when used with selective queries for filtering on one or more sort key columns in logs.

Data loading and Vacuum based operations for table maintenance are slower while using interleaved sort key because it contains a number of columns. It is useful when the table contains 100 million or more rows. If data has to be loaded in sort order then interleaved sort keys are not recommended because they would not preserve this order.

In the given figure below is the query for the table having interleaved sort key. This query contains filters; therefore, it is not ideal for executing this query for a single sort key defined table.

```
select
o_orderkey, o_custkey, o_orderdate
from
ordersinterleaved
where o_orderkey = '28014917'
      and o_custkey = '147679618'
      and o_orderdate between '1992-01-01'
      and '1997-01-15';
```

Figure 5-05: Query for a Table having Interleaved Sort Key

When the same query is in three types of order table, i.e., with single column sort key (o_orderdate), compound sort key (o_orderdate and o_orderkey) and interleaved sort key (o_orderdate, o_orderkey, and o_ordercustkey) are executed. The first query on single sort key table takes about 6 seconds, the second query on compound sort key table takes about 5 seconds and the third query on interleaved sort key table takes 1.5 seconds. This shows that using interleaved sort key table for a query with different filters is much faster than others.

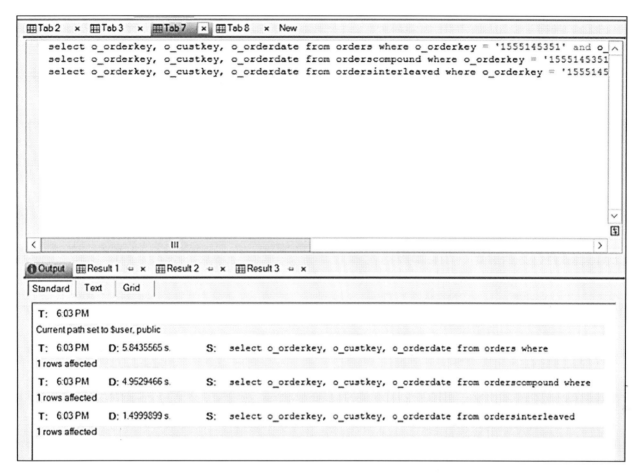

Figure 5-06: Comparison of the types using different Sort Keys

How to choose sort keys

- TIMESTAMP column for recent data: Time base query can be executed faster because it skips the data that is out of time range.
- Columns that are used in between conditions or equality operators.
- Columns that are involved in a JOIN then the same column can be used for the distribution key and sort key.

Note:

- Sort Keys and distribution styles are important in table design that can affect the performance level.
- AWS Admin scripts on GitHub provide tools to check your table design

RedShift Table Design - Data Types

BIGINT, INTEGER, NUMERIC, etc are the different data types. Defining data type is important because it represents the type of data stored in the column.

Supported Data Types

Data Type	Aliases
SMALL INT	INT2
INTEGER	INT, INT4
BIGINT	INT8
DECIMAL	NUMERIC
REAL	FLOAT4
DOUBLE PRECISION	FLOAT8, FLOAT
BOOLEAN	BOOL
CHAR	CHARACTER, NCHAR, BPCHAR
VARCHAR	CHARACTER VARYING, NCHARVAR, TEXT
DATE	
TIMESTAMP	TIMESTAMP WITHOUT TIME ZONE
TIMESTAMPTZ	TIMESTAMP WITH TIME ZONE

Table 5-02: Data Types

Correct use of data type is very important. For example:

- If you are loading data having YYYY/MM/DD, then you have to select 'DATE' data type.
- For comments, you should select 'VARCHAR' because comments can contain both numbers and letters. Therefore, it is the most suitable data type.
- If there is data regarding FLAG, which uses only 'Y' or 'N,' then you should select 'CHAR' as it is a fixed length data type.
- If there is data related to pricing, use 'DECIMAL.'

CHAR and VARCHAR

In RedShift, they are defined as bytes, not characters. For example, if you have a VARCHAR(12) column, it can contain the following:

- 12 single-byte characters
- 6 two-byte characters
- 4 three byte characters
- 3 four-byte characters

Name	Range (Width of Column) bytes
CHAR, CHARACTER or NCHAR	4096
VARCHAR, CHARACTER VARYING, or NVARCHAR	65535
BPCHAR	256
TEXT	260

Table 5-03: Character Ranges

Consider column size while designing the table. If the columns are wider than the required width, then this will affect the performance. For example, if the column size of CHAR is increased from 25 to 2500 and of VARCHAR from 44 to 4400, this will create issues especially when large queries are executed and they will occupy more disk space.

EXAM TIP: Remember the range limits. Wider column when not needed will affect performance.

RedShift Table Design - Compression

Compression is the process, which reduces data storage size on disk results in minimizing ownership cost of RedShift cluster. RedShift compressed the data approximately 3 times than the original data size.

Storing data size is less; therefore, execution requires less number of I/O operations on disk, which will boost the performance.

Each column can have compression encoding in RedShift.

Why Compression Helps?

Consider the compression algorithm that is connected to the RedShift cluster.

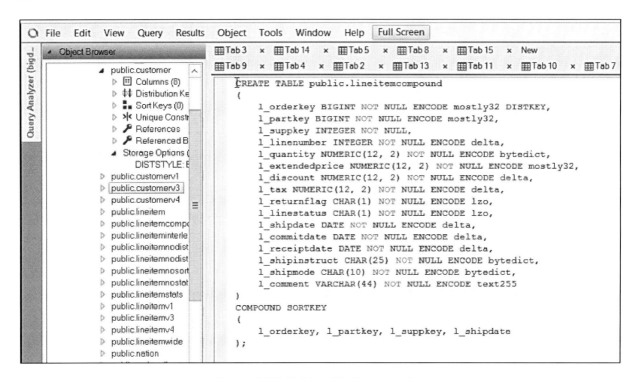

Figure 5-07: Table with Compression

And the mentioned query is executed.

```
select
100.00 * sum(case
when p_type like 'PROMO%'
then l_extendedprice*(1-l_discount)
else 0
end) / sum(l_extendedprice * (1 - l_discount)) as promo_revenue
from
lineitem,
part
where
l_partkey = p_partkey
and l_shipdate >= date '1996-01-01'
and l_shipdate < date '1997-01-01' + interval '1' month;
```

Figure 5-08: Query

It took approximately 298 seconds. The same query is when running on the two tables where compression is not applied takes 406 seconds approximately. It shows that the performance is 25% slower without compression.

Working of Compression

Compression can be performed automatically or manually.

Automatic compression is done by RedShift, and manual compression requires an extra step of running and analyzing compression command, enabling the DDL, creating the table and loading the data. AWS recommends automatic compression.

<u>Automatic Compression</u>

For illustrating the work given figure containing a thermostat_logs table, no compression encodings are defined in Table DDL.

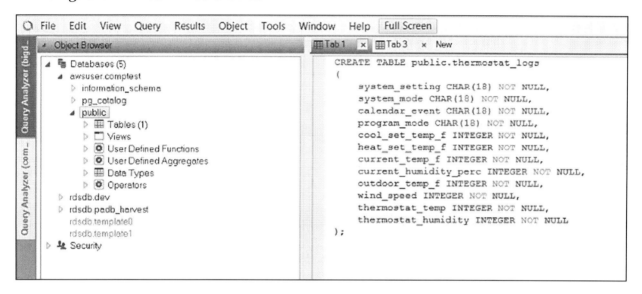

Figure 5-09: Automatic Compression

After table creation 134604 records data is loaded.

DDL is modified using automatic compression

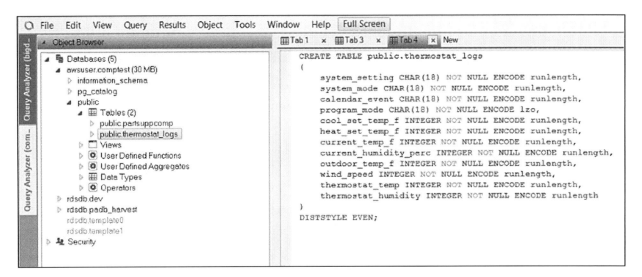

Figure 5-10: Automatic Compression

Automatic compression requires the following steps:

- Table creation
- Loaded data into the table
- Run the copy command when the data is loaded in a new table in RedShift.
- 100 thousand rows are loaded, and at the back end, it analyzes the compression command, selecting the type of encoding.
- Drop the table after the sampling of rows already loaded to see how much compression is required.
- Tables are then recreated with those compression encodings, and all the data is loaded.

Manual Compression

Create the table and Load some data.

In Automatic compression, compression encodings were automatically added, but for manual compression, we have to add comp update to turn off automatic compression in the COPY command.

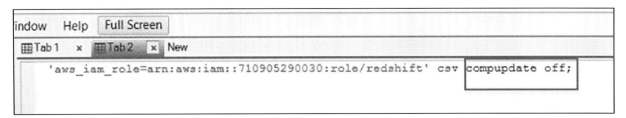

Figure 5-11: Loading Data without Compression

Open the DDL in a new Tab. No compression encodings are applied

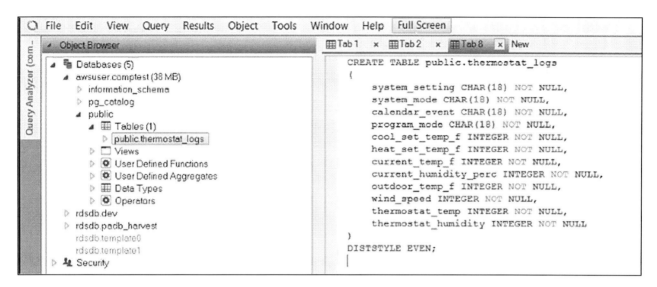

Figure 5-12: DDL without Compression Encodings

Execute "analyze compression thermostat_logs." It provides recommended compression encodings.

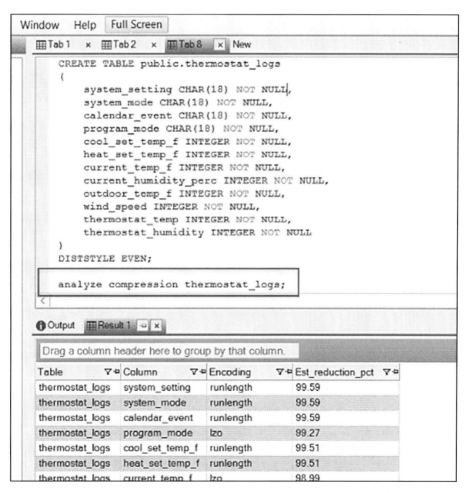

Figure 5-13: Recommended Compression Encodings

Insert them in DDL and then load the data again.

Manual compression requires more steps, therefore Automatic compression is recommended.

RedShift Table Design - Constraints

Constraints can be defined as: rules applied to the type of data that can be loaded into the table. Constraints help maintain the data integrity. For example, there is a transactional table, and an order has been taken. Two tables are order table and customer table. When the order is placed, its data is added into both tables so that the data matches and particular integrity can be maintained. Similarly, if the customer makes changes, then both tables are updated.

Column-level Constraints

RedShift offers column-level constraints, which includes:

<u>PRIMARY KEYS</u>

Primary keys are the column designated. They are uniquely identified in all table records. For example, a primary key can be a unique customer id.

<u>UNIQUE</u>

A unique constraint is not compulsory to apply, but it is useful in order to avoid data duplication.

<u>NOT NULL/NULL</u>

RedShift provides not null or null constraint. This constraint enforces that the column must contain any value, i.e., it cannot be empty.

<u>REFERENCE</u>

Reference constraint is used when a primary key of the table is referenced as a foreign key of another table. For example, the primary key of order table is order id and it is referenced to the order id of the customer table, which is a foreign key, then reference constraint will be used to link them together.

Table-Level Constraints

Table-level constraints include:

- PRIMARY KEY
- FOREIGN KEY
- UNIQUE
- REFERENCES

All of these constraints are not enforced except Not Null constraint.

Constraints are recommended to use only when it is necessary as if there is an application which demands constraints. They can be used for information purposes to generate efficient query plans.

 EXAM TIP:

- Primary keys and Foreign keys can be defined but not enforced.
- They are for performance or information purposes

RedShift Table Design - Design Review

Table design can be reviewed on RedShift by using some scripts that are provided by Amazon on GitHub. Table inspector script is one of the scripts that is used to review the table design.

By running this script on the table, the output is shown below which indicates the table having sort keys, distribution keys, and compression encoding.

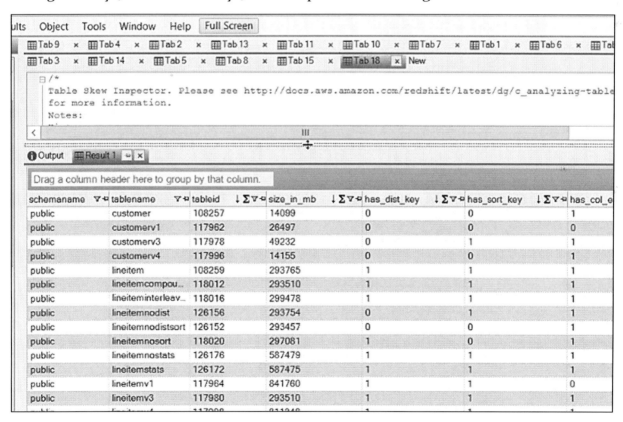

Figure 5-14: Table Design Review

RedShift Workload Management

Long-running queries and short-running queries are managed through RedShift workload management. Workload assign queries to the matching queues on the basis of rules. It enables to configure memory allocation to queues. It helps in improving performance and experience for users after running queries.

Limits

- 500 concurrent user connections are supported. (Connections not queries)
- Up to 50 concurrent queries can be run on RedShift at a time.
- Total of 8 user-defined queues is allowed.
- 1 superuser queue: this queue is reserved for any emergency solution if the administrator needs to take an action, all other queues are taken by 50 queries then the administrator can work with this reserved queue.
- Default concurrency per queue is 5.

Workload Management setup (Demo)

1. For illustrating this, we have a basic RedShift cluster

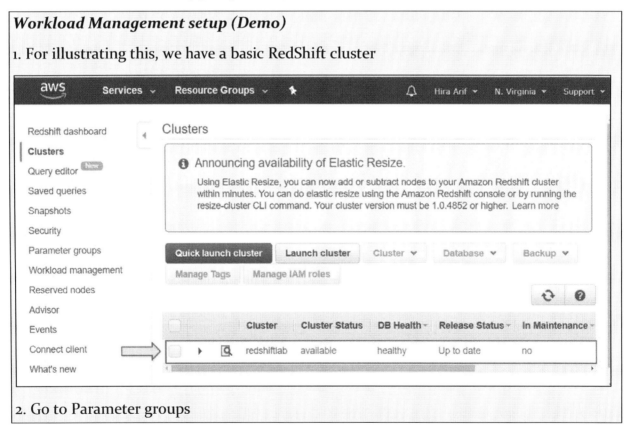

2. Go to Parameter groups

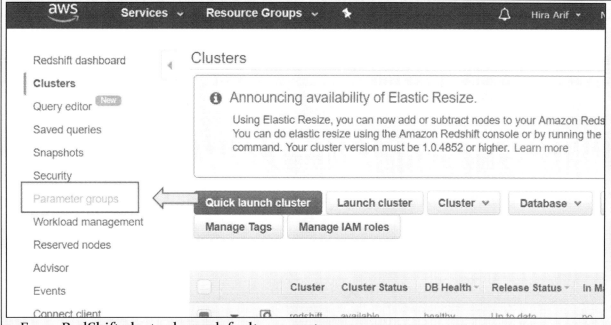

3. Every RedShift cluster has a default parameter group

4. Parameter group allows defining various database settings. Default parameter group is not in editable form.

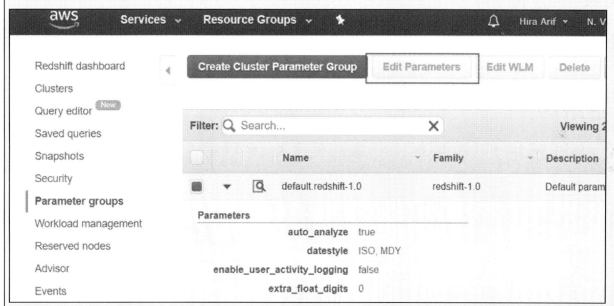

5. Create a new parameter group to change the default settings (If applicable) select 'Create Cluster Parameter Group'

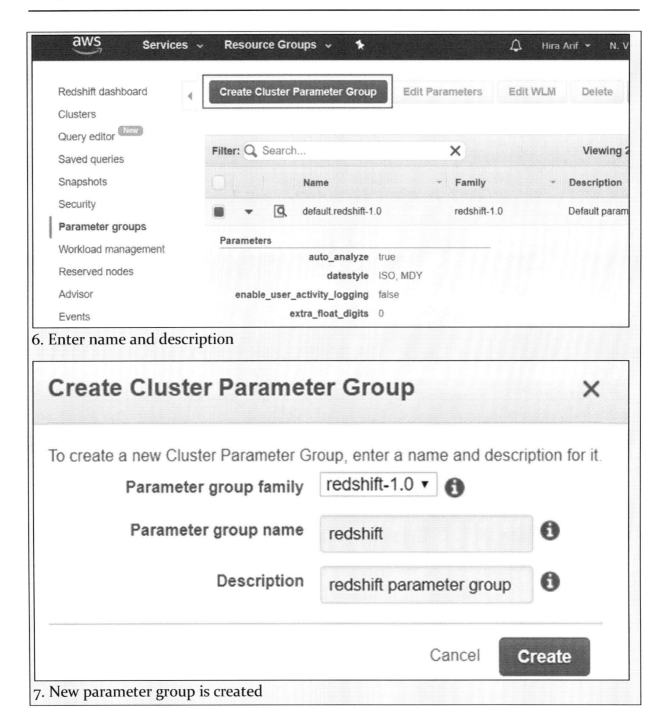

6. Enter name and description

7. New parameter group is created

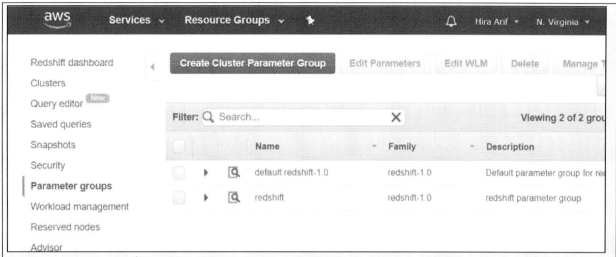

8. Go to the WLM (Workload Management) Tab.

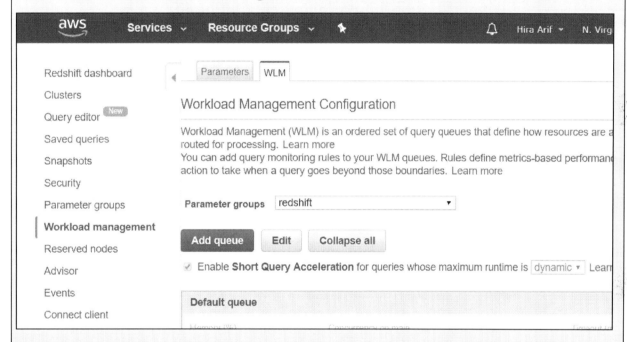

9. In our scenario, there are two types of queries: Large queries and small, fast queries. We have to ensure that large queries should not not occupy all queues so that small queries are also able to execute.

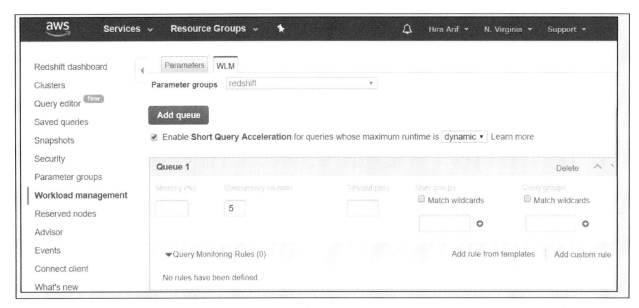

Two types of groups can be set in Workload Management i.e., User Groups (RedShift users can be placed in a group, and the user of that group query will be routed to the created queue) and Query Group (when a query is executed, it is set to be run in a particular query group).

The memory can be allocated for the groups you have created. For example, you can allocate 30% of memory for small queries and 70% of memory for large queries.

There are two types of Work Load Management parameters, i.e., static and dynamic. For example, the memory change is a dynamic parameter that means rebooting of the cluster is not required because this change will occur immediately whereas creating the groups is a static parameter, and it requires rebooting the cluster.

After saving the Workload Management configuration, to check whether the created groups are attached to the cluster or not, go to your cluster and modify the cluster with a new parameter group and then reboot your cluster.

For running the queries that take a long time and wants to run in the "largequeries" group created before inserting the command,"set query_group to largequeries". Similarly, if you attach the small queries to the "smallqueries" group then whenever that query is executed it uses the queue of "smallqueries" group.

Static WLM parameters

As discussed before, the cluster requires a reboot for static parameter

- User Groups
- User Groups Wildcard
- Query Groups

- Query Groups Wildcard

Dynamic WLM Parameters

No rebooting is required, the change occurs immediately

- Concurrency (set the number of concurrent queries executed in each queue)
- Percentage of memory to use per queue (percentage of memory allocated for the different queue)
- Timeout (for force stop of query execution after a certain amount of time)

> **Note:**
>
> The priority is more on the queue base rather than task or query based.
>
> The user can create timeouts to limit long run queries

RedShift has WLM queue assignment rules. For example, if a user logs in as a superuser, then the query is assigned to the superuser queue, or if the user belongs to the particular query group then the query is assigned to that specific group queue. If the query is not matched with any specific queue then it is assigned to the default queue.

Workload Management supports query queue hopping, means that if the query is a timeout in any queue, it will automatically be transferred to the matching queue for further execution.

RedShift Loading Data

The services that allow copying data directly into RedShift by using copy command are as follows:

- S3 (most common and fastest way of copying data into RedShift)
- EC2
- EMR
- DynamoDB

Some of the services can ingest data into RedShift using S3:

- Amazon Kinesis Firehose
- Amazon Kinesis enabled app
- AWS Database Migration Service

If the user wants to load data into RedShift by using Lambda, then data would follow the below steps:

- Files are ingested into an S3 bucket
- Lambda function is triggered and uses the copy command

- The data is then copied into RedShift from S3

Amazon RedShift Database Loader is a utility provided by AWS, which is available on GitHub.

Moving Data to AWS

If the user wants to transfer data from any on-premises to AWS, then:

- Data can be transferred to AWS through S3 by using CLI
- DirectConnect
- AWS Import/Export
- AWS Import/Export snowball when data is large.

A copy command can be used for loading data to RedShift from S3 which is the most common, efficient, and in a fast way.

---

copy (table name) from 's3://(bucket name)/(file that contains the data)' credentials '(role)';

If a 15 GB file is generated for a table name "lineitem" then it is split into 8 files. Now to compare the difference between loading data serially and parallelly, we will load the whole 15 GB file and then split files into RedShift.

Creating a table "lineitem" in SQL client

Figure 5-15: Creating Table

Now copying the data of "lineitem.tbl" file from S3 into RedShift. This data load is serial because we have only one file.

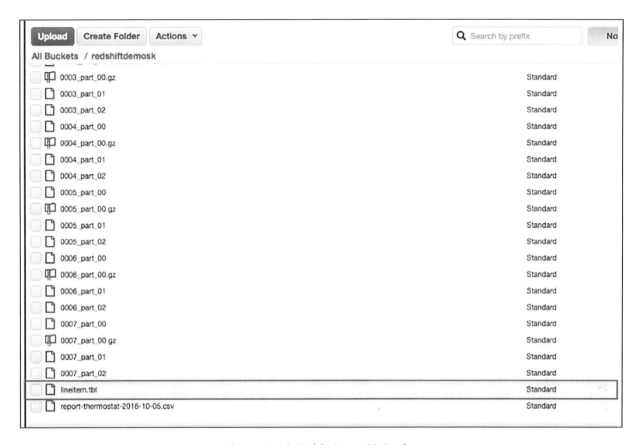

Figure 5-16: Table in an S3 Bucket

It takes approximately 514 seconds to upload the data into RedShift

Now 8 split files have to be loaded parallel into RedShift.

Drop the previous lineitem table and create a new lineitem table in RedShift. There is no need to change the copy command because the split files have the same prefix and only "001-008" appended, therefore, the command will automatically extract these files and load them in parallel. This loading takes approximately 280 seconds.

Conclusion:

The same amount of data is loaded in half of the time in parallel loading.

Loading Data and Node slices

Each compute node in a RedShift cluster has node slices containing nodes memory and disk space.

For example, a cluster has dc1.large 2 nodes, and AWS provides 2 slices per node for dc1.large node type as given in Table 5-05.

Dense Storage Node Types

Node size	vCPU	ECU	RAM(GiB)	Slices Per Node	Storage Per Node	Node Range	Total Capacity
ds1.xlarge	2	4.4	15	2	2 TB HDD	1-32	64 TB
ds1.8xlarge	16	35	120	16	16 TB HDD	2-128	2 PB
ds2.xlarge	4	13	31	2	2 TB HDD	1-32	64 TB
ds2.8xlarge	36	119	244	16	16 TB HDD	2-128	2 PB

Table 5-04: Dense Storage Node Types

Dense Compute Node Types

Node size	vCPU	ECU	RAM(GiB)	Slices Per Node	Storage Per Node	Node Range	Total Capacity
dc1.large	2	7	15	2	160GB SSD	1-32	5.12 TB
dc1.8xlarge	32	104	244	32	2.56 TB SSD	2-128	326 TB

Table 5-05: Dense Compute node types

To see the number of slices, a system table can also be queried, i.e. "stv_slices." Here are two nodes (0-1) and four slices (0-3).

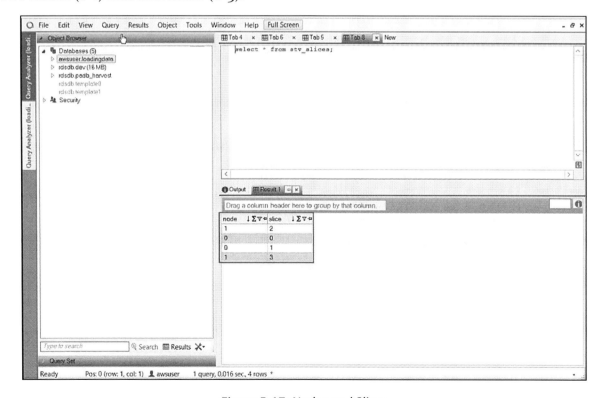

Figure 5-17: Nodes and Slices

The data files to be created should be equal to the number of slices or their multiple. So, in the discussed example, 2 slices per node means 4 slices for 2 nodes then the file can be split in the number of files that are 4 or 4x files. This splitting of files into multiple files according to the number of slices is required whenever the file size is large.

To increase the speed of data load of large files is by compressing. For compressing these files gzip, Izop, bzip2 can be used.

For the efficient loading of data, keep the file size even, that no file would wait for the other to complete and all of them are loaded at the same time.

Try to keep the file size between 1 MB to 1 GB after compression.

Three example commands to transfer data from DynamoDB, EMR, and S3 to RedShift are as follows:

Figure 5-18: COPY Commands

The First command is copying data from DynamoDB into orders table. "readratio 50" specifies that the 50% of read capacity units are allocated to this table in DynamoDB will be assigned to the data being read from DynamoDB into RedShift.

The Second command is for copying data from EMR into RedShift. And the Third command is for copying data from S3 into RedShift.

Manifest

RedShift supports the use of a manifest. Manifest is in JSON format and helps in the following purposes:

- Loading the demanded files only
- The user can load files from different buckets
- Different prefixes files can be loaded

Scenario 1: loading files by using a manifest file

Code of the manifest file when the table is split into 4 files

```
{
  "entries": [
    {"url":"s3://bigdataanalysislab/RedShiftdata/orders.tbl.0000", "mandatory":true},
    {"url":"s3:// bigdataanalysislab /RedShiftdata/orders.tbl.0001", "mandatory":true},
    {"url":"s3:// bigdataanalysislab /RedShiftdata/orders.tbl.0002", "mandatory":true},
    {"url":"s3:// bigdataanalysislab /RedShiftdata/orders.tbl.0003", "mandatory":true}
  ]
}
```

Here "mandatory": true means that if the file is not found, an error is generated.

In this scenario, a table "lineitemmanifest" is created, and a copy command is used, i.e., "copy lineitemmanifest from 's3://RedShiftdemosk/lineitem.manifest' credentials 'aws_iam_role=arn:aws:iam: :accountnumber:role/RedShift' manifest;" this command provides the s3 path of the lineitem manifest file.

The S3 bucket contains the 8 files and also the manifest file but only lineitem.tbl.001-lineitem.tbl.004 file will be uploaded because manifest contains these four files.

Figure 5-19: Manifest File

Approximately 60 million records are uploaded

For counting the number of records in full file of line item table, the command used is "select count(*) from lineitem;" and the number of records is approximately 120 million.

Conclusion:

Manifest file loaded approximately 60 million records, i.e., the half records of the full file that contains 120 million records. It shows that manifest file only loaded the files that were mentioned in it from the S3 bucket.

Scenario 2: Loading files from two different buckets

This manifest file "lineitem2.manifest" in the figure is for loading the files from two different buckets, i.e., RedShiftdemosk and RedShiftdemosk2. Lineitem.tbl.001-lineitem.tbl.004 from bucket "RedShiftdemosk" and lineitem.tbl.005-lineitem.tbl.008 from the bucket "RedShiftdemosk2".

```
[[ec2-user@ip-172-31-56-86 data]$ cat lineitem2.manifest
{
  "entries": [
    {"url":"s3://redshiftdemosk/lineitem.tbl.001", "mandatory":true},
    {"url":"s3://redshiftdemosk/lineitem.tbl.002", "mandatory":true},
    {"url":"s3://redshiftdemosk/lineitem.tbl.003", "mandatory":true},
    {"url":"s3://redshiftdemosk/lineitem.tbl.004", "mandatory":true},
    {"url":"s3://redshiftdemosk2/lineitem.tbl.005", "mandatory":true},
    {"url":"s3://redshiftdemosk2/lineitem.tbl.006", "mandatory":true},
    {"url":"s3://redshiftdemosk2/lineitem.tbl.007", "mandatory":true},
    {"url":"s3://redshiftdemosk2/lineitem.tbl.008", "mandatory":true}
  ]
}
[ec2-user@ip-172-31-56-86 data]$
```

Figure 5-20: Manifest File for files in a different Bucket

By using command "copy lineitemmanifest2 from 's3://RedShiftdemosk2/lineitem2.manifest' credentials 'aws_iam_role=arn:aws:iam::accountnumber:role/RedShift' manifest;" the command is providing the S3 path of "lineitem2.manifest" file.

The loaded data have approximately 120 million records that are equal to the records of 8 files.

Conclusion:

Data can be uploaded from more than one S3 bucket by using manifest files.

Data Format

Data format supported by RedShift, using copy command are as follows:

- CSV (Data is separated by ",")
- Delimited (Data is separated by "|")
- Fixed width (Data is separated by equal spaces)
- JSON
- Avro

Error Checking

There are some system tables in RedShift:

- STL_LOAD_ERRORS
- STL_LOADERROR_DETAIL

When an error is generated while running a copy command, the user can query these tables.

UPSERT

UPSERT is used to insert any record or update an existing record. UPSERT is not supported by RedShift. In RedShift, any new data can be inserted into any existing table by using UPDATE and INSERT from staging tables. Staging tables are the temporary tables and can be used by two different methods:

Method 1: Replace existing rows

- When all the data in the target table is needed to be replaced.
- When the user wants to use all rows in the staging table to merge into the target table
- When the situation occurs where Target and staging tables match

A table "supplier" contains small data. By using command "select * from the supplier;" we can view the data in that table.

Note: Select * in RedShift is not recommended. Here the data is small; therefore, it is used.

There are six suppliers, and if the company wants to replace five suppliers with the new suppliers, then the RedShift data directory needs to update.

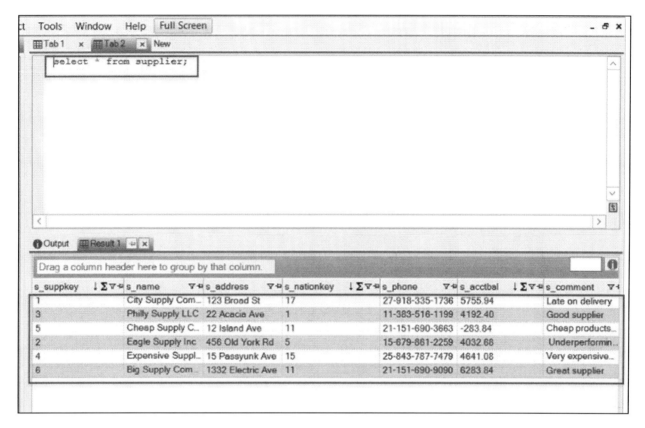

Figure 5-21: Old Record of Supplier

Considering that the ETL process has fetched the file from the transactional system of the company and the copy command is executed, new rows containing new suppliers from the transactional system are copied into the staging table.

To view the suppliers in the staging table, execute the command "select * supplierstage;"

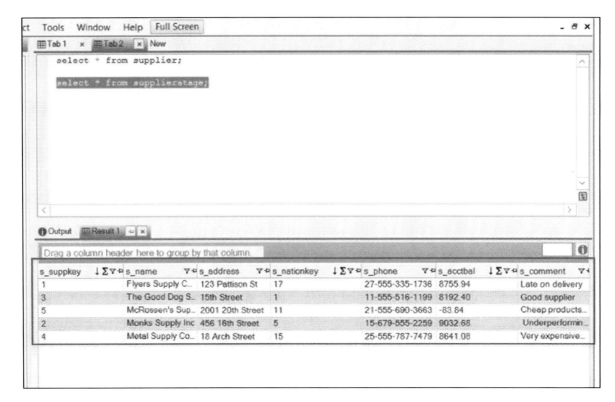

Figure 5-22: New Supplier Table

To replace the five suppliers in the supplier table with the supplier in the staging table, the mentioned commands in the figure are executed one by one.

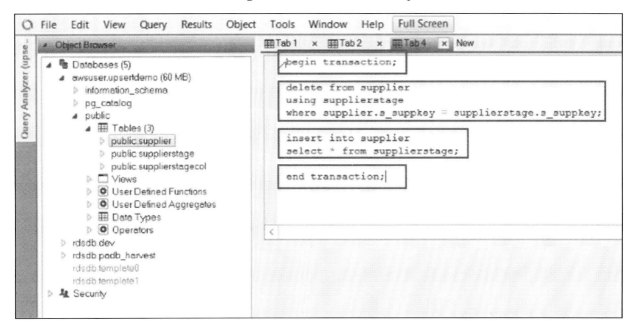

Figure 5-23: Updating Table

New suppliers are added into supplier table

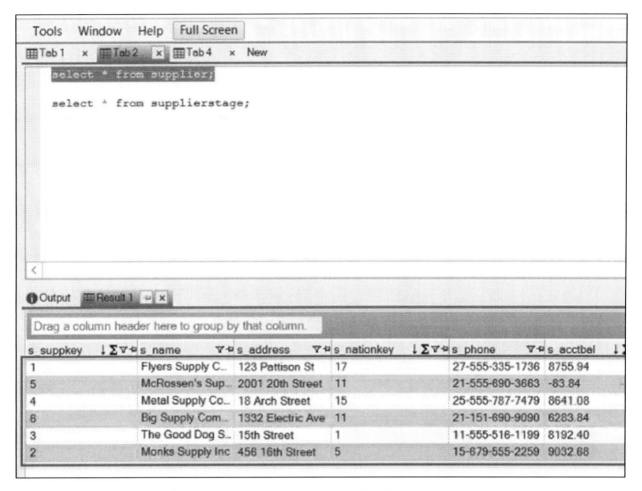

Figure 5-24: Updated Table

Method 2: Specify a Column list

This method is used:

- To update specific columns in the target table
- For the situation where most rows in the staging table will not be used to update the target table.

The company wants to update a single column, i.e., Account balance column

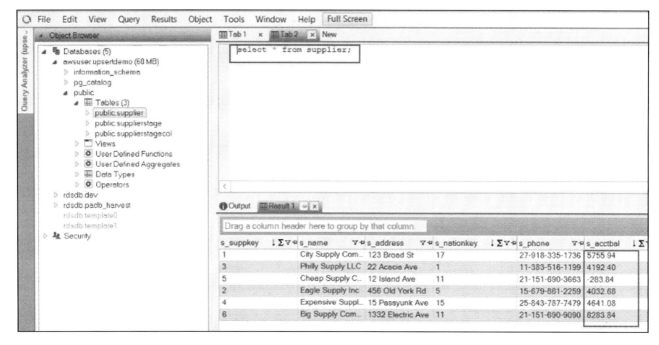

Figure 5-25: Account Balance Column

For this method, a separate stage table "supplierstagecol" is created. This table contains the updated account balance table.

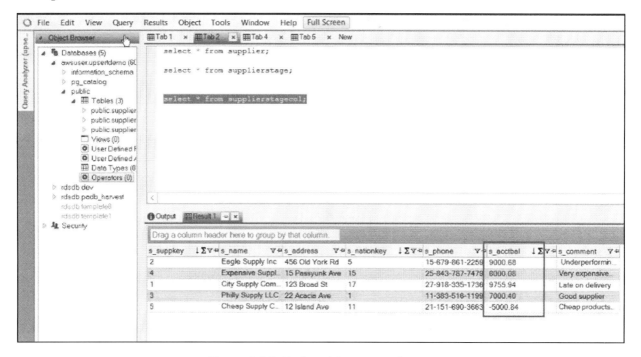

Figure 5-26: Updated Account Balance

The commands in the figure are executed to update the column

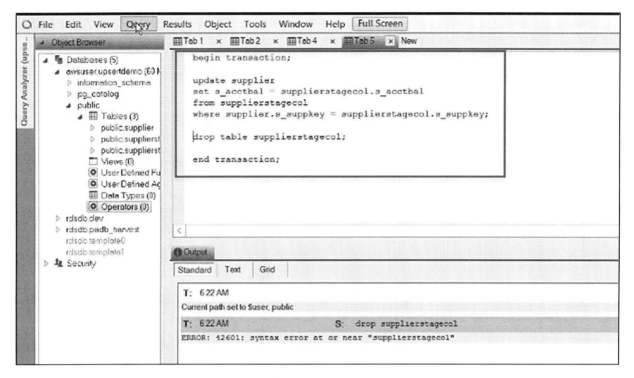

Figure 5-27: Query

The column is updated

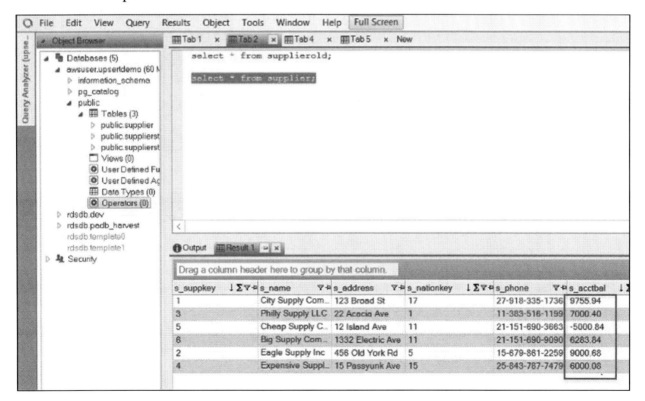

Figure 5-28: Updated Column

Loading Encrypted Data

For loading, encrypted files from S3 by using the "copy" command can be used for the following encryptions:

- Server-Side Encryption with S3 managed keys (SSE-S3)
- Server-Side Encryption with KMS managed keys (SSE-KMS)
- Files using client-side encryption having a client-side symmetric master key

Note: "COPY" command is able to automatically recognize and load the encrypted files using SSE-S3 and SSE-KMS encryption type.

"COPY" command does not support files that are encrypted by using the following encryptions:

- Server-Side Encryption with Customer-provided keys (SSE-C)
- Client-side Encryption using a KMS managed customer master key
- Client-side Encryption using a customer-provided asymmetric master key

Unloading Data

For unloads, query results into single or multiple files from RedShift to S3, UNLOAD command is used.

When this command is executed, files are automatically created by using SSE-S3.

executing the command mentioned in the Figure below to unload the data

Figure 5-29: Unload Data

The Encryption is automatically applied

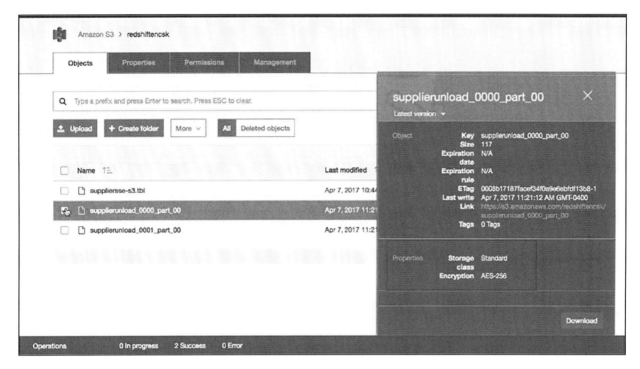

Figure 5-30: Automatic Encryption

By using the KMS key ID parameter and adding the "encrypted" option in the UNLOAD command, SSE-KMS can be applied to the file. Unload also supports Client-side Encryption with a customer-managed key. UNLOAD command does not support SSE-C (Service-side Encryption using a customer-supplied key).

RedShift Maintenance and Operations

This topic involves launching cluster, resizing cluster, vacuum, backup, Restore, and monitoring.

Launching clusters (Demo)

1. Go to Clusters

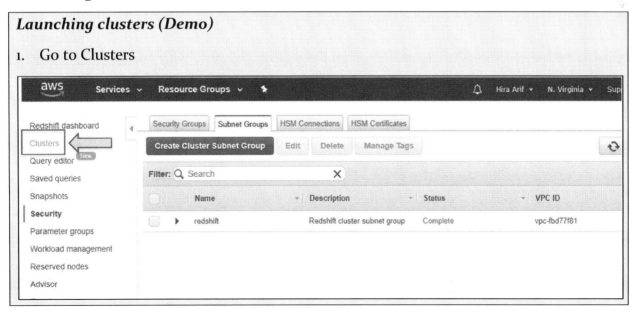

2. Click "Launch cluster."

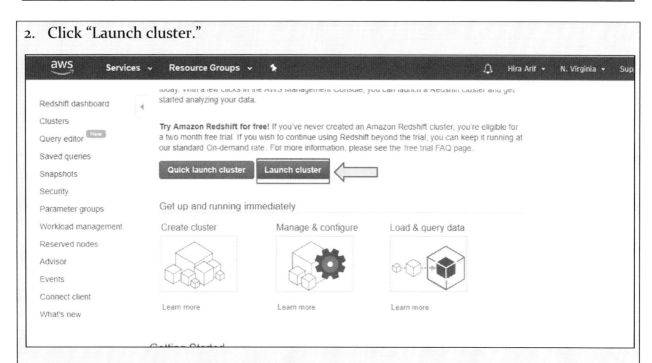

3. Enter any cluster identifier and Database name. Leave the Database port as it is.
4. Enter a Master user name and password

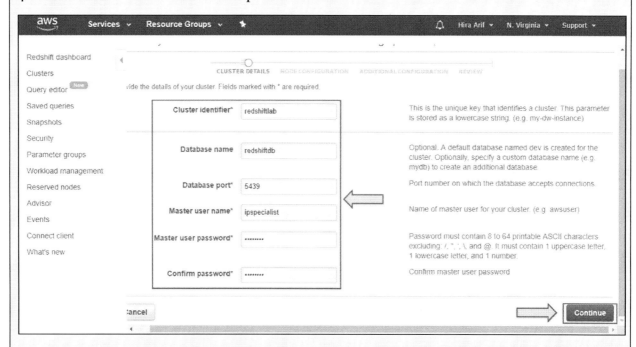

5. Select the node type. If the data is large, then select ds2 node types, and for higher IO dc1 node types are recommended.

While selecting the nodes consider the following:

- The cluster should have free space worth of 2 to 2.5 times larger than the table size which is used when some temporary tables are created due to executing queries and for the maintenance operations like vacuum
- For the number of nodes in a cluster according to your node type, refer Table
6. Select the cluster type, i.e., single node or multi-node and click continue.
7. Select parameter group if already created otherwise a default parameter group will be associated with the cluster

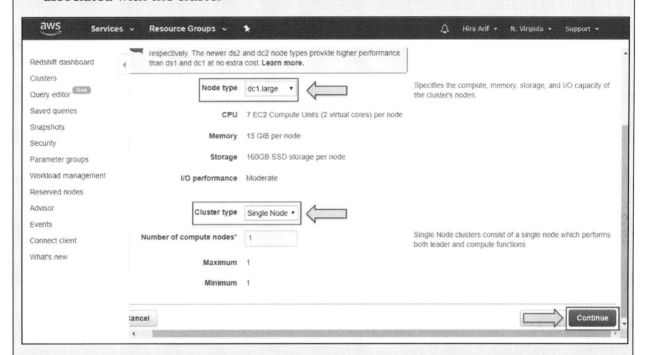

8. Here the data is not selected to encrypt. You can choose as per requirement.
9. Select VPC
10. Select the Cluster Subnet Group

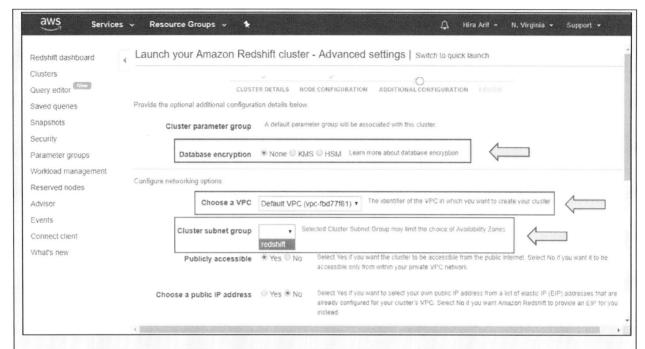

11. Decide whether the cluster would be publicly accessible or not. If you want to ingest your data from Kinesis Firehose to RedShift, then it should be publicly accessible. If the publicly accessible option is selected "yes" then you can select your EIP, and if you don't select your elastic IP, then RedShift will configure an elastic IP for the VPC which can be managed by the RedShift service only. If Enhanced VPC routing is enabled, then this would not allow the traffic from S3 to RedShift over the internet.

12. Select your VPC security group (CloudWatch alarm can also be created)

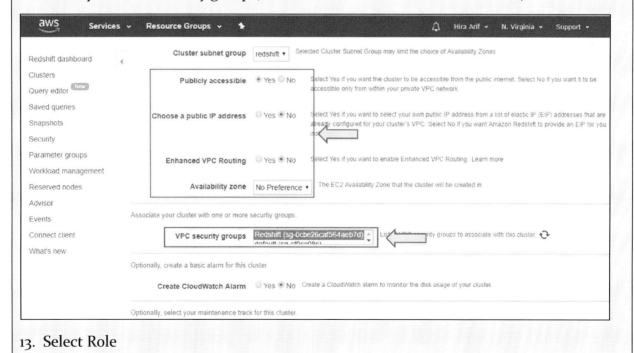

13. Select Role

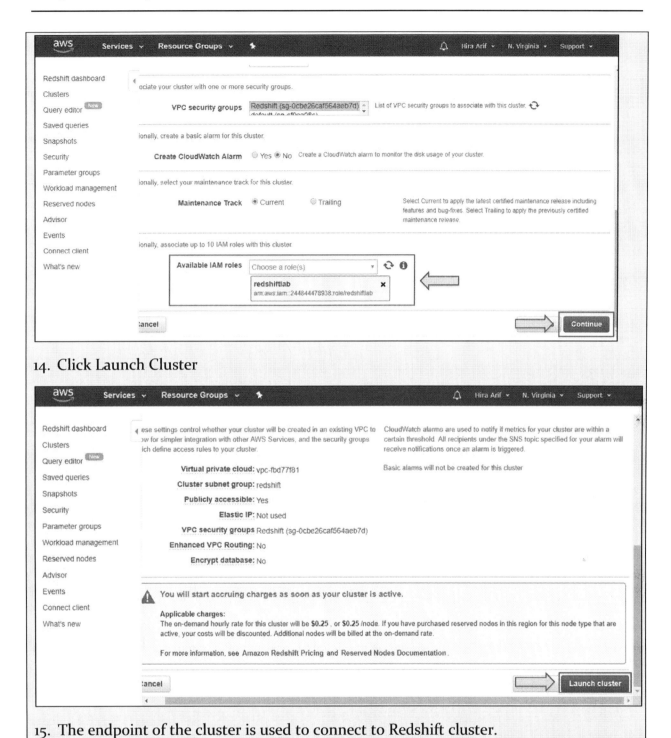

14. Click Launch Cluster

15. The endpoint of the cluster is used to connect to Redshift cluster.

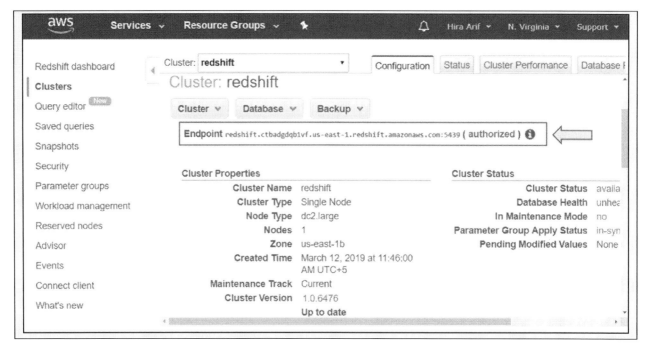

Resizing Cluster

It depends on the data stored in the cluster and amount of data added to the cluster. Resizing a cluster is much simpler than creating a new cluster and copying the data into it.

1. Dropdown Cluster and select Resize cluster

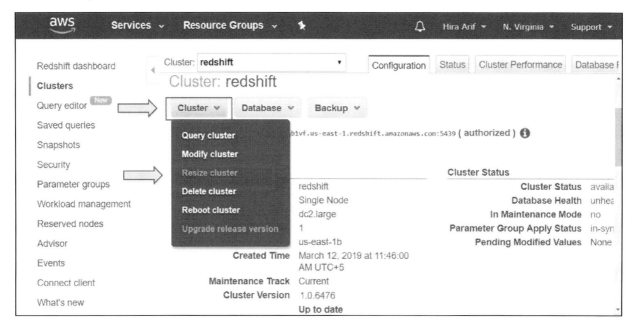

Figure 5-31: Resizing the Cluster

2. You can change node type as well as the number of nodes and then click Resize

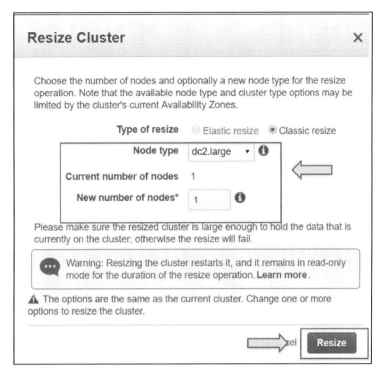

Figure 5 32: Resizing cluster configuration

When Resize is clicked:

- A notification is sent for the creation of the target cluster.
- The existing cluster (source cluster) is restarted and changed into read-only mode.
- All queries and connections are terminated.
- Reconnection can possibly run queries in read-only mode.
- Copying of data from the source cluster to the target cluster starts.
- After the completion of data copying, DNS endpoint of the target cluster is replaced by the DNS endpoint of the source cluster through RedShift.
- Source cluster is then deleted.

Vacuum

RedShift blocks cannot be changed once they are created. Results get updated in new blocks, and deleted rows are not removed from the disk, which means that disk space is occupied by the older rows and the query is executed on them. This results in the wastage of disk space and reduction of performance.

Vacuum command is used to recover the space occupied by the deleted rows; it also restores the sort order.

Vacuum Command Options

VACUUM FULL

Executes the vacuum command on all tables in a database. To run the vacuum command on a specific table the command is "VACUUM FULL *tablename.*"

VACUUM SORT ONLY

Sorts all tables in a database.

VACUUM DELETE ONLY

This will only recover the disk space occupied by the deleted or updated rows.

VACUUM REINDEX

It analyzes the distribution of values in interleave sort keys column and then performs the full vacuum operations.

Execute the vacuum command when a large number of rows are deleted, updated, or added. Vacuum command is I/O intensive, which may affect the query performance therefore, run this command during lower periods of activity or during the windows maintenance.

AWS provides RedShift utilities (Analyze & Vacuum Schema Utility) on GitHub, which would notify whenever the vacuum is required. Ideally, avoid running the vacuum operation by loading data in sort key order and by using time series table.

Performing Deep Copy

Executing vacuum command on large tables is slow, so the recommendation is to perform a deep copy, which involves the recreation and repopulation of tables with a bulk insert that automatically sorts the table. A deep copy is faster than the vacuum command. Vacuum is not a good option for a table size of more than 700 GB.

Ways to perform a Deep Copy

Using original DDL

In this way, the first copy of a table is created, where the table name is "parts" and the copy of the table name is "partscopy."

Then use the INSERT INTO and SELECT statement to populate the copy of the table with the original table data.

Then use the statement "ALTER TABLE" to rename the copied table name with the original table name.

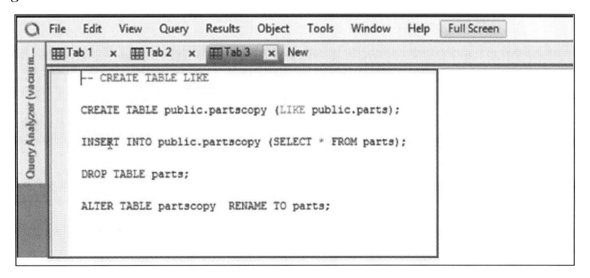

Figure 5-33: Original DDL

Using CREATE TABLE LIKE

This method uses the "CREATE TABLE" statement to create a table and LIKE statement to create it the same way as the original table. INSERT INTO and then SELECT statement populates the copy of the table with the data in the original table. DROP TABLE deletes the original table, and ALTER TABLE RENAME TO renames the copied table name to the original table name.

Figure 5-34: CREATE TABLE LIKE

Using CREATE TEMP TABLE and TRUNCATE original table

CREATE TEMP TABLE will create a temporary (temp) table as an original table. TRUNCATE the original table INSERT INTO SELECT will populate the temp table and the DROP TABLE is used to delete the original table.

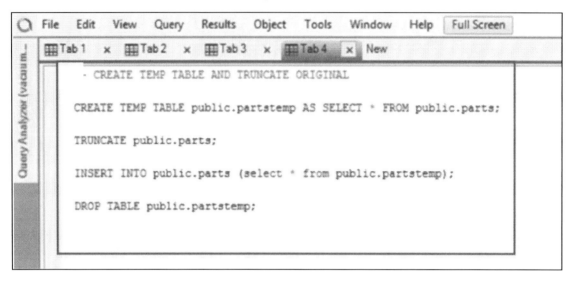

Figure 5-35: CREATE TEMP TABLE and TRUNCATE ORIGINAL

The first method of creating a table using DDL is the fastest method.

Backup and Restore

RedShift snapshots are of two types, i.e., automated or manual

Automated Snapshots

In the modify cluster, go to snapshot settings. Default retention period of snapshots is 1 day, which can be configured up to 35 days. These are incremental and continuous. RedShift takes snapshots at every 8 hours or data change of 5GB.

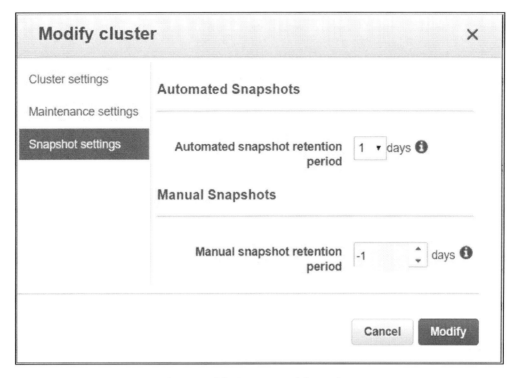

Figure 5-36: Automated Snapshots

Manual snapshots

Manual snapshots can be created at any time. Click Backup and then select Take Snapshot.

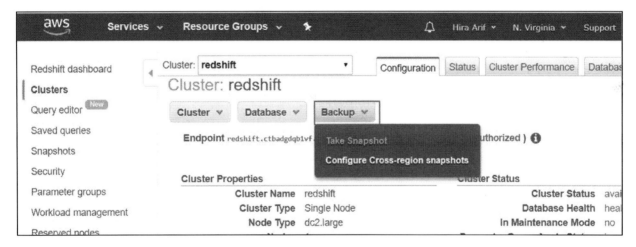

Figure 5-37: Manual Snapshot

Insert any snapshot identifier and click create

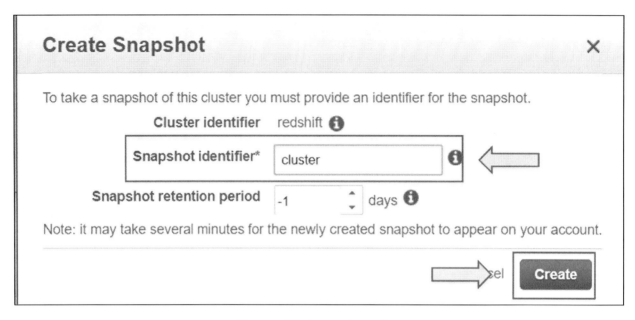

Figure 5-38: Create Snapshot

An automated snapshot can be copied and retained as a manual snapshot

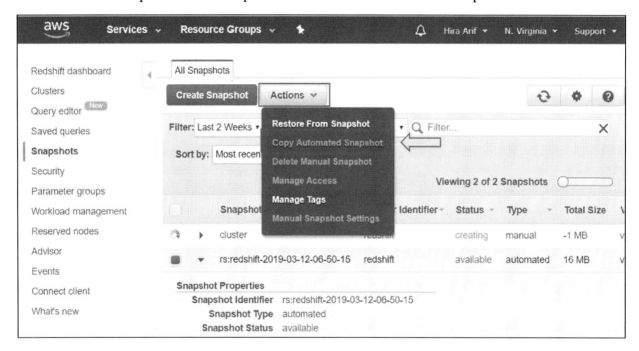

Figure 5-39: Copy Automated Snapshot

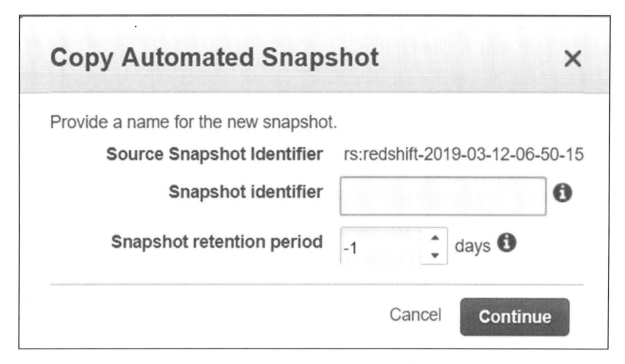

Figure 5-40: Copy Automated Snapshot

For a cross-region snapshot, Click Backup and select Configure Cross-region snapshots

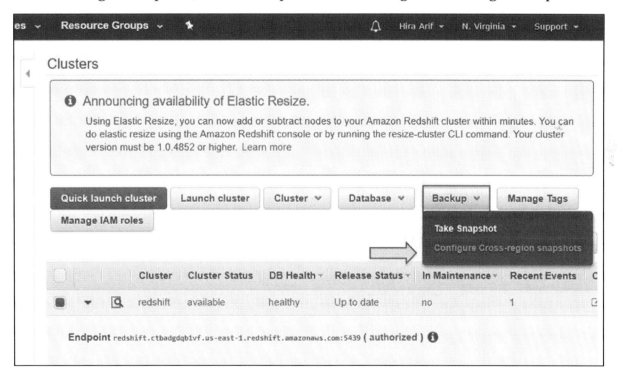

Figure 5-41: Configure Cross-region snapshot

Click "yes" and select the destination region then click "save."

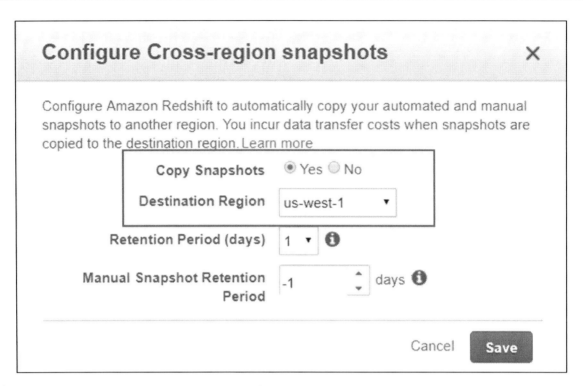

Figure 5-42: Configure Cross-region Snapshot

If the cluster is KMS encrypted, then the snapshots are also encrypted, and the KMS key would be region specific.

To configure snapshots for cross region, go to "Configure Cross-region snapshots", select copy snapshot and click "Yes" then click "No" in existing snapshot copy grant, select the KMS key and type the name.

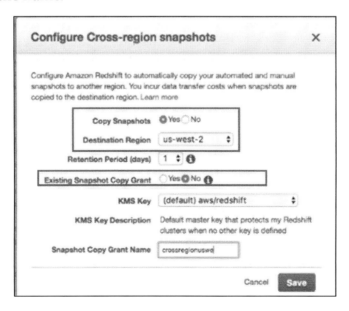

Figure 5-43: Encrypted Cluster Snapshot

For restoring, select Snapshots then go to Actions and select Restore From Snapshot.

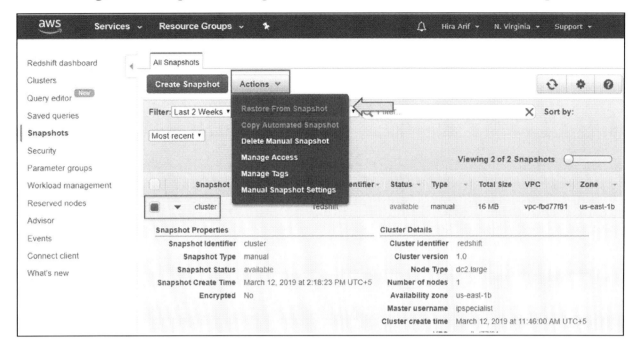

Figure 5-44: Restore Cluster

The configuration of the cluster would be similar to the original cluster.

A single table can also be restored by selecting the cluster then moving into "Table restore" tab and clicking the "Restore table."

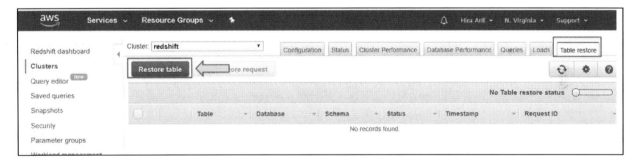

Figure 5-45: Restore Table

Monitoring

RedShift can be monitored by using CloudWatch Metrics. In Cluster, there is a tab called "Performance" which provides graphical monitoring and the Queries tab monitors any running query. The loads tab is to monitor data loading performance.

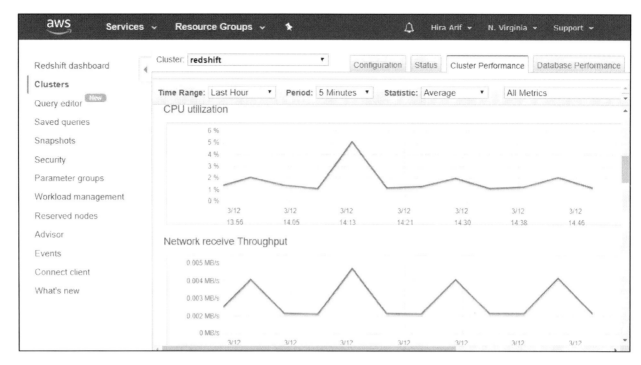

Figure 5-46: Monitoring

AWS provides utilities for monitoring which provides top tuning performance techniques. These utilities introduce custom graphs in CloudWatch.

Lab 5-01: Generating Dataset

For this lab, following features are required:

- An SQL client is required. There are two free SQL clients available:
- Aginity Workbench for Amazon RedShift (Windows only)

Link: https://www.aginity.com/main/RedShift-download-link/

- SQL Workbench/J (Windows or Mac)

Link: http://www.sql-workbench.eu/index.html

- For security purpose, enable MFA
- Create a role with the Administrator Access policy
- Linux Instance in us-east-1 or us-west-2 region with instance type t2.micro to m4.large and attach the created role. (m4.large is recommended)
- Root volume for 100 GB

Scenario

An Instructor wants to demonstrate on Big Data using AWS.

Solution

Generate a random data set by using EC2 instance and loading it to S3.

1. Launch an EC2 instance (m4.large)
2. Enter the command "sudo yum install make git."

```
ec2-user@ip-172-31-47-11:~                                    —    □    ✕

login as: ec2-user
Authenticating with public key "imported-openssh-key"

      __|  __|_  )
      _|  (     /    Amazon Linux AMI
     ___|\___|___|

https://aws.amazon.com/amazon-linux-ami/2018.03-release-notes/
10 package(s) needed for security, out of 15 available
Run "sudo yum update" to apply all updates.
[ec2-user@ip-172-31-47-11 ~]$ sudo yum install make git
```

3. Clone   the   repository   by   using   command   "git   clone
   https://github.com/IPSpecialist/BigDataAnalysis."

```
ec2-user@ip-172-31-47-11:~                                    —    □    ✕

[ec2-user@ip-172-31-47-11 ~]$ git clone https://github.com/IPSpecialist/BigDataA
nalysis
```

4. Move into the directory "cd BigDataAnalysis/tpch-kit/dbgen"

```
ec2-user@ip-172-31-47-11:~                                    —    □    ✕

[ec2-user@ip-172-31-47-11 ~]$ git clone https://github.com/IPSpecialist/BigDataA
nalysis
Cloning into 'BigDataAnalysis'...
remote: Enumerating objects: 22, done.
remote: Counting objects: 100% (22/22), done.
remote: Compressing objects: 100% (20/20), done.
remote: Total 126 (delta 1), reused 0 (delta 0), pack-reused 104
Receiving objects: 100% (126/126), 129.13 KiB | 10.76 MiB/s, done.
Resolving deltas: 100% (26/26), done.
[ec2-user@ip-172-31-47-11 ~]$ cd BigDataAnalysis/tpch-kit/dbgen
```

5. Install GCC by using the command "sudo yum install gcc."

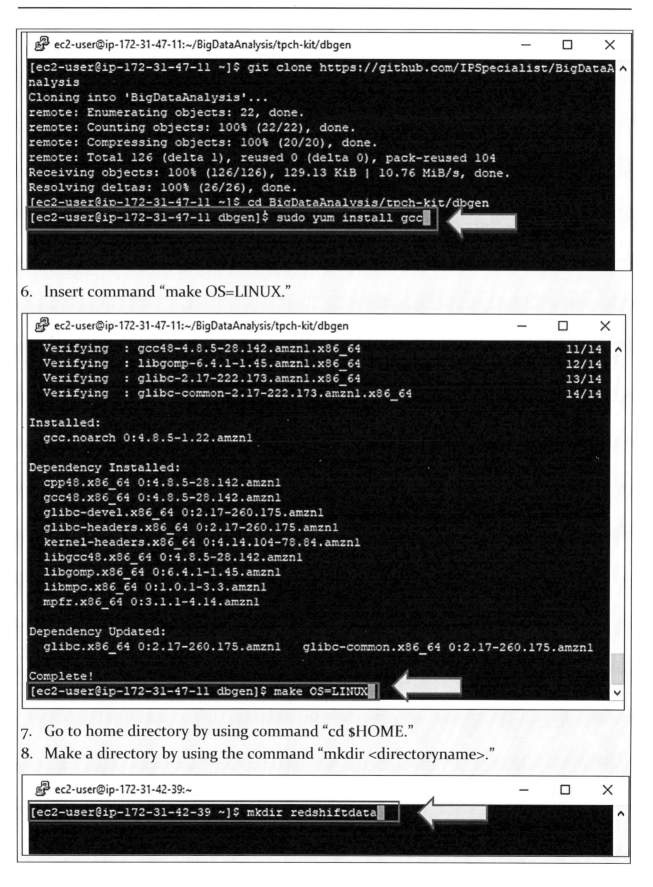

6. Insert command "make OS=LINUX."

7. Go to home directory by using command "cd $HOME."

8. Make a directory by using the command "mkdir <directoryname>."

9. Type command "export DSS_PATH=$HOME/RedShiftdata" so that the generated data will move into the directory.

10. Move into dbgen directory "cd BigDataAnalysis/tpch-kit/dbgen"

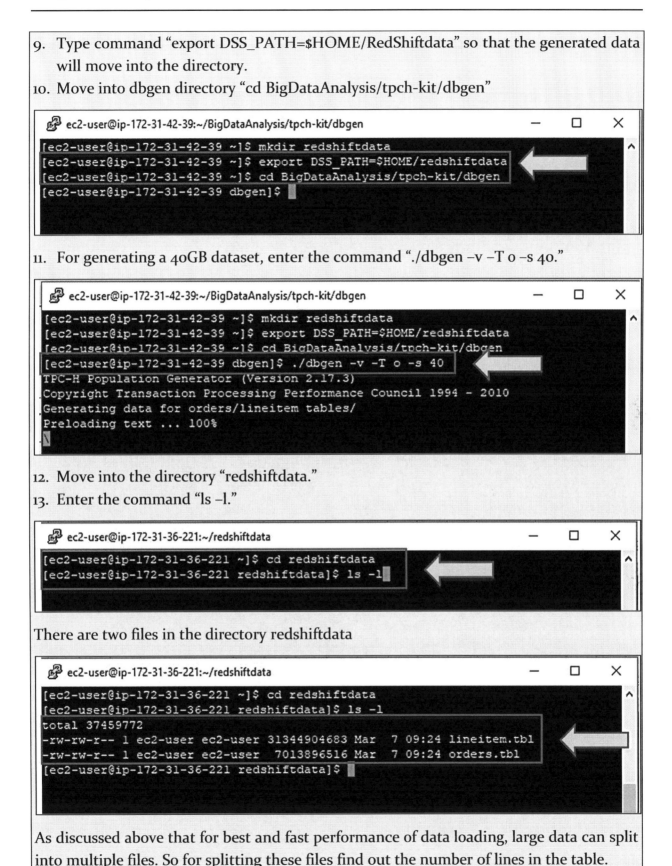

```
ec2-user@ip-172-31-42-39:~/BigDataAnalysis/tpch-kit/dbgen          —  □  ×

[ec2-user@ip-172-31-42-39 ~]$ mkdir redshiftdata
[ec2-user@ip-172-31-42-39 ~]$ export DSS_PATH=$HOME/redshiftdata
[ec2-user@ip-172-31-42-39 ~]$ cd BigDataAnalysis/tpch-kit/dbgen
[ec2-user@ip-172-31-42-39 dbgen]$
```

11. For generating a 40GB dataset, enter the command "./dbgen –v –T o –s 40."

```
ec2-user@ip-172-31-42-39:~/BigDataAnalysis/tpch-kit/dbgen          —  □  ×

[ec2-user@ip-172-31-42-39 ~]$ mkdir redshiftdata
[ec2-user@ip-172-31-42-39 ~]$ export DSS_PATH=$HOME/redshiftdata
[ec2-user@ip-172-31-42-39 ~]$ cd BigDataAnalysis/tpch-kit/dbgen
[ec2-user@ip-172-31-42-39 dbgen]$ ./dbgen -v -T o -s 40
TPC-H Population Generator (Version 2.17.3)
Copyright Transaction Processing Performance Council 1994 - 2010
Generating data for orders/lineitem tables/
Preloading text ... 100%
```

12. Move into the directory "redshiftdata."

13. Enter the command "ls –l."

```
ec2-user@ip-172-31-36-221:~/redshiftdata          —  □  ×

[ec2-user@ip-172-31-36-221 ~]$ cd redshiftdata
[ec2-user@ip-172-31-36-221 redshiftdata]$ ls -l
```

There are two files in the directory redshiftdata

```
ec2-user@ip-172-31-36-221:~/redshiftdata          —  □  ×

[ec2-user@ip-172-31-36-221 ~]$ cd redshiftdata
[ec2-user@ip-172-31-36-221 redshiftdata]$ ls -l
total 37459772
-rw-rw-r-- 1 ec2-user ec2-user 31344904683 Mar  7 09:24 lineitem.tbl
-rw-rw-r-- 1 ec2-user ec2-user  7013896516 Mar  7 09:24 orders.tbl
[ec2-user@ip-172-31-36-221 redshiftdata]$
```

As discussed above that for best and fast performance of data loading, large data can split into multiple files. So for splitting these files find out the number of lines in the table.

14. For lines in orders.tbl table enter command "wc -l orders.tbl"

There are 60000000 lines in orders.tbl

```
ec2-user@ip-172-31-36-221:~/redshiftdata                    —    □    ×

[ec2-user@ip-172-31-36-221 ~]$ cd redshiftdata
[ec2-user@ip-172-31-36-221 redshiftdata]$ ls -l
total 37459772
-rw-rw-r-- 1 ec2-user ec2-user 31344904683 Mar  7 09:24 lineitem.tbl
-rw-rw-r-- 1 ec2-user ec2-user  7013896516 Mar  7 09:24 orders.tbl
[ec2-user@ip-172-31-36-221 redshiftdata]$ wc -l orders.tbl
60000000 orders.tbl
[ec2-user@ip-172-31-36-221 redshiftdata]$
```

15. Now, splitting this table into 4 files by using command "split –d –l 15000000 –a 4 orders.tbl orders.tbl."

```
ec2-user@ip-172-31-36-221:~/redshiftdata                    —    □    ×

   -l, --lines=NUMBER      put NUMBER lines per output file
   -n, --number=CHUNKS     generate CHUNKS output files; see explanation below
   -u, --unbuffered        immediately copy input to output with '-n r/...'
       --verbose           print a diagnostic just before each
                            output file is opened
       --help     display this help and exit
       --version  output version information and exit

SIZE is an integer and optional unit (example: 10M is 10*1024*1024).  Units
are K, M, G, T, P, E, Z, Y (powers of 1024) or KB, MB, ... (powers of 1000).

CHUNKS may be:
N       split into N files based on size of input
K/N     output Kth of N to stdout
l/N     split into N files without splitting lines
l/K/N   output Kth of N to stdout without splitting lines
r/N     like 'l' but use round robin distribution
r/K/N   likewise but only output Kth of N to stdout

GNU coreutils online help: <http://www.gnu.org/software/coreutils/>
For complete documentation, run: info coreutils 'split invocation'
[ec2-user@ip-172-31-36-221 redshiftdata]$ split -d -l 15000000 -a 4 orders.tbl o
rders.tbl.
```

16. Find the number of lines in the table lineitem.tbl by using command "wc –l lineitem.tbl"

There are total 240012290 number of lines in lineitem.tbl

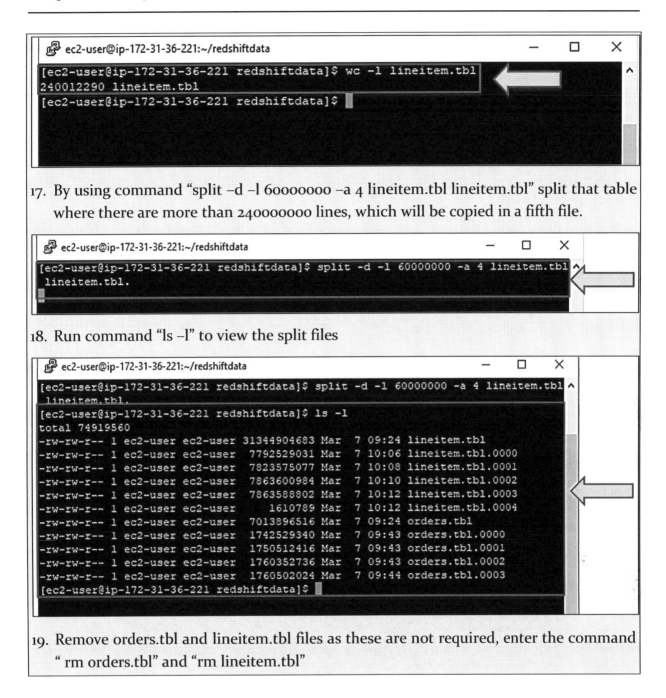

17. By using command "split –d –l 60000000 –a 4 lineitem.tbl lineitem.tbl" split that table where there are more than 240000000 lines, which will be copied in a fifth file.

18. Run command "ls –l" to view the split files

19. Remove orders.tbl and lineitem.tbl files as these are not required, enter the command " rm orders.tbl" and "rm lineitem.tbl"

```
ec2-user@ip-172-31-36-221:~/redshiftdata                    —    □    ×

[ec2-user@ip-172-31-36-221 redshiftdata]$ split -d -l 60000000 -a 4 lineitem.tbl
  lineitem.tbl.
[ec2-user@ip-172-31-36-221 redshiftdata]$ ls -l
total 74919560
-rw-rw-r-- 1 ec2-user ec2-user 31344904683 Mar   7 09:24 lineitem.tbl
-rw-rw-r-- 1 ec2-user ec2-user  7792529031 Mar   7 10:06 lineitem.tbl.0000
-rw-rw-r-- 1 ec2-user ec2-user  7823575077 Mar   7 10:08 lineitem.tbl.0001
-rw-rw-r-- 1 ec2-user ec2-user  7863600984 Mar   7 10:10 lineitem.tbl.0002
-rw-rw-r-- 1 ec2-user ec2-user  7863588802 Mar   7 10:12 lineitem.tbl.0003
-rw-rw-r-- 1 ec2-user ec2-user     1610789 Mar   7 10:12 lineitem.tbl.0004
-rw-rw-r-- 1 ec2-user ec2-user  7013896516 Mar   7 09:24 orders.tbl
-rw-rw-r-- 1 ec2-user ec2-user  1742529340 Mar   7 09:43 orders.tbl.0000
-rw-rw-r-- 1 ec2-user ec2-user  1750512416 Mar   7 09:43 orders.tbl.0001
-rw-rw-r-- 1 ec2-user ec2-user  1760352736 Mar   7 09:43 orders.tbl.0002
-rw-rw-r-- 1 ec2-user ec2-user  1760502024 Mar   7 09:44 orders.tbl.0003
[ec2-user@ip-172-31-36-221 redshiftdata]$ rm orders.tbl
[ec2-user@ip-172-31-36-221 redshiftdata]$ rm lineitem.tbl
[ec2-user@ip-172-31-36-221 redshiftdata]$
```

20. Create an S3 bucket by using the command "aws s3api create-bucket --bucket bigdataanalysislab --region us-east-1."

```
ec2-user@ip-172-31-36-221:~/redshiftdata                    —    □    ×

[ec2-user@ip-172-31-36-221 redshiftdata]$ aws s3api create-bucket --bucket bigda
taanalysislab --region us-east-1
{
    "Location": "/bigdataanalysislab"
}
[ec2-user@ip-172-31-36-221 redshiftdata]$
```

21. Copy data files into s3 by using the command """

```
ec2-user@ip-172-31-36-221:~/redshiftdata                    —    □    ×

[ec2-user@ip-172-31-36-221 redshiftdata]$ aws s3api create-bucket --bucket bigda
taanalysislab --region us-east-1
{
    "Location": "/bigdataanalysislab"
}
[ec2-user@ip-172-31-36-221 redshiftdata]$ aws s3 cp $HOME/redshiftdata s3://bigd
ataanalysislab/redshiftdata --recursive
```

22. To check that the files are copied or not, go to the console and check the S3 bucket

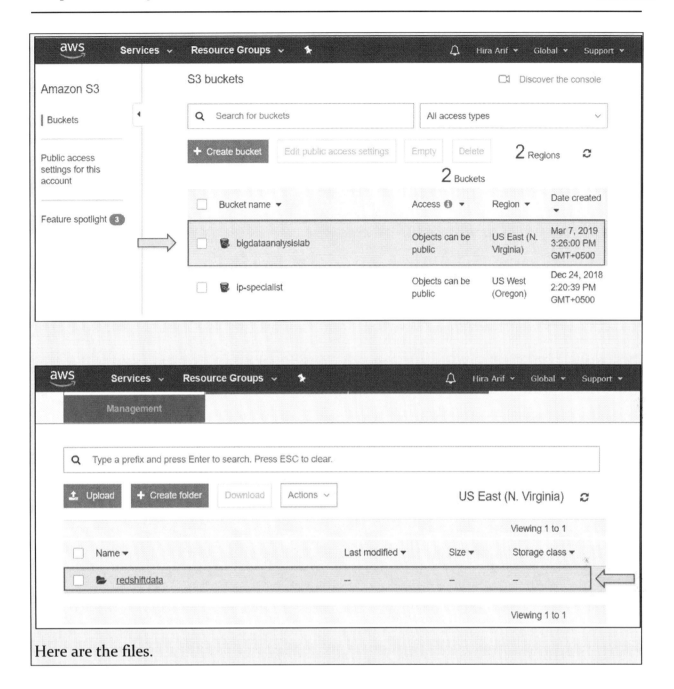

Here are the files.

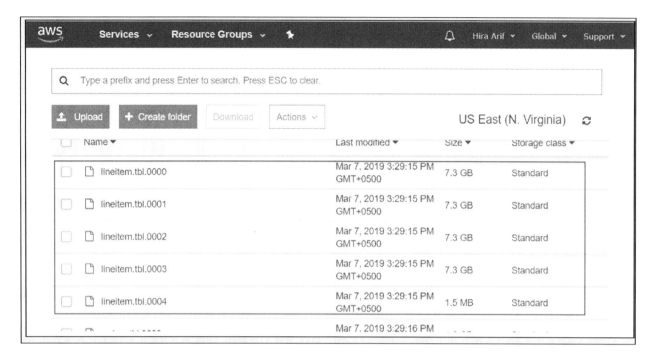

Lab 5-02: RedShift

Scenario

You are a data engineer in an organization that wants to store and manage its 40 GB dataset related to shipment and run several queries on it. The dataset contains two tables, i.e., lineitem and orders. The organization wants to analyze the difference in the loading time of tables with compression encoding, without compression encoding, with and without distribution style and sort keys. They want to set an infrastructure using Cloud services.

Solution

The organization can launch a RedShift cluster and then by using an SQL client they can connect to the RedShift and run the required queries.

1. Go to EC2 in the console
2. Go to the security group

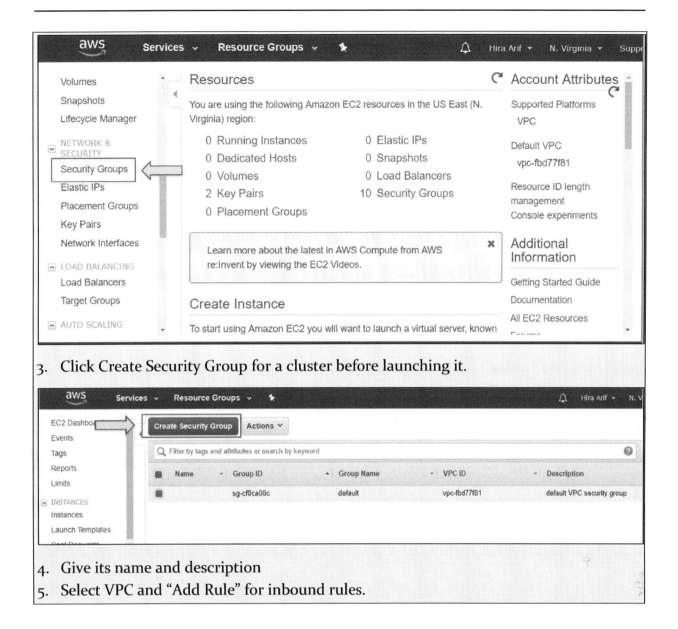

3. Click Create Security Group for a cluster before launching it.

4. Give its name and description
5. Select VPC and "Add Rule" for inbound rules.

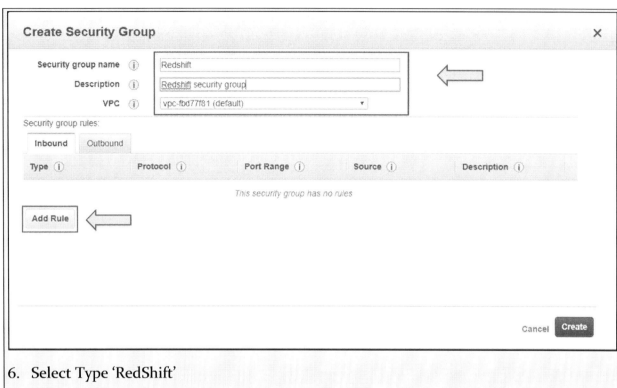

6. Select Type 'RedShift'
7. The source is either the personal computer or EC2 instance of the SQL client Here we have selected "Anywhere"
8. Click 'Create'

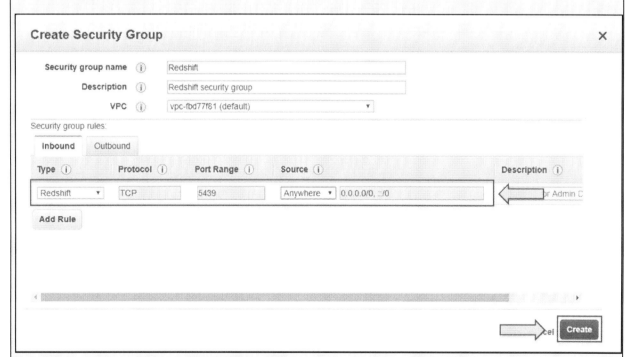

9. Go to IAM console Create a new role
10. Select 'RedShift'

11. Select 'Redshift – customizable' and click 'Next Permission.'

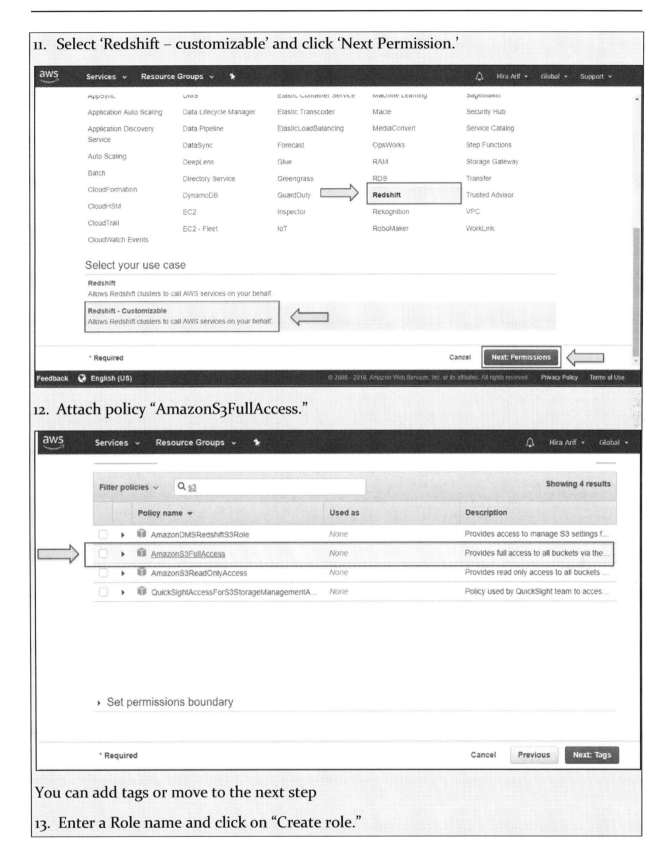

12. Attach policy "AmazonS3FullAccess."

You can add tags or move to the next step

13. Enter a Role name and click on "Create role."

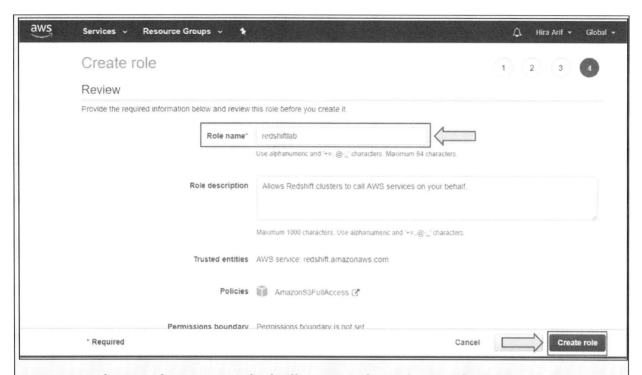

To create a cluster subnet group which allows specifying the set of subnets in your VPC:

14. Go to RedShift in the AWS console and click 'Security.'

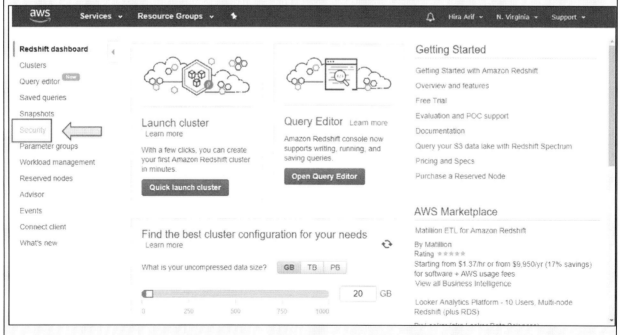

15. Click " Create Cluster Subnet Group" in Subnet Groups

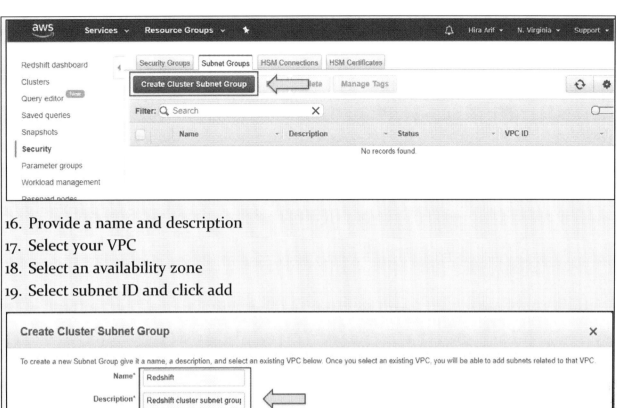

16. Provide a name and description
17. Select your VPC
18. Select an availability zone
19. Select subnet ID and click add

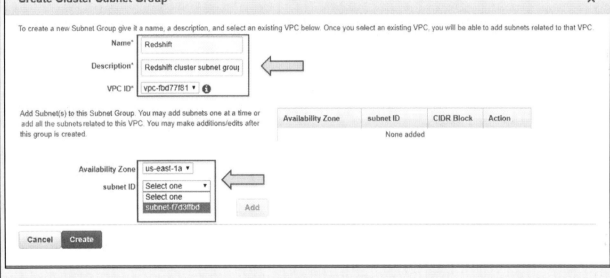

20. You can add more availability zone and then click Create

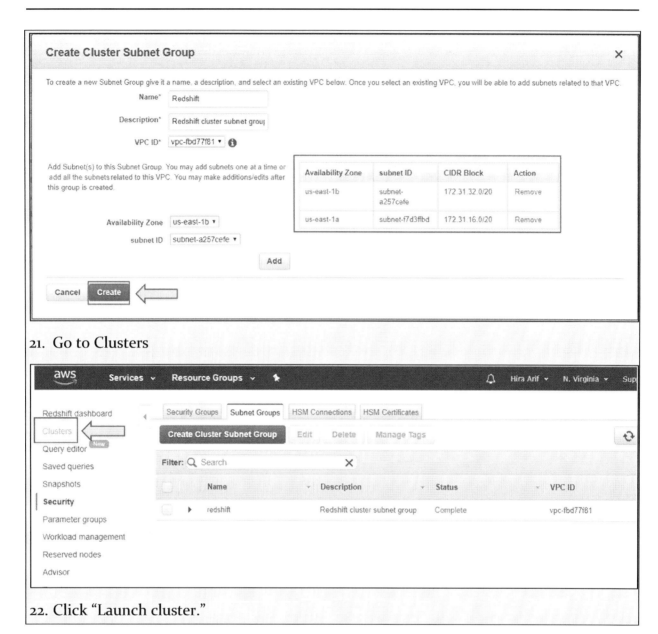

21. Go to Clusters

22. Click "Launch cluster."

23. Enter any cluster identifier and Database name. Leave the Database port as it is.
24. Enter any Master user name and password
25. Click Continue

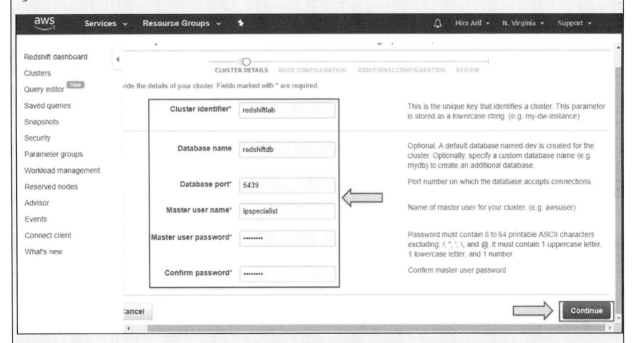

26. Select "dc1.large" node type and cluster type "single node." Leave the other fields default and click Continue

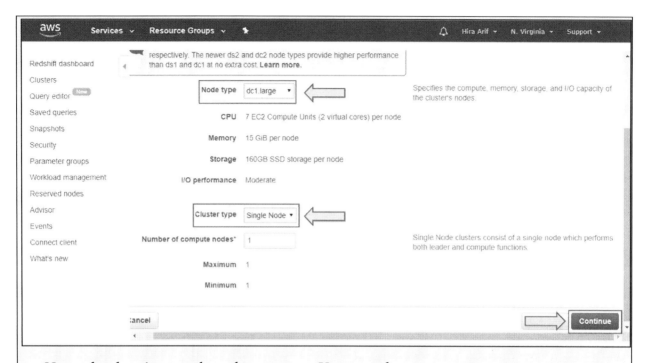

27. Here, the data is not selected to encrypt. You can choose as per requirement.
28. Select VPC
29. Select the Cluster Subnet Group

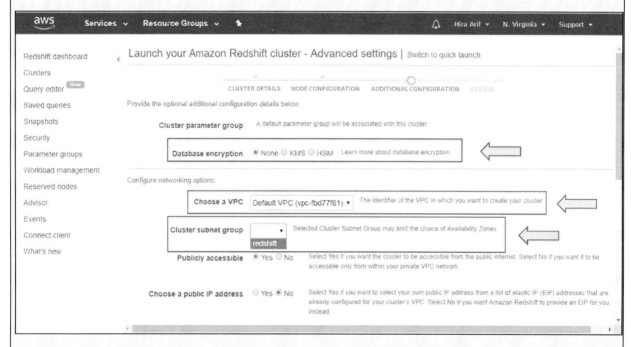

30. Leave publicly accessible, public IP address, Enhanced VPC Routing and Availability zone options as default. You can change it as required.
31. Select your VPC security group

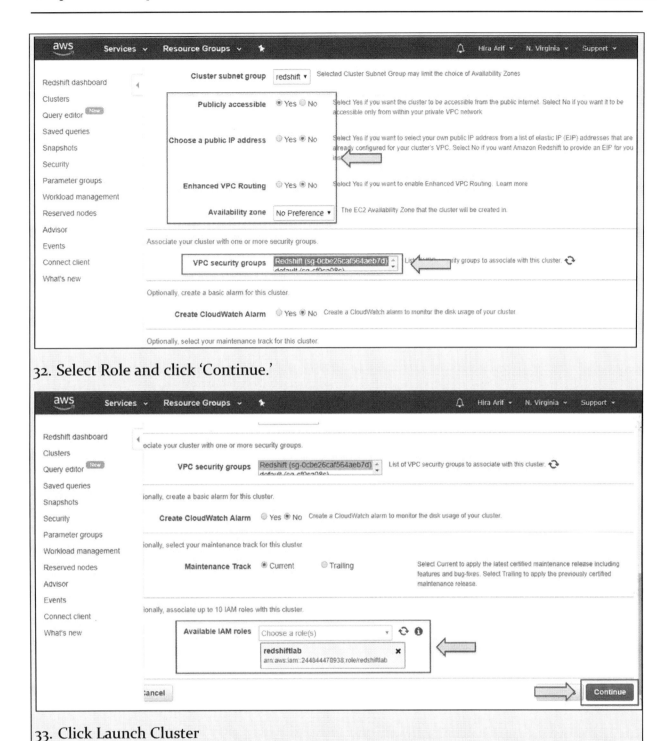

32. Select Role and click 'Continue.'

33. Click Launch Cluster

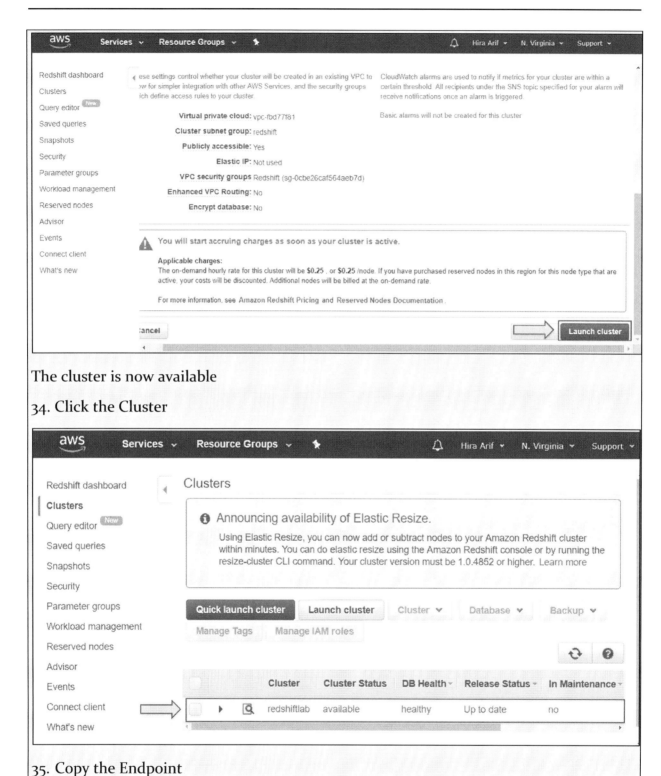

The cluster is now available

34. Click the Cluster

35. Copy the Endpoint

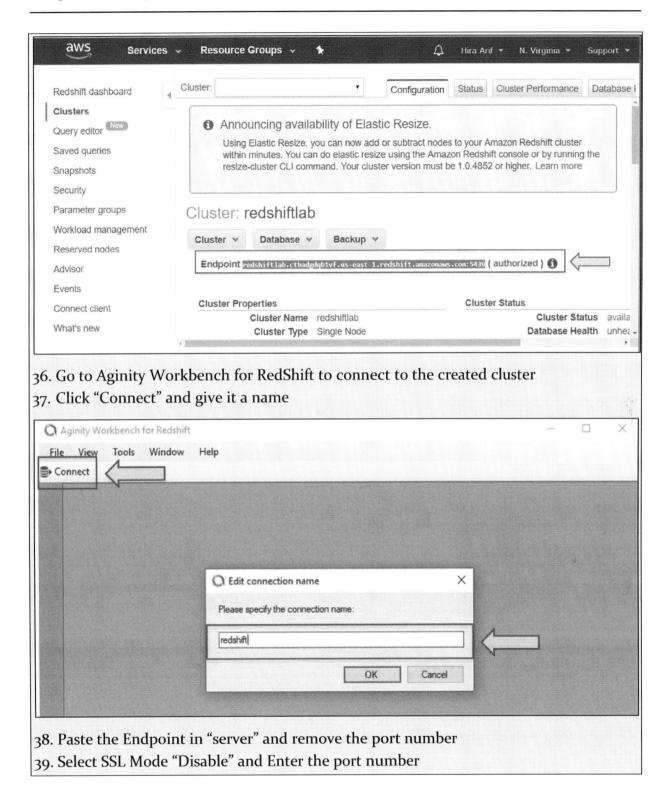

36. Go to Aginity Workbench for RedShift to connect to the created cluster

37. Click "Connect" and give it a name

38. Paste the Endpoint in "server" and remove the port number

39. Select SSL Mode "Disable" and Enter the port number

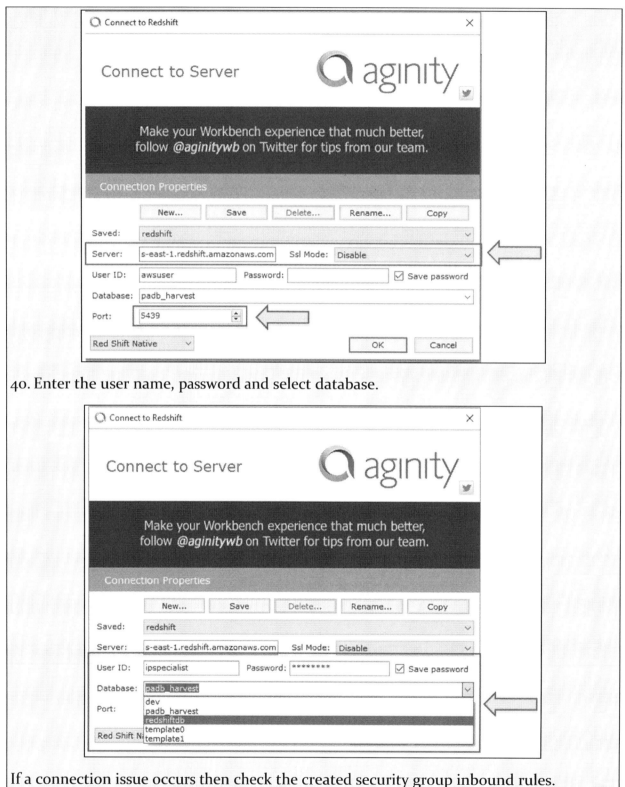

40. Enter the user name, password and select database.

If a connection issue occurs then check the created security group inbound rules.

The connection is successfully built.

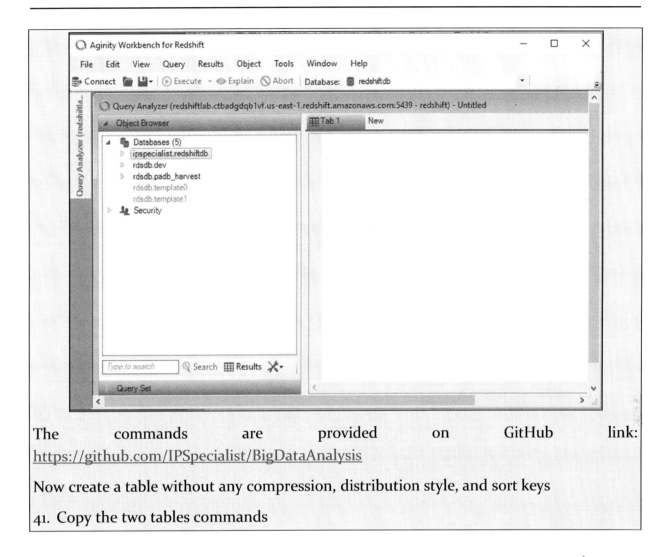

The commands are provided on GitHub link: https://github.com/IPSpecialist/BigDataAnalysis

Now create a table without any compression, distribution style, and sort keys

41. Copy the two tables commands

```
1    -- Create tables without compression, distribution style or sort keys:
2
3    CREATE TABLE orders_nocomp
4    (
5            o_orderkey BIGINT NOT NULL,
6            o_custkey BIGINT NOT NULL,
7            o_orderstatus CHAR(1) NOT NULL,
8            o_totalprice NUMERIC(12, 2) NOT NULL,
9            o_orderdate DATE NOT NULL,
10           o_orderpriority CHAR(15) NOT NULL,
11           o_clerk CHAR(15) NOT NULL,
12           o_shippriority INTEGER NOT NULL,
13           o_comment VARCHAR(79) NOT NULL);
14
15
16   CREATE TABLE lineitem_nocomp
17   (
18           l_orderkey BIGINT NOT NULL,
19           l_partkey BIGINT NOT NULL,
20           l_suppkey INTEGER NOT NULL,
21           l_linenumber INTEGER NOT NULL,
22           l_quantity NUMERIC(12, 2) NOT NULL,
23           l_extendedprice NUMERIC(12, 2) NOT NULL,
24           l_discount NUMERIC(12, 2) NOT NULL,
```

42. Paste it in Aginity
43. Click Execute

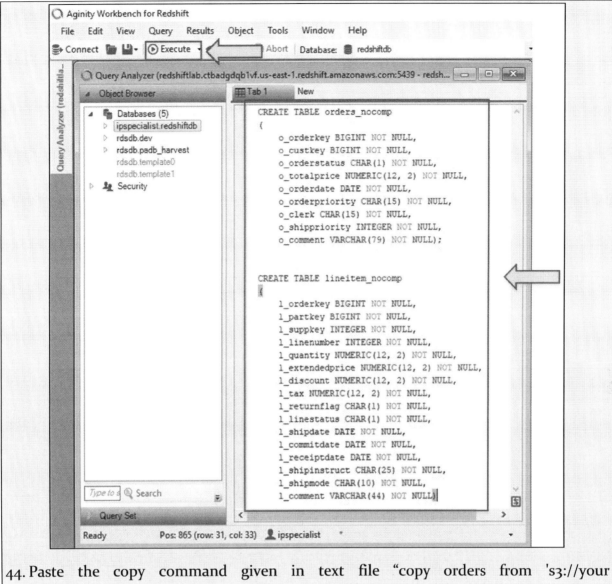

44. Paste the copy command given in text file "copy orders from 's3://your bucket/RedShiftdata/orders.manifest' iam_role 'arn:aws:iam::your account number:role/your role' delimiter '|' manifest;"

"copy lineitem from 's3://your bucket/RedShiftdata/lineitem.manifest' iam_role 'arn:aws:iam::your account number:role/your role' delimiter '|' manifest;"

Replace the S3 bucket path with your S3 path, and insert your Role ARN

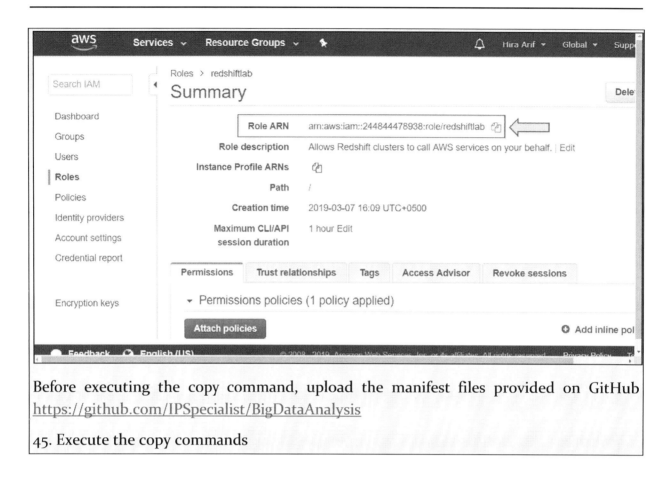

Before executing the copy command, upload the manifest files provided on GitHub https://github.com/IPSpecialist/BigDataAnalysis

45. Execute the copy commands

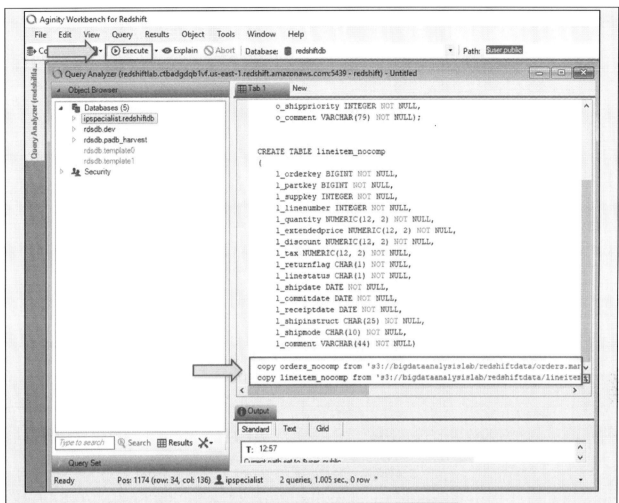

Note: Cluster performance of two same nodes can also be different

When a query is run for the first time, RedShift compiles the code and sends it to the compute node; therefore, the first query always takes more time than other queries.

46. Copy the code of Query for tables without compression from RedShift.txt file

```
40   -- Query for tables without compression, distribution style or sort keys:
41
42   SELECT
43       l_shipmode,
44       sum(case
45           when o_orderpriority = '1-URGENT'
46               OR o_orderpriority = '2-HIGH'
47               then 1
48           else 0
49       end) as high_line_count,
50       sum(case
51           when o_orderpriority <> '1-URGENT'
52               AND o_orderpriority <> '2-HIGH'
53               then 1
54           else 0
55       end) AS low_line_count
56   FROM
57       orders_nocomp,
58       lineitem_nocomp
59   WHERE
60       o_orderkey = l_orderkey
61       AND l_shipmode in ('AIR', 'SHIP')
62       AND l_commitdate < l_receiptdate
63       AND l_shipdate < l_commitdate
64       AND l_receiptdate >= date '1992-01-01'
```

47. Paste it in Aginity and execute it

It takes approximately 31 secs

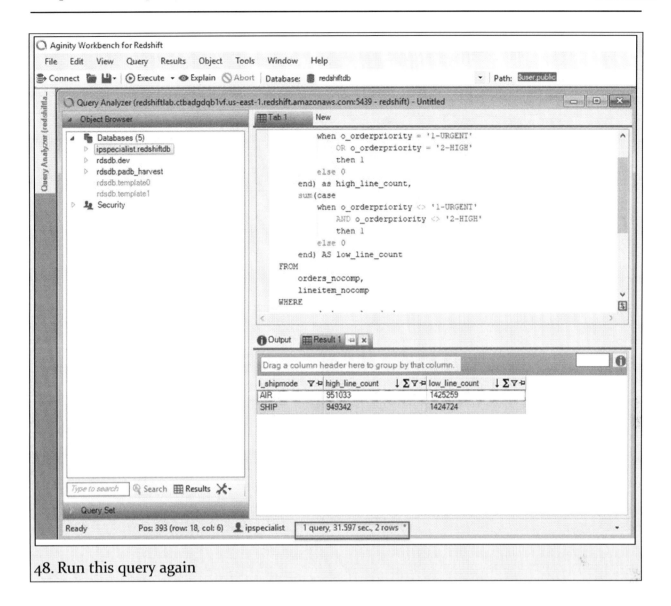

48. Run this query again

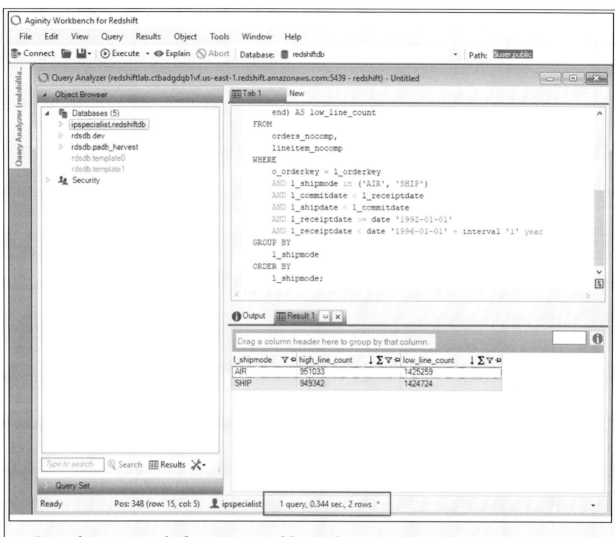

49. Copy the commands for creating tables with compression, but no distribution and sort keys from RedShift.txt file and execute it in Aginity

```
72   -- Create tables WITH compression, NO distribution style or sort keys:
73
74   CREATE TABLE orders_comp
75   (
76          o_orderkey BIGINT NOT NULL,
77          o_custkey BIGINT NOT NULL,
78          o_orderstatus CHAR(1) NOT NULL,
79          o_totalprice NUMERIC(12, 2) NOT NULL,
80          o_orderdate DATE NOT NULL,
81          o_orderpriority CHAR(15) NOT NULL,
82          o_clerk CHAR(15) NOT NULL,
83          o_shippriority INTEGER NOT NULL,
84          o_comment VARCHAR(79) NOT NULL);
85
86
87   CREATE TABLE lineitem_comp
88   (
89          l_orderkey BIGINT NOT NULL,
90          l_partkey BIGINT NOT NULL,
91          l_suppkey INTEGER NOT NULL,
92          l_linenumber INTEGER NOT NULL,
93          l_quantity NUMERIC(12, 2) NOT NULL,
94          l_extendedprice NUMERIC(12, 2) NOT NULL,
95          l_discount NUMERIC(12, 2) NOT NULL,
```

Tables are created with compression

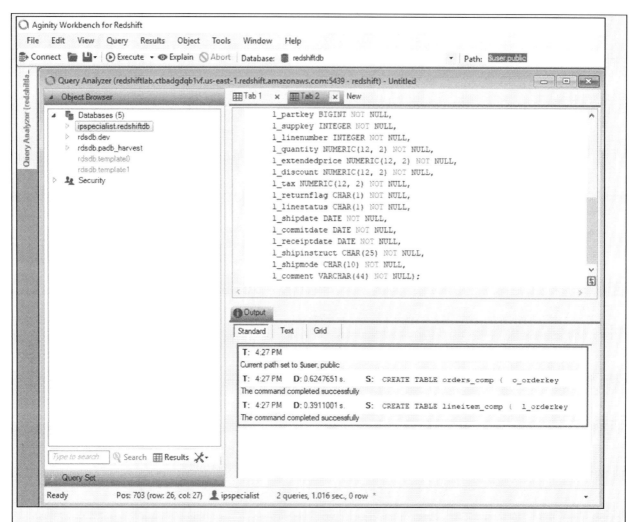

50. Now load the data into these tables from S3 by using the copy command where comupdate off is removed.

"copy orders_comp from 's3://bigdataanalysislab/RedShiftdata/orders.manifest' iam_role 'arn:aws:iam::244844478938:role/RedShiftlab' delimiter '|' manifest;"

"copy lineitem_comp from 's3://bigdataanalysislab/RedShiftdata/lineitem.manifest' iam_role 'arn:aws:iam::244844478938:role/RedShiftlab' delimiter '|' manifest;"

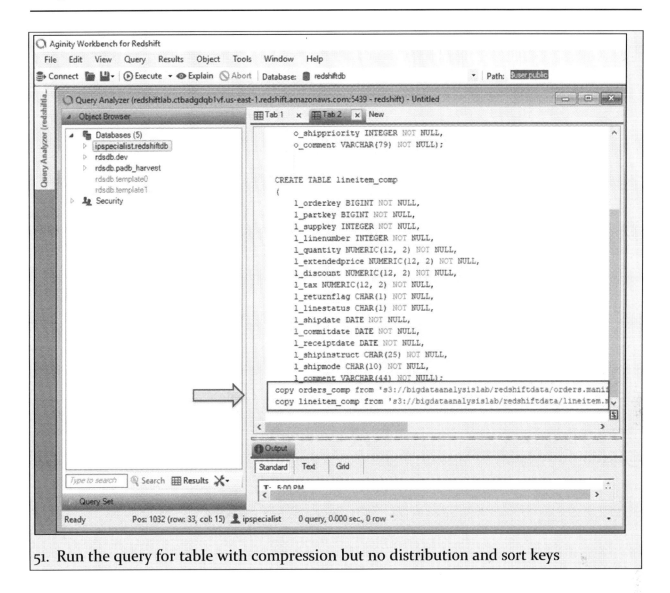

51. **Run the query for table with compression but no distribution and sort keys**

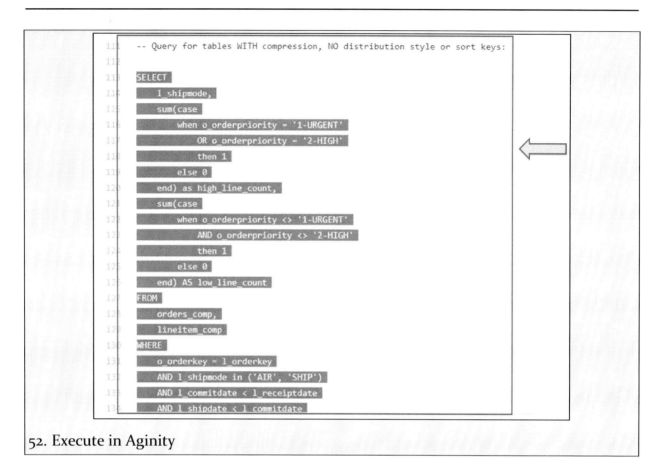

```
-- Query for tables WITH compression, NO distribution style or sort keys:

SELECT
    l_shipmode,
    sum(case
        when o_orderpriority = '1-URGENT'
            OR o_orderpriority = '2-HIGH'
        then 1
        else 0
    end) as high_line_count,
    sum(case
        when o_orderpriority <> '1-URGENT'
            AND o_orderpriority <> '2-HIGH'
        then 1
        else 0
    end) AS low_line_count
FROM
    orders_comp,
    lineitem_comp
WHERE
    o_orderkey = l_orderkey
    AND l_shipmode in ('AIR', 'SHIP')
    AND l_commitdate < l_receiptdate
    AND l_shipdate < l_commitdate
```

52. Execute in Aginity

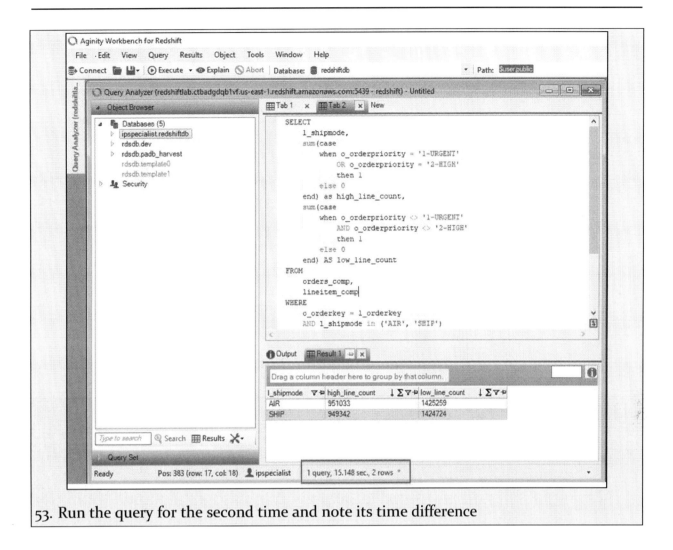

53. Run the query for the second time and note its time difference

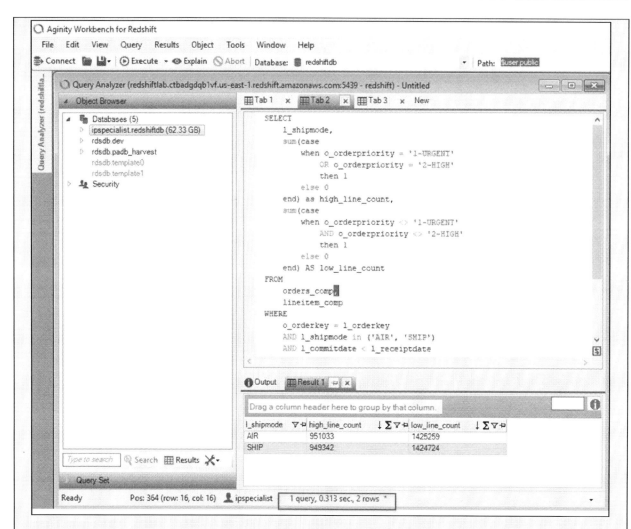

Tables without compression take longer time than tables with compression to execute a query.

54. Copy the commands to create the table with compression, distribution style, and sort keys.

```
138         l_shipmode
139     ORDER BY
140         l_shipmode;
141
142     -- Create tables WITH compression, distribution style and sort keys:
143
144     CREATE TABLE orders
145     (
146             o_orderkey BIGINT NOT NULL DISTKEY,
147             o_custkey BIGINT NOT NULL,
148             o_orderstatus CHAR(1),
149             o_totalprice NUMERIC(12, 2),
150             o_orderdate DATE NOT NULL,
151             o_orderpriority CHAR(15) NOT NULL,
152             o_clerk CHAR(15) NOT NULL,
153             o_shippriority INTEGER NOT NULL,
154             o_comment VARCHAR(79) NOT NULL
155     )
156     SORTKEY
157     (
158             o_orderdate
159     );
160
161     CREATE TABLE lineitem
```

55. Execute the command to create table

56. Copy command in Aginity

"copy orders from 's3://your bucket/RedShiftdata/orders.manifest' iam_role 'arn:aws:iam::your account number:role/your role' delimiter '|' manifest;"

"copy lineitem from 's3://your bucket/RedShiftdata/lineitem.manifest' iam_role 'arn:aws:iam::your account number:role/your role' delimiter '|' manifest;"

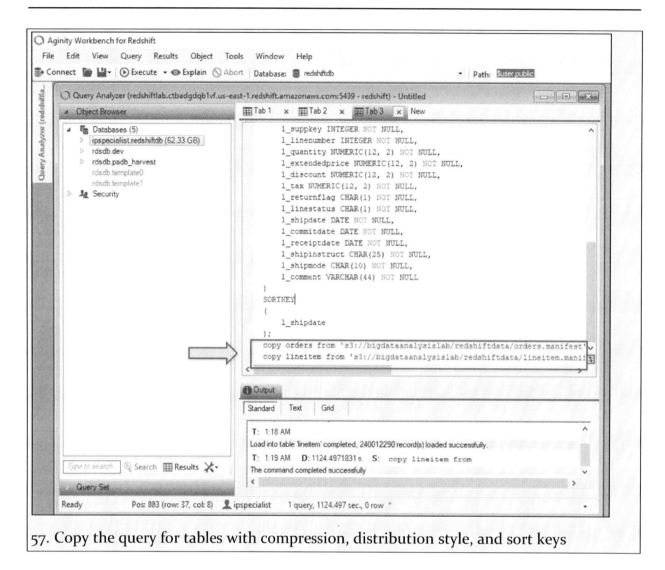

57. Copy the query for tables with compression, distribution style, and sort keys

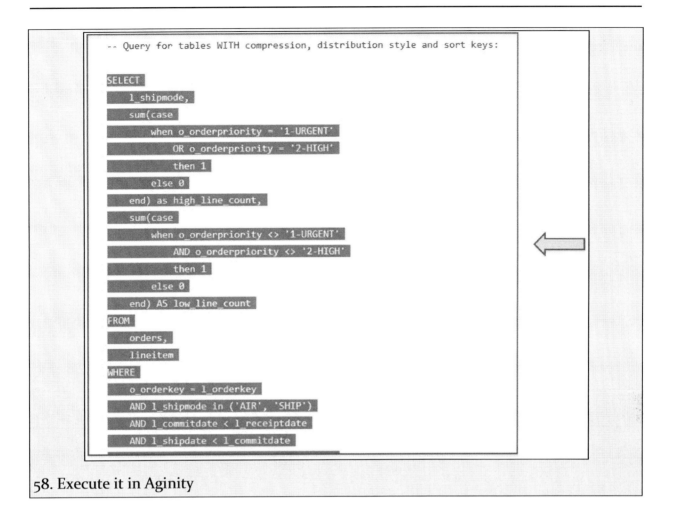

```
-- Query for tables WITH compression, distribution style and sort keys:

SELECT
    l_shipmode,
    sum(case
        when o_orderpriority = '1-URGENT'
            OR o_orderpriority = '2-HIGH'
            then 1
        else 0
    end) as high_line_count,
    sum(case
        when o_orderpriority <> '1-URGENT'
            AND o_orderpriority <> '2-HIGH'
            then 1
        else 0
    end) AS low_line_count
FROM
    orders,
    lineitem
WHERE
    o_orderkey = l_orderkey
    AND l_shipmode in ('AIR', 'SHIP')
    AND l_commitdate < l_receiptdate
    AND l_shipdate < l_commitdate
```

58. Execute it in Aginity

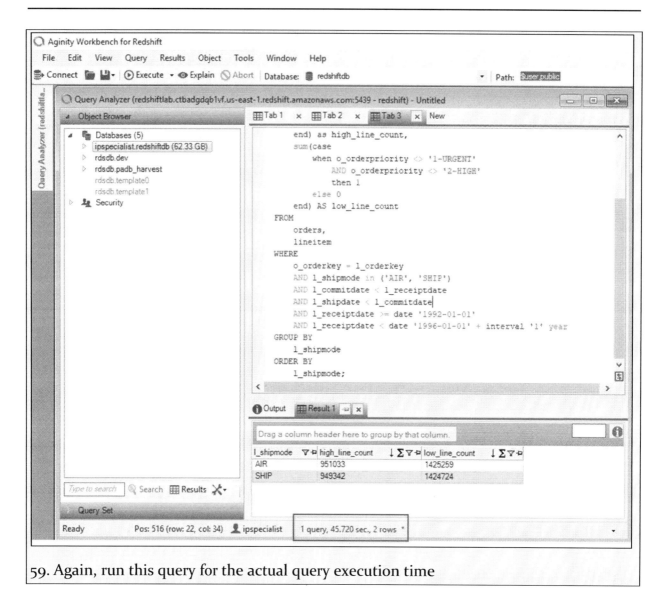

59. Again, run this query for the actual query execution time

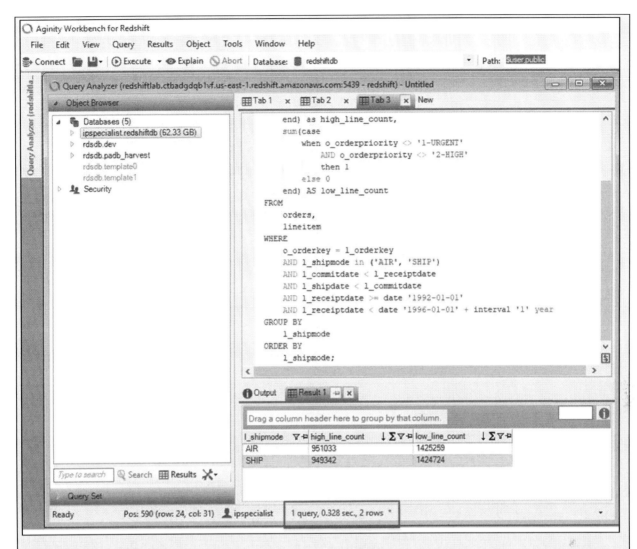

Conclusion:

Tables without compression have maximum query execution time, tables with compression but no distribution style and sort keys have minimum query execution time. Table with compression, distribution style, and sort keys have query execution time more than without distribution style and sort keys table but less than the query execution time of table without compression. Therefore, when working on less number of nodes and not much larger size data, distribution style, and sort keys do not have any significant effect on the query execution time but to keep the proper design in practice, one should have the habit of distribution style and sort keys in the table.

Machine Learning

It is an application of Artificial intelligence, which allows a machine to analyze any situation and learn from its previous situations (percept history) on its own without being programmed or user intervention.

Use Cases

- Fraud detection by the help of a number of data points
- Customer service: when someone is browsing any information and facing difficulty then this situation will be automatically detected and assisted.
- Models can be used to translate legal language into simple language so that it can be helpful in understanding the contracts easily.
- Security related to finding malware files in thousands of documents
- Healthcare: by understanding the patient's data
- Game predictions with the previous dataset with the scores of any team or player

Algorithms

Two mostly used machine learning algorithms are: Unsupervised learning and Supervised learning.

Unsupervised Learning

In this learning, the available data is not labeled, i.e., no tags or no classifications. Therefore, data cannot be sorted, and no columns can be added. It is a self-guided learning algorithm. Unsupervised learning algorithm helps you to figure out data patterns and groupings. AWS Machine learning does not support unsupervised learning so for it use Amazon EMR with spark Machine learning library.

Supervised Learning

The supervised learning algorithm is applied on the datasets containing any labels, tags or classifications. In this algorithm, it is already known which type of data is to be extracted. Training data is also provided for data learning. Training data is the set of data, which assists in the prediction. Supervised learning is used for predictive analytics.

In Figure 5-55 the data is classified and can be used to predict data whereas in Figure 5-56 data is random with no labels and grouping can be performed.

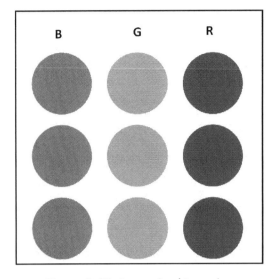

Figure 5-47: Supervised Learning

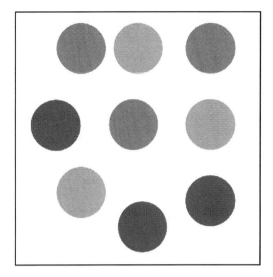

Figure 5-48: Unsupervised Learning

Amazon SageMaker

It is a fully managed Machine Learning service provided by AWS. This service assists data scientists and developers in building and training machine learning models easily and quickly, then deploy these models into a production-hosted environment. In order to access easily to the data sources for analysis and exploration, an integrated jupyter authoring notebook instance is provided by Amazon SageMaker. There is no need to manage servers. SageMaker provides common Machine Learning algorithms, and the user can create their own algorithms.

Note: AWS provides Amazon MachineLearning service which is for the previous customers only whereas it is now replaced by Amazon SageMaker, which is a more advanced service for Machine Learning.

Lab 5-03: Machine Learning

Scenario: A Bank launches a new service 'Certificate of deposit.' A Machine Learning developer of that Bank Marketing Department has to predict how many customers will enrol for this service by using the previous dataset, which indicates if the customer is enrolling in various bank services.

Solution

Use Amazon SageMaker service, which makes it easy to build an ML model.

1. Go to Amazon SageMaker console

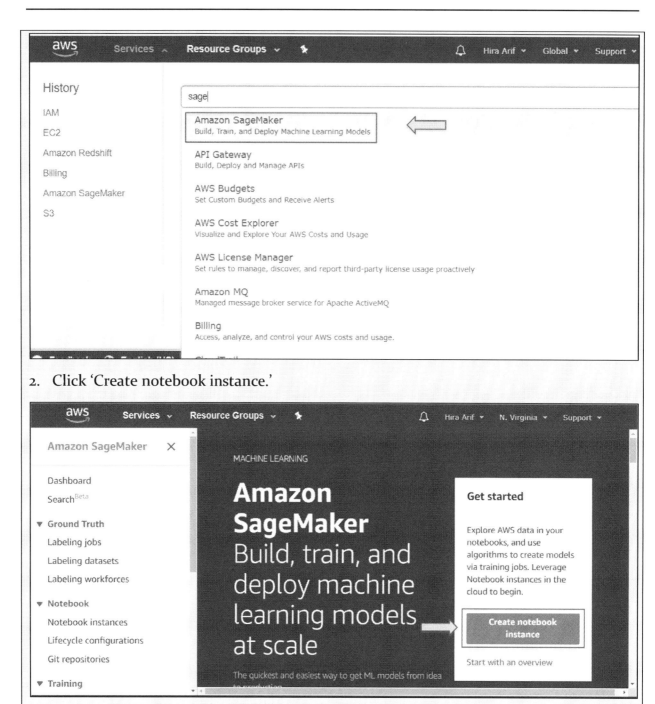

2. Click 'Create notebook instance.'

3. Give this instance a name 'MySageMakerInstance.'

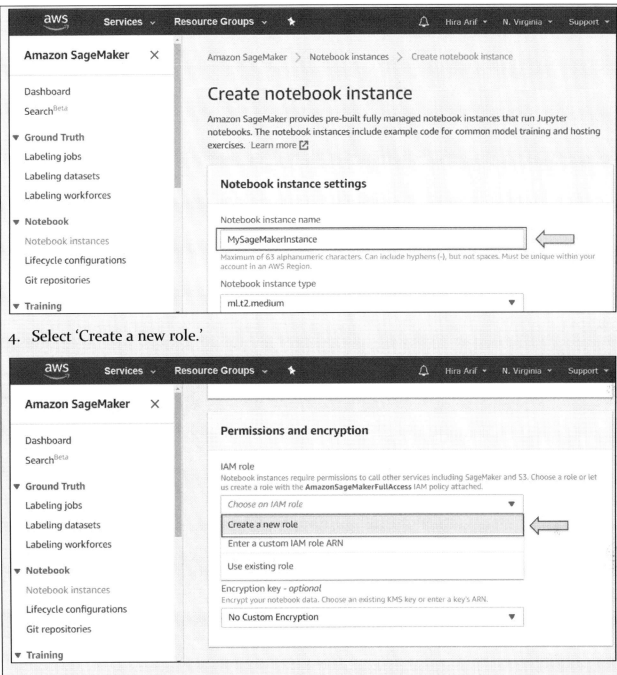

4. Select 'Create a new role.'

5. Select 'Any S3 bucket' so that Amazon SageMaker get access to all S3 buckets. Click 'Create a role.'

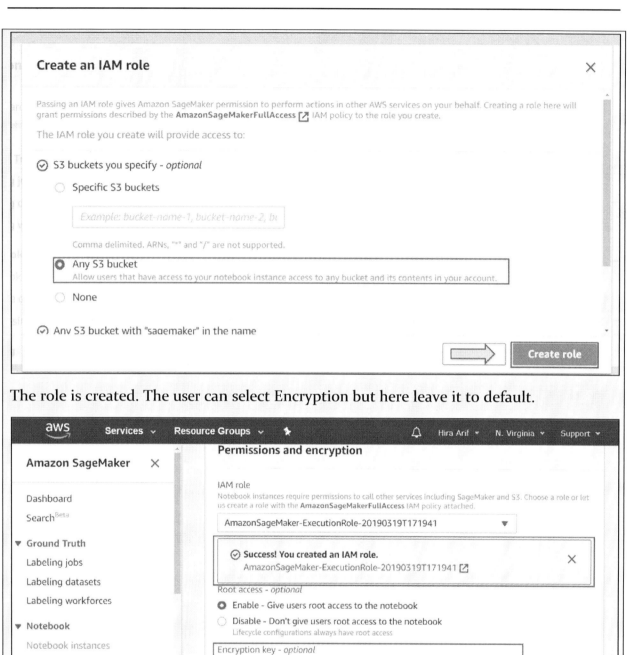

The role is created. The user can select Encryption but here leave it to default.

6. Click 'Create notebook instance.'

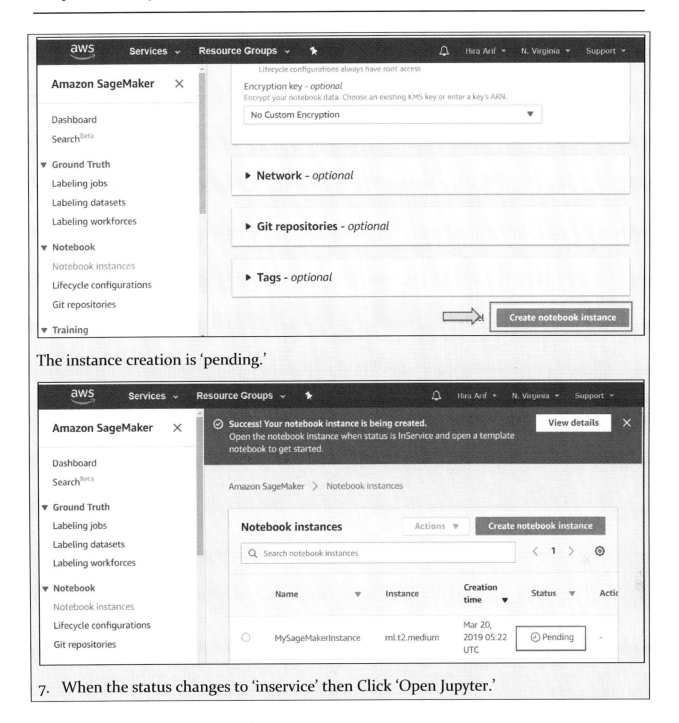

The instance creation is 'pending.'

7. When the status changes to 'inservice' then Click 'Open Jupyter.'

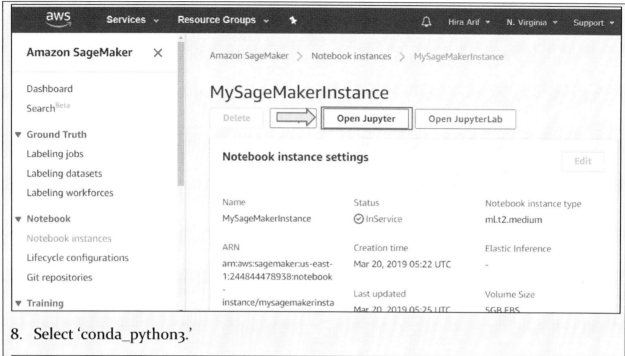

8. Select 'conda_python3.'

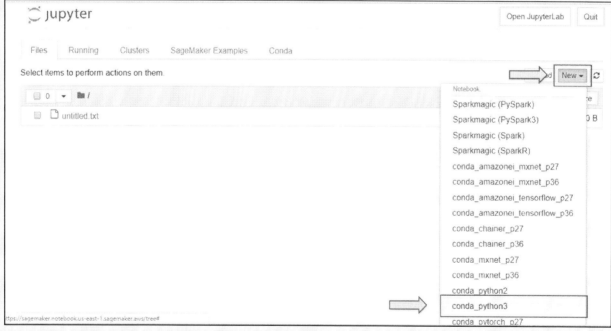

9. Copy the code in it. (Provided in the sagemaker.txt file on GitHub) in order to import libraries and to define new environmental variables

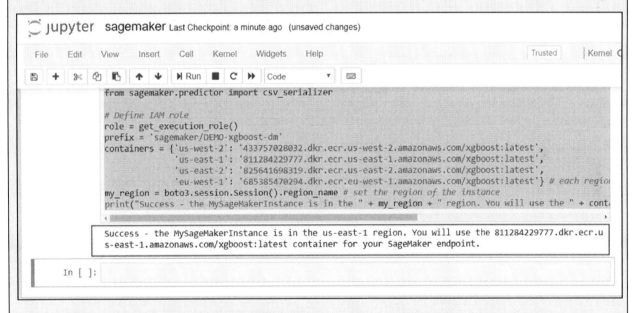

```
# import libraries
import boto3, re, sys, math, json, os, sagemaker, urllib.request
from sagemaker import get_execution_role
import numpy as np
import pandas as pd
import matplotlib.pyplot as plt
from IPython.display import Image
from IPython.display import display
from time import gmtime, strftime
from sagemaker.predictor import csv_serializer

# Define IAM role
role = get_execution_role()
prefix = 'sagemaker/DEMO-xgboost-dm'
containers = {'us-west-2': '433757028032.dkr.ecr.us-west-2.amazonaws.com/xgboost:latest',
              'us-east-1': '811284229777.dkr.ecr.us-east-1.amazonaws.com/xgboost:latest',
              'us-east-2': '825641698319.dkr.ecr.us-east-2.amazonaws.com/xgboost:latest',
              'eu-west-1': '685385470294.dkr.ecr.eu-west-1.amazonaws.com/xgboost:latest'} # each regio
my_region = boto3.session.Session().region_name # set the region of the instance
print("Success - the MySageMakerInstance is in the " + my_region + " region. You will use the " + cont
```

10. Run the code

```
from sagemaker.predictor import csv_serializer

# Define IAM role
role = get_execution_role()
prefix = 'sagemaker/DEMO-xgboost-dm'
containers = {'us-west-2': '433757028032.dkr.ecr.us-west-2.amazonaws.com/xgboost:latest',
              'us-east-1': '811284229777.dkr.ecr.us-east-1.amazonaws.com/xgboost:latest',
              'us-east-2': '825641698319.dkr.ecr.us-east-2.amazonaws.com/xgboost:latest',
              'eu-west-1': '685385470294.dkr.ecr.eu-west-1.amazonaws.com/xgboost:latest'} # each regio
my_region = boto3.session.Session().region_name # set the region of the instance
print("Success - the MySageMakerInstance is in the " + my_region + " region. You will use the " + cont
```

```
Success - the MySageMakerInstance is in the us-east-1 region. You will use the 811284229777.dkr.ecr.u
s-east-1.amazonaws.com/xgboost:latest container for your SageMaker endpoint.
```

11. Copy the S3 bucket code, change the bucket name and execute this code.

An S3 bucket will be created to store training data

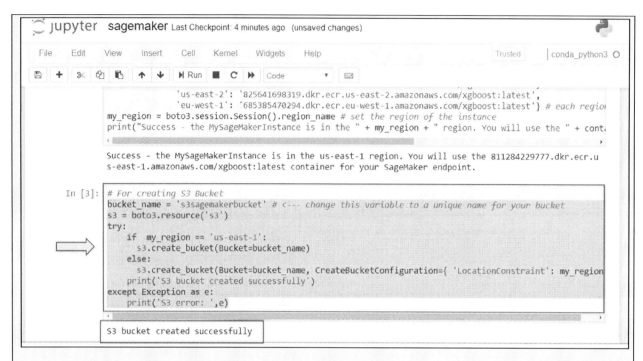

12. Copy the code 'download the data into the instance' for downloading data to the SageMaker instance and to load it into a dataframe.

13. Copy the commands of 'shuffle and split data' and execute it. These commands will shuffle the data and split it into Training data (70%) and Test data (30%)

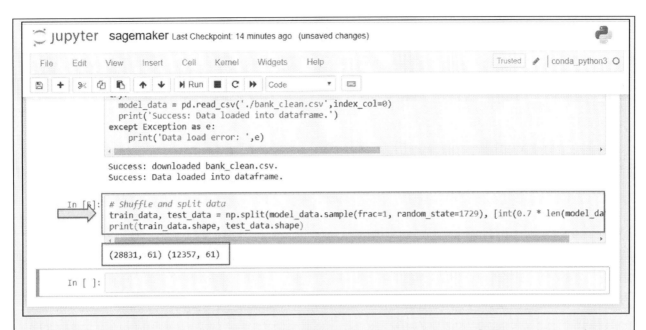

For using pre-built XGBoost model, header and first column of the training data is required to reformat and then load it from S3 bucket.

14. Copy and Run the commands of 'Train the model from data.'

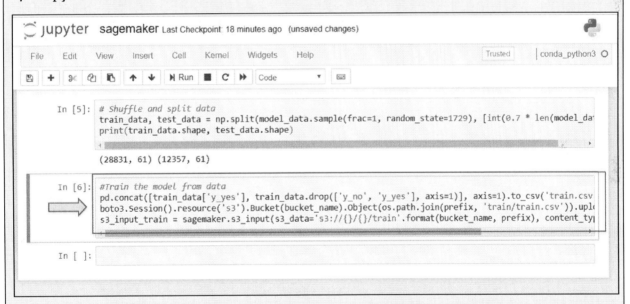

15. Copy and Run the commands of 'Setup the sagemaker session' for setting the sagemaker session, creating an XGBoost model instance and defining the model hyperparameters.

16. Using gradient optimization to train the model, Copy and Run the code of 'gradient optimization.'

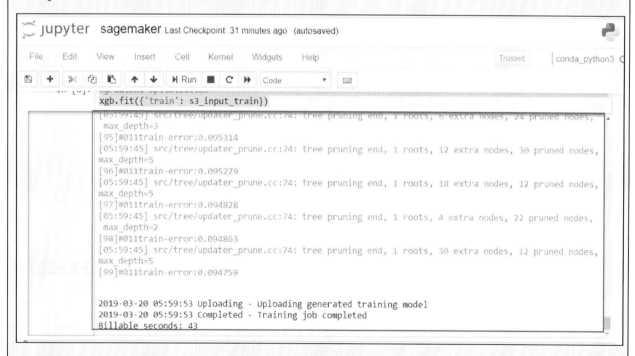

17. Copy and Run the code 'Deploy' to deploy the model on a server and creating the endpoint.

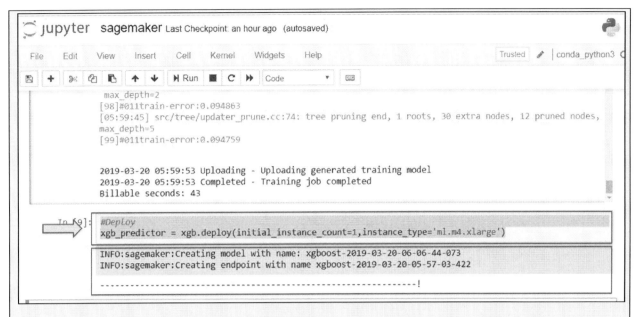

18. Copy the code 'predictions' and Run it. This code will predict whether the customers in test data are enrolled for bank product or not.

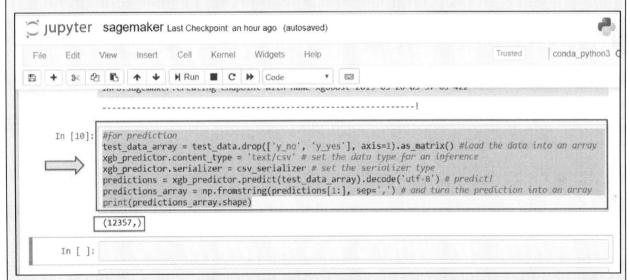

19. For comparing the predicted results with the actual in a matrix called confusion matrix, Run the code 'Evaluate model.'

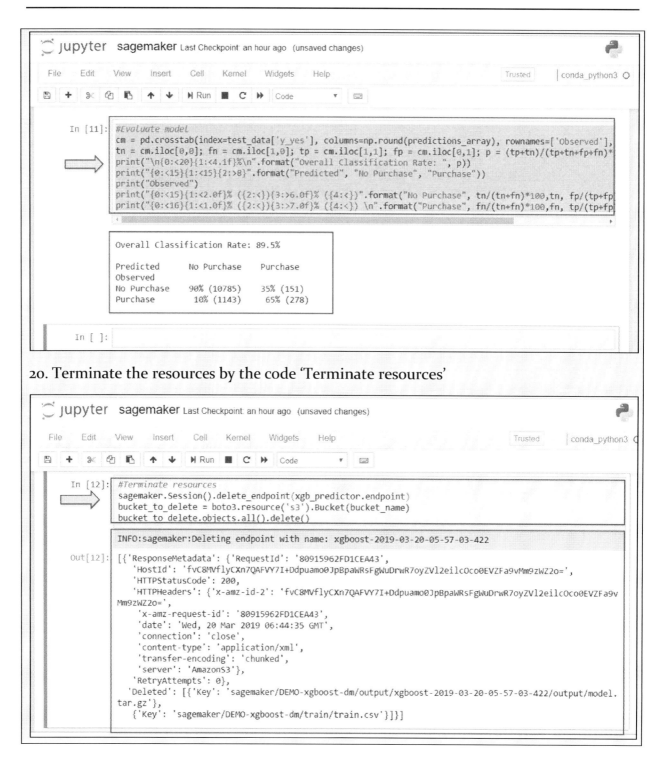

20. Terminate the resources by the code 'Terminate resources'

Elasticsearch

It is a distributed, multitenant-capable full-text search engine. Multitenancy means that this search engine can serve multiple customers. It has an HTTP web interface, and JSON documents are schema-free. Elasticsearch can be integrated with Logstash and Kibana.

Logstash is the data collection and log-praising engine whereas Kibana is an Open-source data visualization and exploration tool. When Elasticsearch is used with Logstash and Kibana, they are referred as ELK stack. Elasticsearch is a versatile tool with many use cases.

Use Cases include:

- Search
- Logging and analysis: Logstash will be used to collect the logs, and Kibana will analyze these logs. This will help in security purpose.
- Distributed document store: User can create applications to store billions of documents.
- Real-time application monitoring: User can use Elasticsearch to capture logs across applications and websites for real-time analysis. For this purpose, Logstash is used to push logs into Elasticsearch where data is indexed and made available for the near Real-time analysis. For visualization and analysis of data, Kibana is used.
- Clickstream weblog ingestion.

Amazon Elasticsearch Service

Amazon provides an Elasticsearch service, which is a fully managed service used for running Elasticsearch. For this, user has to install Elasticsearch on EC2. The compute instances are provisioned with Elasticsearch by using this service, which includes patching of instances, recovery from failure, Backups, Monitoring and security integration with IAM and auditing with CloudTrail.

Integration of Elasticsearch with other AWS services

Elasticsearch can be integrated with other AWS services such as IoT, S3, DynamoDB, Kinesis Streams, CloudWatch.Kinesis Firehose is integrated with Elasticsearch via Lambda Function. Lambda functions process the data received by these services and then stream it to Elasticsearch.

Amazon Elasticsearch Service Domain

It is the collection of all resources needed to run the Elasticsearch cluster. To create a domain, user should configure the cluster, which includes:

- A number of instances and types that depend on the number of applications and number of events.
- The dedicated master node, which is used to increase cluster stability. It is a cluster node for performing cluster management tasks but does not hold data or upload data on request

- Distribution of nodes across availability zones can be set
- Storage and snapshot settings
- Index settings
- IAM policy to control access of domain

Dedicated Master Nodes

Dedicated master nodes are used for cluster management tasks that include tracking all nodes in the cluster, a number of indices in the cluster, how many charges belong to each index, cluster state changes, etc. At least 3 dedicated master nodes allocation is recommended by AWS for each Elasticsearch domain.

Indices and Shards

Indices are similar to the table in Relational databases. An index is a logical namespace, and it maps to primary shards and replica shards. There can be one or more primary shards and 0 or more replica shards. Schema-free JSON documents are stored in a shard. First, the document is stored in a primary shard then it is stored in a replica shard. Replica shard serves as a backup in case of any issue with primary shard and also helps in performance. Replica shards are on different nodes.

Zone Awareness

Zone Awareness can be set up by using Amazon Elasticsearch Service, which involves the allocation of nodes across two availability zones in the same region. Primary shards can be in one one-availability zone and replica shards in another availability zone. Zone Awareness can affect network latency. For zone Awareness, even number of instances are required.

Loading of data into Elasticsearch

The given diagram below is for the illustration of the loading of data into an Elasticsearch using a Lambda function.

1. The user has to enable VPC flow logs in a specific VPC. Flow log data is posted to Amazon CloudWatch Logs by VPC. The data is then streamed to Lambda.
2. The data is passed to Firehose via Lambda ingestor function. The Lambda function is provided by AWS in the GitHub repository.
3. The data is then passed by Firehose to Lambda decorator function.
4. Lambda decorator function performs a number of lookups on data and then transfer it to Firehose with additional fields.
5. The errors are passed to S3, and the data is passed to Amazon Elasticsearch service.

Fields added by Lambda decorator function are as follows:

- The source includes the data results in looking up a free service for geographical lookups. This includes country code, country name, region code, region name, city, location, longitude, and latitude.

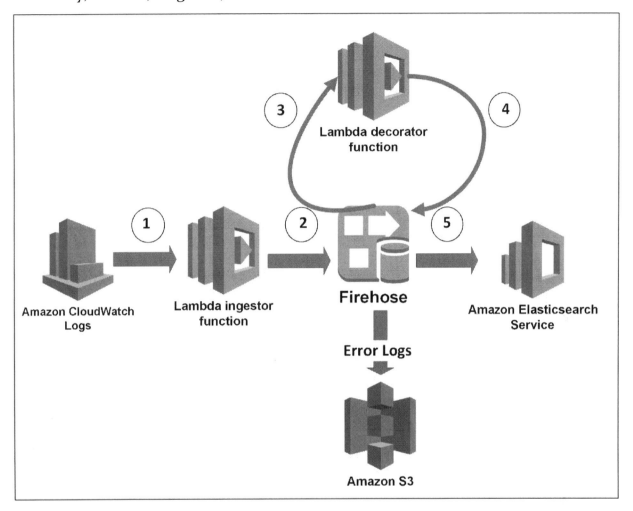

Figure 5-49: Loading Data into Elasticsearch

Logstash

Amazon Elasticsearch service is connected with the Logstash output plugin that is provided by AWS on GitHub. This plugin is installed on the application instance, which helps to push data from instance to Amazon Elasticsearch service domain.

Note: Couple of ways to load data into Elasticsearch are Lambda and Logstash

RStudio

RStudio is a programming language having a free software environment used for statistical computing and graphics. RStudio is widely used for statistical software and analysis among statisticians and data miners.

Characteristics

- It is used for statistical and data analysis.
- Machine learning and predictive analytics.
- It has high quality graphing and charting capabilities.
- It is platform independent.

RStudio is defined as an Open-source IDE for R. Two additions of RStudio are:

- RStudio Desktop.
- RStudio Server allows access of RStudio through a web browser.

RStudio server can integrate with various AWS big data services such as Athena, RedShift, EMR, RDS, and S3. RStudio is integrated with these services by using drivers and packages.

Lab 5-04: RStudio

Scenario

A company wants to fetch and analyze its dataset stored in the S3 bucket.

Solution

Use RStudio to fetch the file and then further data analysis can be obtained by R.

1. Go to EC2 instance console and create a security group

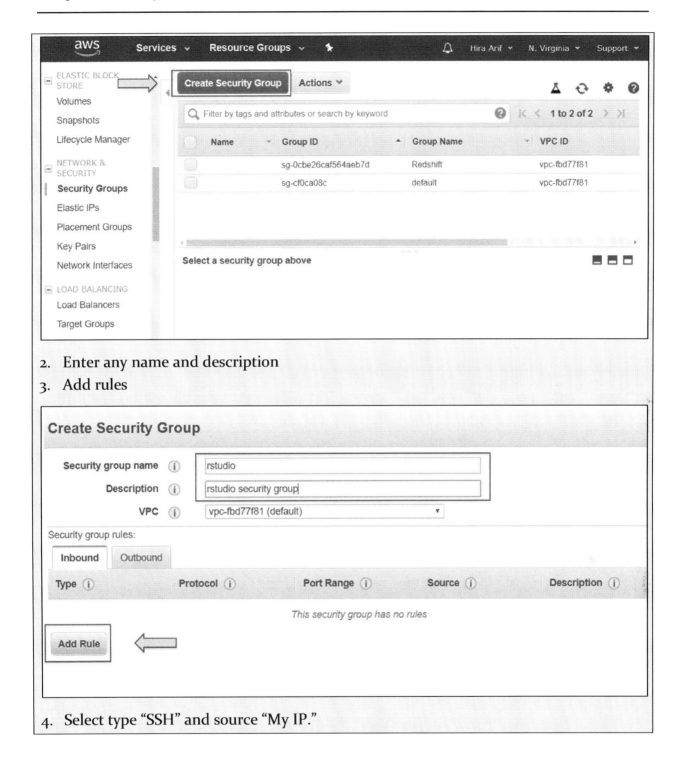

2. Enter any name and description
3. Add rules

4. Select type "SSH" and source "My IP."

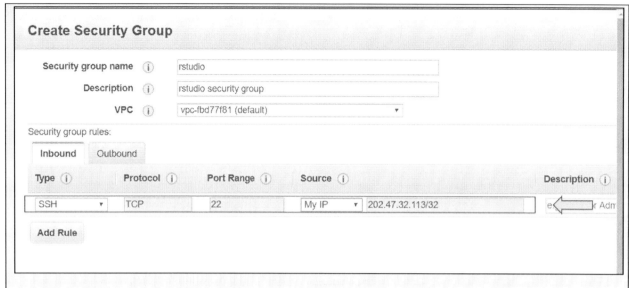

5. Create a custom rule with "8787" port range for RStudio and source "My IP."
6. Create it.

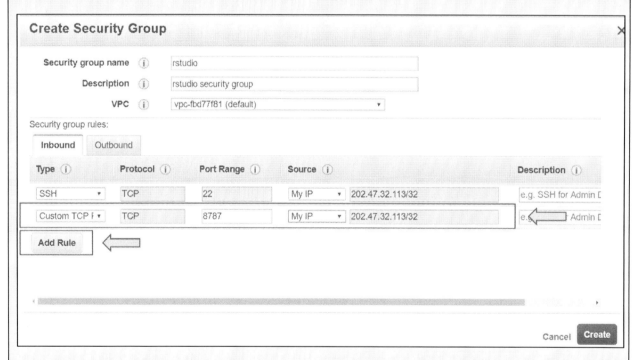

7. Go to the IAM console to create a role with policy "AmazonS3FullAccess."
8. Launch an EC2 instance with the created security group and the role attached.
9. Log in to your EC2 instance and install R by using the command "sudo yum install -y R."

```
    Verifying  : 32:bind-license-9.9.4-73.amzn2.1.1.noarch             7/15
    Verifying  : kernel-4.14.104-95.84.amzn2.x86_64                    8/15
    Verifying  : 32:bind-libs-lite-9.9.4-61.amzn2.1.1.x86_64           9/15
    Verifying  : 32:bind-utils-9.9.4-61.amzn2.1.1.x86_64              10/15
    Verifying  : python2-botocore-1.12.92-1.amzn2.0.1.noarch          11/15
    Verifying  : 32:bind-license-9.9.4-61.amzn2.1.1.noarch            12/15
    Verifying  : 1:openssl-libs-1.0.2k-16.amzn2.0.2.x86_64            13/15
    Verifying  : 1:openssl-1.0.2k-16.amzn2.0.2.x86_64                 14/15
    Verifying  : 32:bind-libs-9.9.4-61.amzn2.1.1.x86_64               15/15

Installed:
  kernel.x86_64 0:4.14.104-95.84.amzn2

Updated:
  bind-libs.x86_64 32:9.9.4-73.amzn2.1.1
  bind-libs-lite.x86_64 32:9.9.4-73.amzn2.1.1
  bind-license.noarch 32:9.9.4-73.amzn2.1.1
  bind-utils.x86_64 32:9.9.4-73.amzn2.1.1
  openssl.x86_64 1:1.0.2k-16.amzn2.0.3
  openssl-libs.x86_64 1:1.0.2k-16.amzn2.0.3
  python2-botocore.noarch 0:1.12.92-2.amzn2.0.1

Complete!
[ec2-user@ip-172-31-38-68 ~]$ sudo yum install -y R
```

10. Download RStudio by using the command "wget https://download2.rstudio.org/rstudio-server-rhel-1.0.153-x86_64.rpm."

```
ec2-user@ip-172-31-44-164:~                                   —  □  ×
    texlive-varwidth.noarch 2:svn24104.0.92-38.24.amznl
    texlive-wasy.noarch 2:svn15878.0-38.24.amznl
    texlive-wasysym.noarch 2:svn15878.2.0-38.24.amznl
    texlive-xcolor.noarch 2:svn15878.2.11-38.24.amznl
    texlive-xdvi.noarch 2:svn26689.22.85-38.24.amznl
    texlive-xdvi-bin.x86_64 2:svn26509.0-38.20130427_r30134.24.amznl
    texlive-xkeyval.noarch 2:svn27995.2.6a-38.24.amznl
    texlive-xunicode.noarch 2:svn23897.0.981-38.24.amznl
    texlive-zapfchan.noarch 2:svn28614.0-38.24.amznl
    texlive-zapfding.noarch 2:svn28614.0-38.24.amznl
    tre.x86_64 0:0.8.0-18.20140228gitc2f5d13.3.amznl
    tre-common.noarch 0:0.8.0-18.20140228gitc2f5d13.3.amznl
    tre-devel.x86_64 0:0.8.0-18.20140228gitc2f5d13.3.amznl
    xorg-x11-proto-devel.noarch 0:7.7-9.10.amznl
    xz-devel.x86_64 0:5.1.2-12alpha.12.amznl
    zlib-devel.x86_64 0:1.2.8-7.18.amznl
    zziplib.x86_64 0:0.13.62-1.3.amznl

Dependency Updated:
  glibc.x86_64 0:2.17-260.175.amznl    glibc-common.x86_64 0:2.17-260.175.amznl

Complete!
[ec2-user@ip-172-31-44-164 ~]$ wget https://download2.rstudio.org/rstudio-server
-rhel-1.0.153-x86_64.rpm
```

11. Install RStudio by using the command "sudo yum install -y --nogpgcheck rstudio-server-rhel-1.0.153-x86_64.rpm"

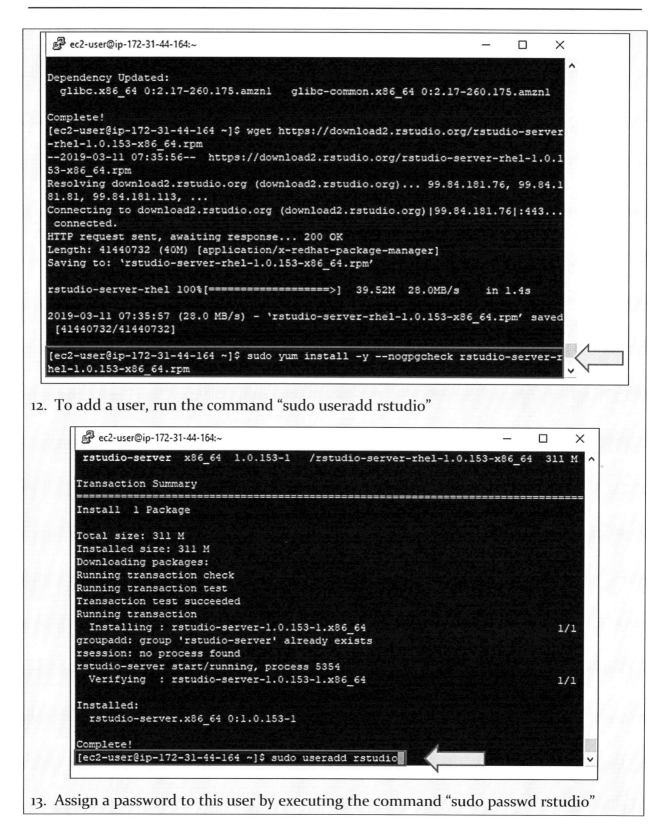

12. To add a user, run the command "sudo useradd rstudio"

13. Assign a password to this user by executing the command "sudo passwd rstudio"

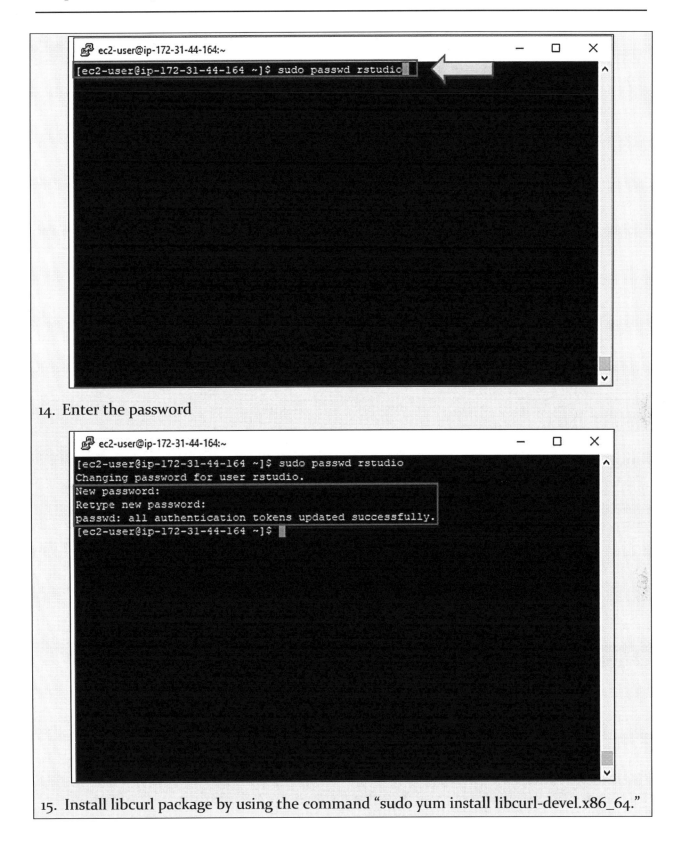

14. Enter the password

15. Install libcurl package by using the command "sudo yum install libcurl-devel.x86_64."

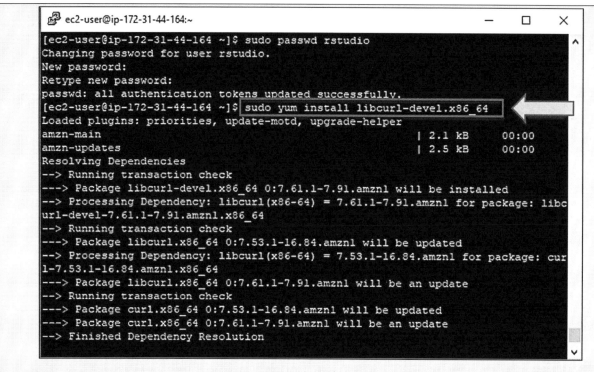

16. Copy the RStudio instance IP or public DNS name in the web browser with RStudio port number (DNS name;8787)

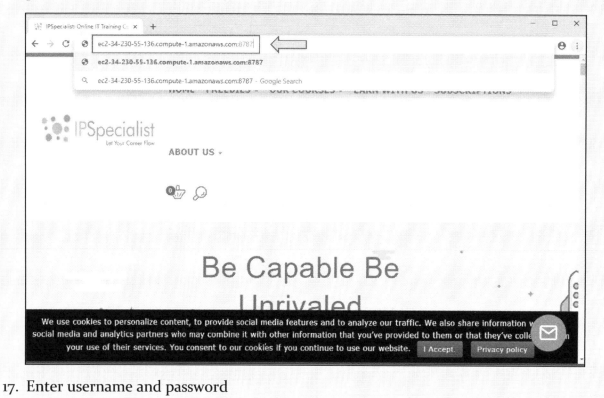

17. Enter username and password

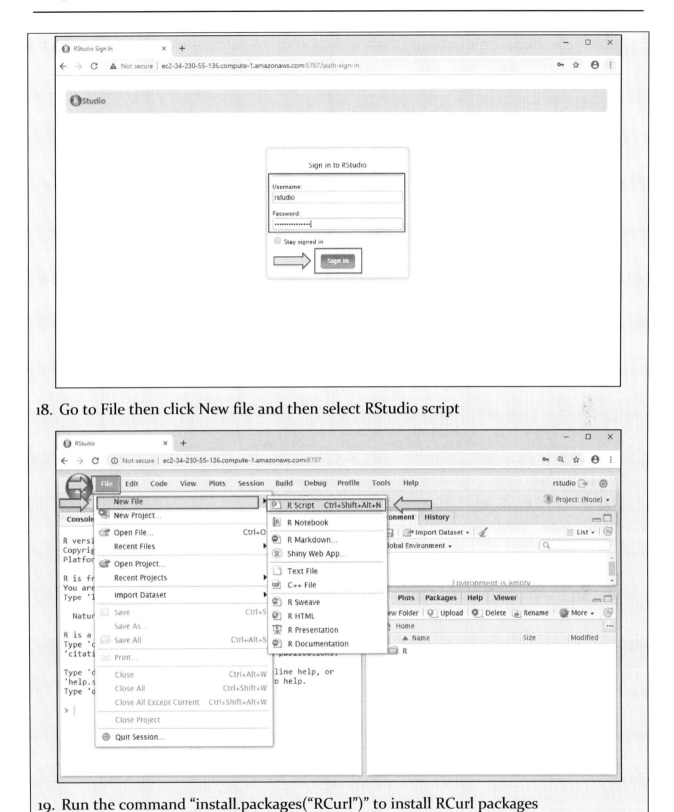

18. Go to File then click New file and then select RStudio script

19. Run the command "install.packages("RCurl")" to install RCurl packages

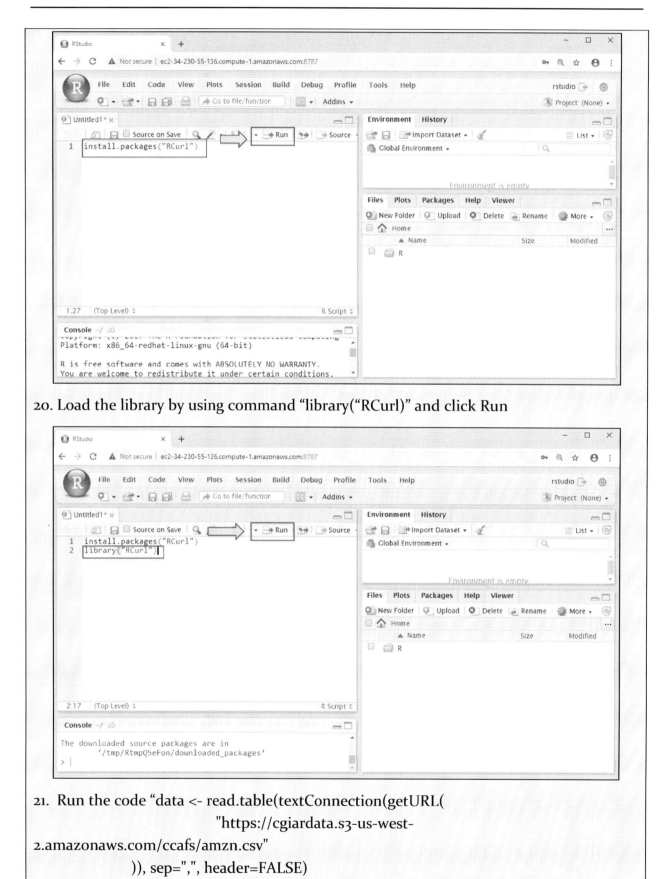

20. Load the library by using command "library("RCurl)" and click Run

21. Run the code "data <- read.table(textConnection(getURL(

"https://cgiardata.s3-us-west-

2.amazonaws.com/ccafs/amzn.csv"

)), sep=",", header=FALSE)

head(data)" which will fetch the data from S3

The URL can be changed according to the file that user wants to fetch

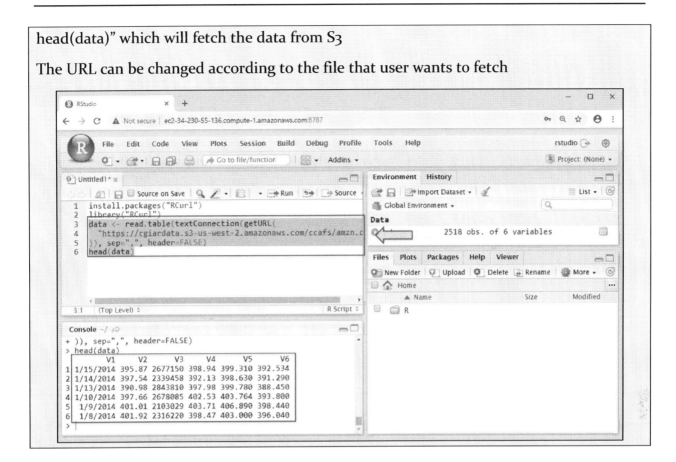

Athena

Athena is a query service, which helps to analyze data in Amazon S3 by using standard SQL. It is a server-less service; therefore, management of infrastructure is not required, and the cost is only based on the query execution.

Server-less refers to the service where administration is not required. It does not need any backups or snapshots, as the data is stored in S3. This feature does not demand any spin up, which means if large data query has to be executed, more nodes spin up will not be necessary.

For example, AWS IoT service processes the data and then transfers it to Amazon Kinesis Firehose. Kinesis Firehose captures and streams the data to Amazon S3. Furthermore, user can analyze data in S3 with Athena using SQL.

Presto and Hive

Athena provide full standard SQL support by using Presto, and it supports DDL by using Hive.

Data Formats

Athena supports CSV, TSV, JSON, Textfiles, ORC, and Parquet. It also supports compressed data in Snappy, Zlib, LZO, and GZIP.

Integration with AWS Glue

AWS Glue is used to categorize your data, clean it, enrich it, and move it reliably between various data stores. This service is fully managed ETL (Extract, Transform and Load). Automatically, AWS Glue Crawlers store the associated metadata in an AWS Glue Data Catalog, entering the database and table schema from your data source. By using AWS Glue crawler, a table can be created in Athena.

Comparison of Athena with other AWS services

Comparing Athena with RedShift, EMR, S3 Select, and Glacier Select.

RedShift

It is used for enterprise reporting, BI or Fast query, which involves complex SQL queries. RedShift is not server-less, as it needs running nodes. The data is extracted from a number of different sources.

EMR

EMR is used to run distributed processing frameworks like Hadoop, Spark, HBase, etc. EMR is a flexible service as the user can run custom applications in code, amount of compute required, take benefit of spot instances, select the required memory and storage, etc. EMR can run Machine Learning and data transform.

S3 Select

It is used for retrieving a subset of data from an object via simple SQL expressions. The performance of the application is increased as the data is only the demanded one.

Glacier Select

Data can be extracted by a Glacier query within a minute. Standard SQL statements can run directly against the Glacier object after the data is retrieved. Restoration to S3 is not required.

Athena is used to run ad-hoc queries in S3. It is a server-less service, and data formatting is not required. It can be integrated with RedShift or EMR.

For example, data has to be ingested into RedShift from S3. Athena can be used to check the data and then ingested into RedShift.

Lab 5-05: Athena

Scenario

A company wants to create a database and tables in that database for the files stored in an S3 bucket. Then they want to execute a query with the help of any server-less infrastructure.

Solution

They can create a database by using Athena.

1. Go to S3 console and select the bucket created for big data

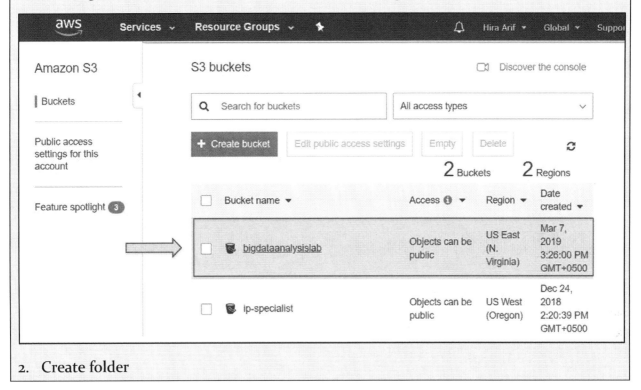

2. Create folder

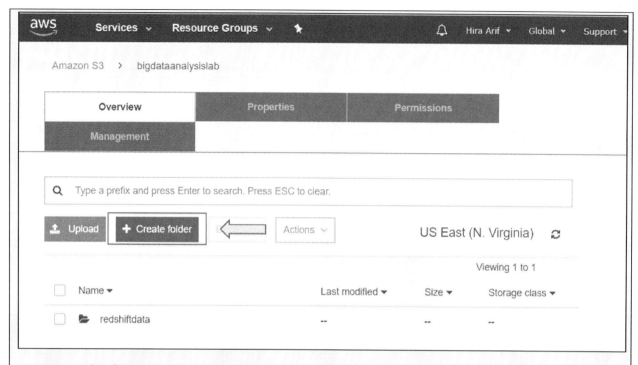

3. Name the folder and save it

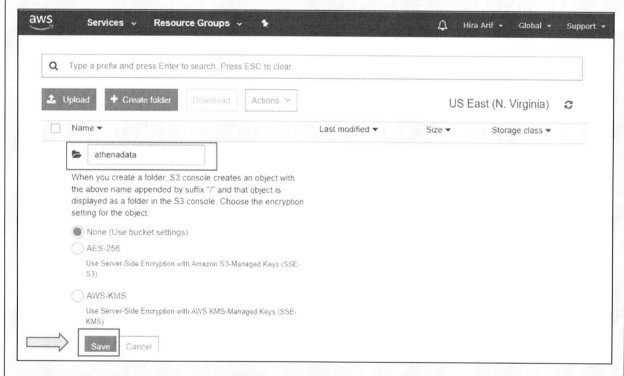

Note: For this lab generate the dataset by following the same procedure as the RedShift data was generated but generate the data of 10 GB by using the command "./dbgen –v –T o –s 10" and move the two files 'lineitem.tbl' and 'orders.tbl' in S3 bucket.

4. Create two more folders in "athenadata" name orders and line item

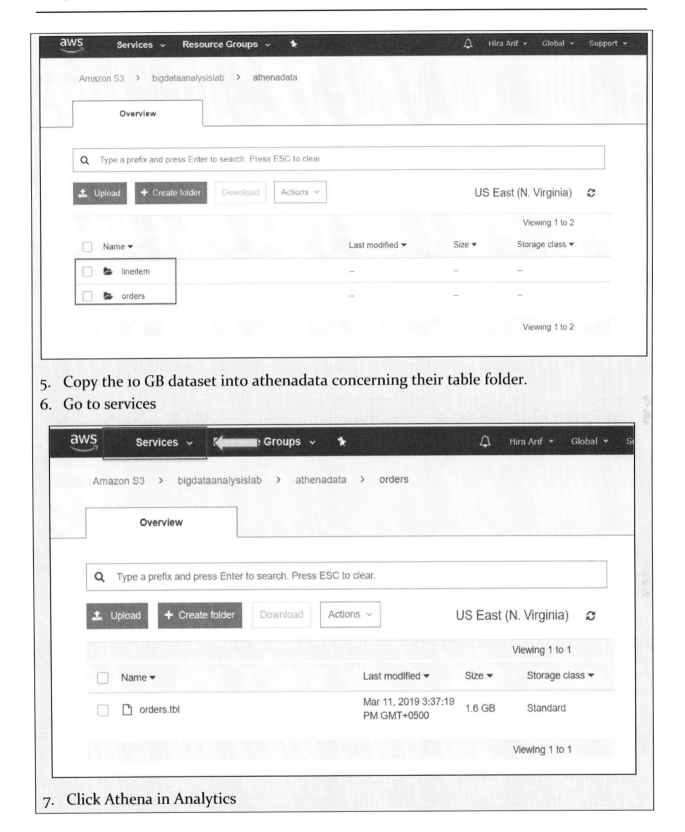

5. Copy the 10 GB dataset into athenadata concerning their table folder.

6. Go to services

7. Click Athena in Analytics

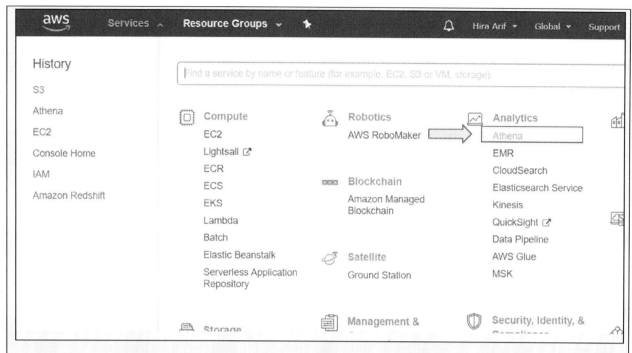

8. Click Get Started

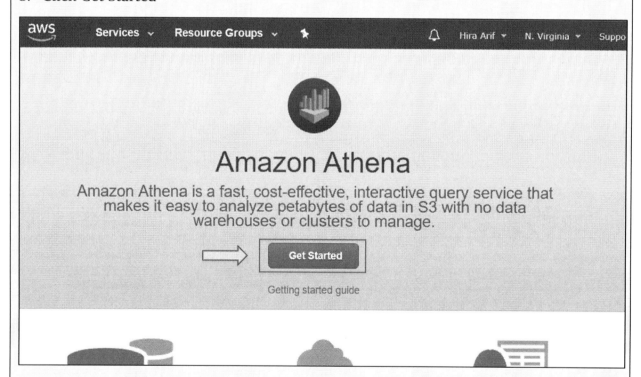

elb_logs are available in the sample database to get started, but in this lab, a new database will be created. This database will store the metadata, not the actual data which is in S3 bucket.

9. Open new tab

10. Run command "create database athenalab;" and click the Run query

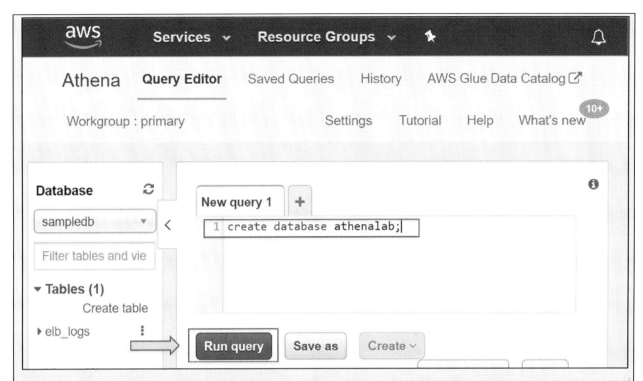

A file name Athenacode.txt is given at the following link. Edit this file with your dataset path of S3.

https://github.com/IPSpecialist/BDS-chap5-lab/blob/master/Athenacode.txt

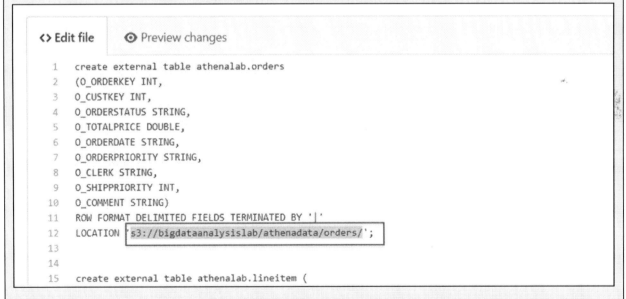

11. Copy these create table commands in Athenacode.txt file and paste in the new query tab

12. Highlight the table for orders and run the query and similarly highlight the second query and run it.

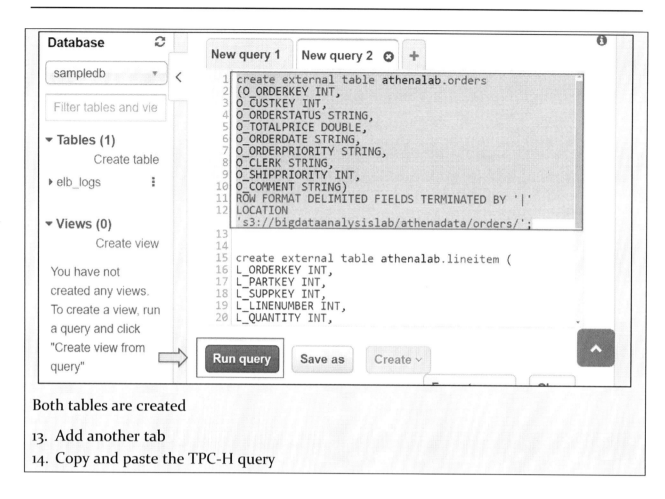

Both tables are created

13. Add another tab
14. Copy and paste the TPC-H query

```
36    TPC-H Query:
37
38    select
39      l_shipmode,
40      sum(case
41        when o_orderpriority ='1-URGENT'
42             or o_orderpriority ='2-HIGH'
43        then 1
44        else 0
45    end
46      ) as high_line_count,
47      sum(case
48        when o_orderpriority <> '1-URGENT'
49             and o_orderpriority <> '2-HIGH'
50        then 1
51        else 0
52    end
53      ) as low_line_count
54    from
55      orders o join lineitem l
56      on
57        o.o_orderkey = l.l_orderkey and l.l_commitdate < l.l_receiptdate
58    and l.l_shipdate < l.l_commitdate and l.l_receiptdate >= '1994-01-01'
59    and l.l_receiptdate < '1995-01-01'
60    where
61      l.l_shipmode = 'MAIL' or l.l_shipmode = 'SHIP'
62    group by l_shipmode
63    order by l_shipmode;
```

15. Run this query

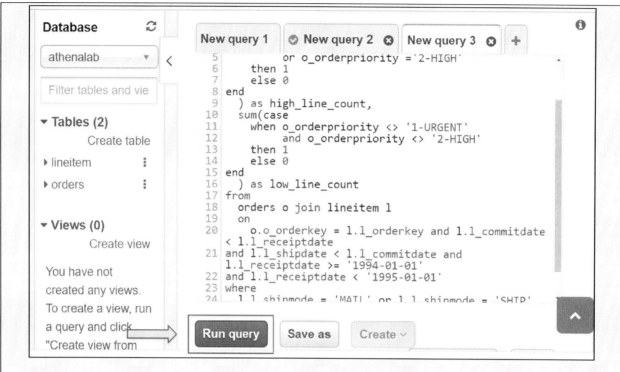

16. Result of query

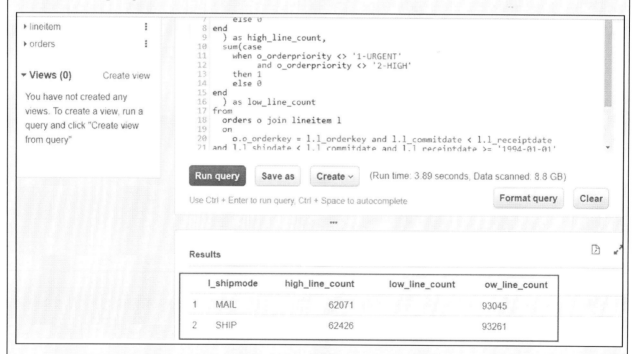

17. Click AWS Glue Data Catalog as the metadata for these tables are stored there.

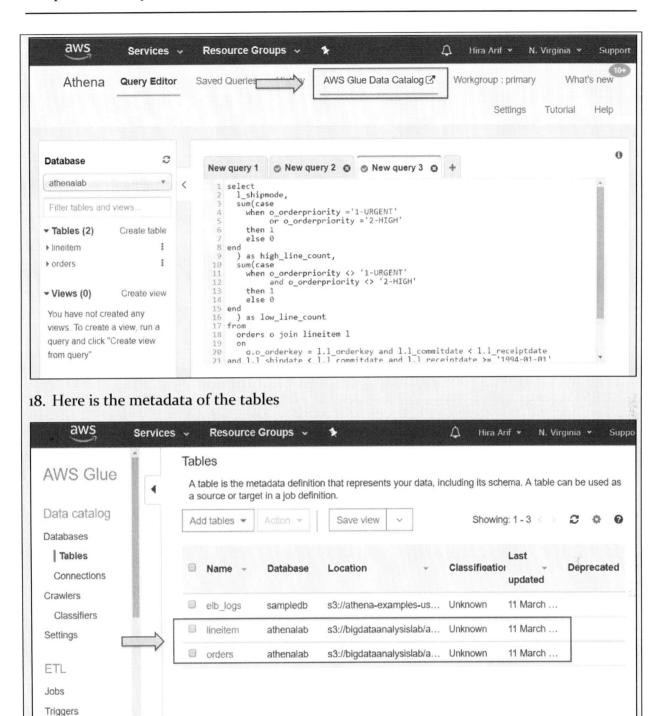

18. Here is the metadata of the tables

Mind Map

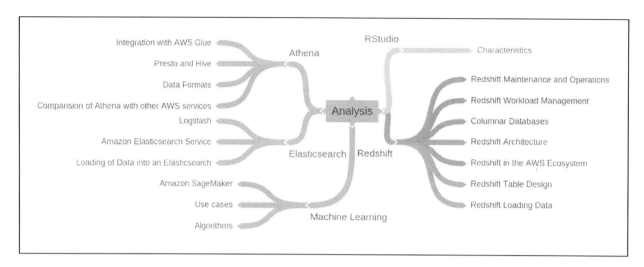

Figure 5-50: Chapter's Mind Map

Practice Questions

1. Choose two machine learning types that are commonly encountered?
   A. Supervised Learning
   B. Unsupervised Learning
   C. Hypervised Learning
   D. Transcoded Learning

2. Choose the fastest and efficient way for loading data into RedShift
   A. By restoring backup data files into RedShift.
   B. By using multi-line INSERTS
   C. By using the COPY command
   D. By using single-line INSERTS

3. How many queries can you execute at the same time on a RedShift cluster?
   A. 20
   B. 30
   C. 40
   D. 50

4. In your RedShift cluster, you have a table, and the data in this table changes rarely. The table has less than 15 million rows, and no other tables JOIN. Choose the appropriate distribution style.
   A. All
   B. Default
   C. KEY
   D. EVEN

5. Which is not a RedShift manifest function?
   A. To load files that have a different prefix
   B. To automatically check files in S3
   C. To load files from different buckets
   D. To load required files only

6. Choose 3 services that integrate directly with RedShift via the COPY command.
   A. EMR/EC2 instances
   B. S3
   C. Data Pipeline
   D. Machine Learning
   E. DynamoDB
   F. Kinesis Stream

7. BI analysts consistently combine two tables in your current data warehouse: the customer table and the order table. Customer_id is the column on which they JOIN

(and common to both tables). Both tables are very large, with more than one billion rows. You are responsible for the design of the tables in RedShift as well as the migration of data. Which style of distribution would you choose when BI analysts run customer_id queries for the JOIN customer table and the order table?

A. All
B. KEY
C. EVEN
D. Default

8. Select the benefits and use cases of Columnar Databases. (Choose 2)

A. Compression, as it helps with performance and provides a lower total cost of ownership.
B. They are ideal for Online Analytical Processing (OLAP)
C. They are ideal for 'needle in a haystack' queries
D. They are ideal for the small amount of data
E. They store binary objects quite well

9. All of the days, your analytics team carries out extensive, long - term automated queries. The results of these important queries are then used for business decisions. However, the analytics team also performs small ad - hoc queries manually. How can you ensure that the large queries do not take up all the resources, preventing the smaller ad-hoc queries from running?

A. Create a query user group for small queries based on the analysts' RedShift user IDs, and create a second query group for the large, long-running queries.
B. Assign each query a priority number
C. Do nothing, because RedShift handles this automatically
D. Setup node affinity and assign large queries and small queries to run specific nodes.

10. Defining primary keys and foreign keys is a major part of the design of RedShift as it ensures data integrity. True or False?

A. True
B. False

11. Indicate the most effective way to merge data into an existing table.

A. Execute an UPSERT
B. Connect the source table and the target RedShift table via a replication tool and run direct INSERTS, UPDATES into the target RedShift table.
C. UNLOAD data from RedShift into an S3, use EMR to merge new data files with the unloaded data files, and copy the data into RedShift.
D. Use a staging table to replace existing rows or update existing rows.

12. Using the RedShift UNLOAD to write data into S3, files are automatically created

using Amazon S3 server-side encryption with SSE - S3 encryption key. Using the RedShift UNLOAD to write data into S3, files are automatically created using Amazon S3 server-side encryption with SSE - S3 encryption key managed by AWS. True or False?

    A. True

    B. False

13. RedShift can be used for Transactional processing. True or False?

    A. True

    B. False

14. Compute node assists the communication between the SQL clients or BI tools and Compute nodes. True or False?

    A. True

    B. False

15. RedShift stores data in:

A. Both Rows and Columns

B. Cells

C. Columns

D. Rows

16. Which of the following is not the distribution style in RedShift?

    A. KEY

    B. ALL

    C. EVEN

    D. ODD

17. Which of the following is the default type of sort key?

    A. Single

    B. Primary

    C. Compound

    D. Secondary

18. Manual compression is easily applicable. True or False?

    A. True

    B. False

19. How many user-defined queues are allowed?

    A. 6

    B. 7

    C. 8

    D. 9

20. You can use UPSERT to update any table in RedShift. True or False?

    A. True

B. False

21. Which command is used to execute a vacuum on all the tables?

   A. VACUUM REINDEX

   B. VACUUM SORT ONLY

   C. VACUUM DELETE ONLY

   D. VACUUM FULL

22. Vacuum commands on large tables are recommended. True or False?

   A. True

   B. False

23. Which of the following Amazon service provides Machine Learning?

   A. CloudWatch

   B. CloudTrail

   C. Elasticsearch

   D. SageMaker

24. Which of the service helps to push data from instance into an Elasticsearch?

   A. Amazon Kinesis

   B. CloudWatch

   C. Logstash

   D. None of the above

25. RStudio is defined as an Open-source IDE for?

   A. Java

   B. Python

   C. C

   D. R

Chapter 06: Visualization

Introduction

This chapter includes the basics of visualization and applications used to perform visualization for the analysis of business insights. Amazon QuickSight service is used to build visualizations and allows you to get better business analysis. This chapter includes the following main topics which cover the bunch of multiple topics:

- Amazon QuickSight Introduction.
- QuickSight Visualization.
- Big Data Visualization.

Amazon QuickSight Introduction

QuickSight is a cloud-based analytics service that permits you to build visualizations and perform Ad-hoc analysis allowing you to get better business insights. Amazon QuickSight is a fast, cloud-powered business intelligence (BI) carrier that makes it smooth and allows you to supply insights to concerned people in the organization.

QuickSight helps you create and submit interactive dashboards that may be accessed from browsers or cellular devices. You can embed dashboards into your programs, imparting your customers with effective self-carrier analytics. QuickSight, without difficulty scales to a lot of customers without any software program to put in, servers to deploy, or infrastructure to manage.

Use Cases

With QuickSight you can analyze marketing data, sales data, financial data, operations data, and any other interesting data that might be there in the data source. First, look at which data source QuickSight supports. With QuickSight you can ingest data from Redshift, Aurora, Athena, as well as the RDS (MariaDB 10.0 and later, SQL Server 2012 or later, MySQL 5.1 or later, and Postgre SQL 9.3.1 or later). You can also ingest data into QuickSight from databases that are EC2 or on-premises. These include SQL Server, MySQL, PostgreSQL. QuickSight can also use files on S3 or on-premises as data sources. These include Excel, text files, common log format (.clf) and extended log format (.elf). QuickSight also supports using objects or reports from the following version of Salesforce; Enterprise, Unlimited, and Developer. The Sales Force support information is more for your general knowledge.

With QuickSight you have a choice of two editions; Standard Edition and Enterprise Edition. Both editions offer a full set of features for creating and sharing data visualizations. In QuickSight Standard Edition, you can invite IAM users and allow them to use their credentials to access QuickSight. You can also invite anyone with an email address to create a QuickSight-only user account. When you are creating a user account, QuickSight emails the user asking them to activate their account. Enterprise edition additionally offers encryption at rest and Microsoft Active Directory (Microsoft Active Directory) integration. In Enterprise Edition, you select a Microsoft Active Directory in AWS Directory Service. You use that active directory to identify and manage your Amazon QuickSight users and administrators. In Enterprise Directory, one or more Microsoft AD groups in AWS Directory Service are used for administrative access. You can also select one or more active directory groups in the AWS Directory service for user access. In both the editions of QuickSight all the data transfers are encrypted. Database connections are secured using SSL, although the transfer is secured using TLS.

In the Enterprise Edition, data addressed in SPICE is encrypted using block role encryption with AWS managed keys. With the Enterprise Edition, there is no automatic notification of QuickSight access; therefore, administrators and users added to enterprise edition are not automatically notified of their access to QuickSight.

Comparing Editions

Features	Standard Edition	Enterprise Edition
Free Author	1	1
Free Trial Authors (60 Days)	4	4
Included SPICE Capacity	10 GB/User	10 GB/User
Readers	N/A	$0.30 /session
Additional SPICE Capacity	$0.25 /GB/month	$0.38 / GB/ month
Connect to spreadsheets, databases, data lakes, and business apps.	●	●
Easily analyze data with Autograph.	●	●
Fast, Scalable Visualization.	●	●
Publish Dashboards for interactive data access.	●	●
Single Sign-On with SAML and Open-ID Connect.	●	●

Web Access and Mobile access.	•	•
Drill down to details and customize filters.	•	•
Enable audit logs with AWS Cloud Trial.	•	•
Reader Role.		•
Securely access data in Private VPCs and On-Prem.		•
Row Level Security.		•
Hourly Refresh of SPICE data.		•
Secure data encryption at rest.		•
Connect to Active Directory.		•
Use Active Directory Groups		•

Table 6-01: Comparison between QuickSight Enterprise and Standard Edition

Data Set

QuickSight has a concept of Data Set, and essentially with these data sets, you are identifying specified data in your defined data sources. If you are connecting to a table in Redshift or connecting to Excel file in S3 as a data source, then you essentially import data set into QuickSight, which does not provide better performance only but if you have done any preparation then you do not have to repeat data preparation when you are using that data for analysis and visualization.

Essentially you are importing the data set into SPICE which stands for Super-fast, Parallel, In-memory Calculation Engine. SPICE allows QuickSight to run anything from small to very large queries to get fast results. AWS creates a SPICE to use accommodation of storage in memory technology which is enabled using the latest hardware innovation machine code generation and data compression. SPICE is measured in GB, and each user is initially allocated to 10GB per user. SPICE is highly available and durable because the data imported into it is replicated.

QuickSight allows you to prepare your data for analysis. So, you are capable of cleaning or transforming your raw data from one of the data sources that you use with QuickSight. The preparation includes changing field names, adding calculated fields and using a SQL query to determine the data that you want to work with. You can also join two or more tables, but they must be from the same data source. You can also change data types except for calculated fields. So, QuickSight can convert the field data according to the

data type you choose. A useful feature of QuickSight is that it provides previously stored data that you want to work with; it can skip rows that are not interpreted properly. You also get a message for how many rows are skipped. Once you have a data set, you can create an analysis, as AWS provide us with some sample analysis as well. Within the analysis, you have the option of creating visuals. You also have an option of creating a story in QuickSight and that Story allows you to preserve multiple iterations of analysis, and run them sequentially to provide the narrative about the analysis of data. For example, if you want to check the sample version of analysis all within the same chart but with different filters applied. You can also create a Dashboard which is the Read-only snapshot of an analysis. You can share it with another QuickSight user for reporting. The data in the Dashboard reflects the data set that is used for analysis. If you share a Dashboard with the user, they can then view and filter the Dashboard data, but they cannot save any of the filters applied to the Dashboard.

QuickSight Visualization

Visuals are the graphical representation of your data. In QuickSight you can create a variety of visuals and then announce them by using different data sets and visual types. In QuickSight, you can have up to 20 visuals per analysis. Creating a visual is fairly very straight forward. QuickSight can also create a visual for you, you decide the fields you want, and by using Autograph, QuickSight will determine the most appropriate visual type. You can modify them in the range of ways to customize your needs including changing, mapped to elements, change in individual type, sorting visual data or applying filters. In the field list, you have two categories, the dimension field (blue icon) and the measured field (green icon) as presented in the picture. In the Fields list pane, dimension fields have blue icons, and measure fields have green icons. The dimensions are generally text or date fields, and they might be items such as products or attributes that relate to measures and can be used to partition themselves. Measures are a numeric value that you could use for measurement, comparison and aggregation. Normally you use the combination of dimension and measure fields to produce a visual.

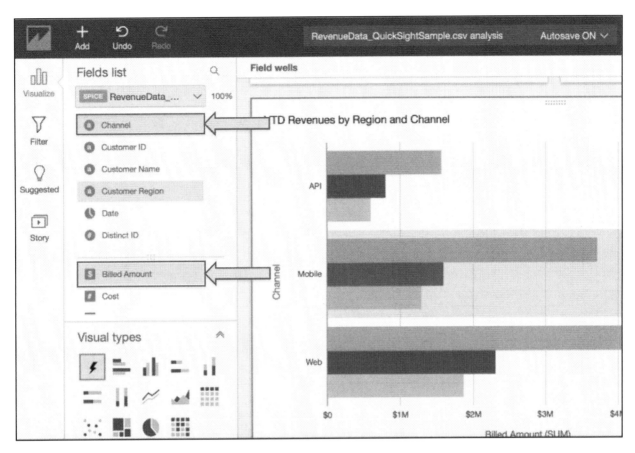

Figure 6-01: Dimension and Measured Field.

Visual Types

Autograph

Autograph isn't a visual kind itself, however alternatively it helps you tell Amazon QuickSight to choose the visual kind for you. While you create a visual through choosing Autograph and then selecting fields, Amazon QuickSight uses the maximum appropriate visual kind for the range and records forms of the fields you select. In case you need QuickSight, it will select a visual type for you, which will be based on your statistics and data.

Bar Chart

QuickSight supports Bar Charts which include horizontal and vertical bar charts. In horizontal bar charts, you have Single Measure bar charts where one measure is for one dimension. You can have Multi-Measure bar charts (two or more measures for one dimension). You have Cluster bar charts where related dimension groups value for dimensions. With the horizontal bar chart, you would use a dimension for the Y-axis. The other option is to create vertical bar charts, and they are similar to horizontal bar charts in terms of measures and dimensions. The difference between horizontal and vertical bar

chart is that, vertical chart uses the dimensions in X-axis and horizontal bar chart uses dimensions for Y-axis.

To perform the visual types on data analysis, you need to create a data set, and then perform visualization for the analysis of data. Then you can select your type of visualization and drag the dimensions and measured values according to the desired axis, and you can find the average statistics of your desired data set.

Line Charts

You can use the Line Chart to compare changes in measured values over the period. Line Charts are better suited for date fields. Line Charts can also be used for a single measure like Gross sales by month. Line Chart can be used for multiple measures like Gross sales and Net sales by a month, or you can use Line Chart for one measure for dimension over the period. For example, flight delays per day by the airline.

For this, you create an analysis, select the line chart from visual type, drag the dimension and measured fields according to the demand and you will get a line chart representing the relation between the different fields of your analysis.

You can also create an Area Line Chart. The difference between the Line Chart and Area Line Chart is that each value is represented by the colored area of chart instead of the line. This makes it easier to evaluate item values related to each other.

Pivot Tables

Pivot Tables are supported in QuickSight. The pivot table is an essential way to summarize data. Pivot Table is used to show measure values for the intersection of two dimensions. After populating a Pivot Table, you can change the row sort order and also apply statistical function for further analysis.

For this purpose, you can use AWS provided sample; you create a Pivot Table using the sample. You can choose the measured and dimension values. You can also specify other additional functions if needed

Scatter Plot Visuals

To visualize two or three measures in a dimension, scatter plots are used. Bubble on the scatter plot represents items in the dimension. The X and Y axes represent one of a kind of measures that apply to the dimension. A bubble seems on the chart at the point in which the values for the two measures for an item inside the dimension intersect. Optionally, you may additionally use bubble size to represent an additional measure.

TreeMap

TreeMap is a diagram representing hierarchical data using nested rectangles. Each rectangle responds to its numerical value. With QuickSight, you can use treemaps to visualize one or more measures for a dimension.

Pie Chart

Pie Charts are used to compare the values of the items in a dimension. A wedge in a pie chart represents one single item in the dimension. Wedge size represents the share of the value for the selected measure that the item represents as compared to the complete value of the dimension. Pie charts are exceptional when precision is not critical, and there are few items inside the measurement.

Heat Map

Heat Map is the graphical representation of data with individual values contained in a matrix, represented as colors. You can use heat maps to identify trends and outliers. You use heat maps to expose a degree for the intersection of dimensions, with coloration-coding to differentiate wherein values fall within the range. Heat maps can also be used to show the count of values for the intersection of the two dimensions.

Stories

In QuickSight, you also have the option of creating a story. QuickSight allows you to preserve multiple iterations of an analysis and then play them sequentially to provide a narrative about the analysis of data. Over time you may use the same chart but apply different filters but still be able to get to the previous chart.

You select the story and then capture the scene. You can capture the scene by clicking on the capture button which takes the snapshot.

As an instance, you may want to look at numerous versions of the analysis, all with the same charts but with exclusive filters carried out. A captured new release of iteration is referred to as a scene. A scene preserves the visuals which can be inside the analysis on time you create it, inclusive of such things as filtering and type order. The information inside the visuals is not captured as a portion of the scene. When you run the story, visuals will reflect the current information within the data set.

Dashboard

QuickSight also supports the creation of Dashboard. You can create a dashboard which is a Read-only snapshot of an analysis that you can share with other Amazon QuickSight users for reporting purposes. A dashboard preserves the configuration of the analysis at the time you publish it, including such things as filtering, parameters, controls, and sort

order. The data used for the analysis is not captured as part of the dashboard. When you view the dashboard, it reflects the current data in the data sets used by the analysis.

For creating a Dashboard, you simply go to share and select Create Dashboard. The dashboard can be shared with other users who have access to QuickSight. The data in the dashboard reflects the data that is used in the analysis. And if you share dashboard with users, they can view and filter the dashboard data but cannot save any filters applied to the dashboard.

When you share a dashboard, you specify which users have access to it. Users who are dashboard viewers can view and filter the dashboard data. Any selections to filters, controls, or sorting that users apply while viewing the dashboard exist only while the user is viewing the dashboard, and are not saved once it is closed. Users who are dashboard owners can edit and share the dashboard, and optionally can edit and share the analysis. If you want them to edit and share the data set, you can set that up in the analysis.

A shared dashboard can also be embedded in a website or an app if you are using Enterprise edition.

Big Data Visualization

Apache Zeppelin

Zeppelin is an open source web-based notebook that enables interactive data analysis and collaboration. With Zeppelin, you can use Scala, Python, Spark SQL, and HiveQL to manipulate data and visualize the result. Zeppelin allows you to collaborate with other users by sharing Zeppelin notebook. You can also publish visualization to the dashboard. It also uses your Spark setting on EMR. Zeppelin also integrates with S3. Zeppelin notebooks may be shared amongst numerous customers, and visualizations can be posted to outside dashboards. Zeppelin uses the Spark settings in your cluster and can use Spark's dynamic allocation of executors to let YARN estimate the optimal resource consumption.

To install the Apache Zeppelin first go to the AWS Console and select EMR. Now select Zeppelin and Spark. Now click on Enable Web Connection link. Now you have some instruction on how to create an SSH tunnel on EMR cluster node, or you have an option to configure a proxy management tool. Once the cluster is up and you set up everything, you click on Zeppelin, and you are ready to use it.

You can download the notebook in JSON format and import it to Apache Zeppelin, and notebook URL can be shared among collaborators. Zeppelin can broadcast any changes in

real time just like collaboration in google docs. When launching the EMR Cluster, you can configure Zeppelin to store the configure notebook in S3.

Use Cases

- Zeppelin, Spark SQL and ML lib on EMR can be used together for exploratory data science and recommendation engines.
- Kinesis Stream, Zeppelin, and Spark Streaming can be used together for analyzing real-time data.
- There are two AWS Big Data Blogs that are worth reading. Building a Recommendation engine with Spark ML on Amazon EMR using Zeppelin and Analyze real-time data from Amazon Kinesis Stream using Zeppelin and Spark Streaming.

Jupyter Notebook

Jupyter Notebook is also a web-based notebook that enables interactive data analysis and collaboration. It contains live code in languages like Python, R, Julia, and Scala. Technically Jupyter can support up to 40 programming languages, but these are the popular ones. You can collaborate with other users by sharing Jupyter notebooks using GitHub, Dropbox, email or the Jupyter Notebook Viewer. In terms of used cases, Jupyter Notebook is heavily used for data science.

To install Jupyter on EMR, you need to run a custom bootstrap action when launching your cluster. BootStrap Action install custom software in your cluster. Essentially, they are the scripts that just run on cluster nodes when EMR launches, when you select the applications provided to you by EMR that is installing Hive, Pig, Spark, Hue and setting up those applications for you.

Jupyter notebook (previously IPython) is one of the most popular user interfaces for strolling Python, R, Julia, Scala, and other languages to produce and visualize data, perform the statistical evaluation, teach and run machine studying models. Jupyter notebooks are self-contained files that may include live code, charts, narrative textual content, and more. The notebooks may be without any problem transformed into HTML, PDF, and different codecs for sharing. Amazon EMR is a popular hosted big facts processing carrier that lets in users to effortlessly run Hadoop, Spark, Presto, and other Hadoop ecosystem applications, together with Hive and Pig.

Python, Scala, and R offer assistance to Spark and Hadoop, and run them in Jupyter on Amazon EMR making it smooth to take benefit of:

- The big information processing capabilities of Hadoop programs.
- The huge choice of Python and R packages for analytics and visualization.

Comparison between Notebooks

Both Zeppelin and Jupyter have similar functionalities. However, there is some contrast if you are a heavy user of Zeppelin or a heavy user of Jupyter. Heavy Spark users tend to favor Zeppelin as the Sparks turn over work with Zeppelin very well. Heavy Python user tends to like Jupyter as the front-end interpreter. So, keep this main difference in mind for the exam.

D3.js (Data-Driven Documents)

D3.js is a javascript library used for producing dynamic, interactive data visualizations in a web browser. D3.js can read data from CSV, TSV or JSON files and can generate HTML tables, SVG bar charts and other visualization like real-time dashboards, interactive graph and interactive maps that work in a browser.

D3 lets you bind arbitrary records to a document object model (DOM), and then follow data-driven transformation to the record. As an example, you could use D3 to generate an HTML desk from an array of numbers. Or, use the same information to create an interactive SVG bar chart with smooth transitions and interaction.

D3 is not a monolithic framework that seeks to provide every attainable characteristic. Rather, D3 solves the crux of the problem: effective manipulation of files based on the information. This avoids proprietary representation and presents extraordinary flexibility, exposing the overall capabilities of web standards such as HTML, SVG, and CSS. With minimum overhead, D3 is extraordinarily rapid, helping big datasets and dynamic behaviors for interaction and animation. D3's practical style allows code reuse through the various collection of respectable and community-developed modules.

MicroStrategy

MicroStrategy is the provider of Business Intelligence tools and analytics software. The software helps businesses make a better decision and transform the way to your business through the ability to create a dashboard, scorecards, reports, queries, and more. You can access the software by a browser, desktop application, and mobile devices. There are some products including MicroStrategy Enterprise Platform that can run on EC2 through the AWS Market Place. You can integrate MicroStrategy with Athena, Aurora, connect to a high job flow running on EMR, and Redshift.

Mind Map

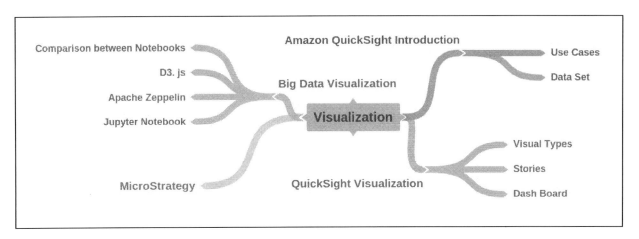

Figure 6-02: Chapter's Mind Map.

Practice Question

1. SPICE stands for:
   A. System Performance Inline Collaboration Engine.
   B. Sponsored Parallel In-Memory Corporate Engine.
   C. Super-Fast Parallel In-Memory Calculation Engine.
   D. Super Performance Intelligent Compass Engine.

2. _____ is a cloud-based analytics service that allows you to build visualizations.
   A. Amazon QuickSight.
   B. Apache Zeppelin.
   C. D3.js
   D. Jupyter.

3. With QuickSight you have a choice of _____ Editions.
   A. One.
   B. Two.
   C. Three.
   D. Four.

4. In which of the QuickSight Edition you can invite an IAM user and allow them to use their credentials to access QuickSight?
   A. Standard.
   B. Enterprise.
   C. Both.
   D. None.

5. In which of the following QuickSight Edition, you select a Microsoft Active Directory in AWS Directory Service?
   A. Standard.
   B. Enterprise.
   C. Both.
   D. None.

6. In which edition of QuickSight the data transfer is encrypted?
   A. Standard.
   B. Enterprise.
   C. Both.

D. None.

7. In which of the QuickSight Edition, data addressed in SPICE is encrypted using block role encryption with AWS managed keys?
    A. Standard Edition.
    B. Enterprise Edition.
    C. Both Editions.
    D. None of the Above.

8. _____ are the graphical representation of your data.
    A. Visuals.
    B. Data Set.
    C. Stories.
    D. Dashboard.

9. In QuickSight you can have up to _____ visuals per analysis.
    A. 10.
    B. 30.
    C. 20.
    D. 50.

10. In the field list, how many categories do you have in QuickSight Visualization?
    A. Five.
    B. Four.
    C. Three.
    D. Two.

11. A client needs an assistant in data visualization, and the client is fluent in Python and wants to integrate well with Python. Which is best for this assistant?
    A. Jupyter Notebook.
    B. Apache Zeppelin.
    C. Hue.
    D. D3.js

12. The QuickSight dashboard contains Read-only view into the data.
    A. False.
    B. True.

13. Jupyter Notebook contains live code.
    A. True.
    B. False.

14. D3.js is used for: (Choose 2)
    A. Data Storage.
    B. To generate HTML tables, SVG bar charts, and other visualizations like the real-time dashboard, as well as interactive graph and charts that work in the browser.
    C. To produce dynamic, interactive data visualization in web browsers.
    D. To migrate data from documents to data store.

15. QuickSight can select the best appropriate style of visualization based on the properties of data?
    A. True.
    B. False.

16. How many SPICE per GB are allocated initially?
    A. 10 GB.
    B. 20GB.
    C. 50 GB.
    D. 100 GB.

17. QuickSight supports _____ which include horizontal and vertical bar charts.
    A. Line Chart.
    B. Bar Chart.
    C. Pivot Table.
    D. Heat Map.

18. Which chart is used to compare changes in measured values over the period?
    A. Line Chart.
    B. Bar Chart.
    C. Pivot Table.
    D. Heat Map.

19. _____ is an essential way to summarize data.
    A. Line Chart.
    B. Bar Chart.
    C. Pivot Table.

D. Heat Map.

20. _____ is used to visualize two or three measures in a dimension.
   A. Heat Map,
   B. Pivot Table.
   C. Scatter Plot Visuals.
   D. Pie Chart.

21. _____ is a diagram representing hierarchical data using nested rectangles.
   A. Heat Map.
   B. Pie Chart.
   C. Pivot Table.
   D. TreeMap.

22. In which of the following chart, the concept of the wedge is used?
   A. Pie Chart.
   B. Bar Chart.
   C. Line Chart.
   D. Autograph.

23. _____ is the graphical representation of data with individual values contained in a matrix, represented as colors.
   A. TreeMap.
   B. Scatter Plot Visuals.
   C. Heat Map.
   D. Autograph.

24. QuickSight allows you to preserve multiple iterations of an analysis and then play them sequentially to provide a narrative about the analysis of data by using:
   A. Stories.
   B. Dashboard.
   C. Visuals.
   D. MicroStrategy.

25. _____ is the provider of Business Intelligence tools and analytics software.
   A. Stories.
   B. Dashboard.
   C. Visuals.

D. MicroStrategy

Chapter 07: Security

Introduction

In this Chapter, Big Data Security is discussed in detail. Big data security consists of EMR and RedShift security. Here, we will discuss the methods of introducing security of data storage and transfer using EMR and Redshift clusters. The ways for Encryption of data in-transit and at-rest are also included.

EMR Security

For EMR security, Security groups, IAM roles, Private Subnet, Encryption at rest and Encryption in-transit should be considered.

Security Group

Following are the two types of security groups that can be used with EMR:

- EMR Managed Security Groups
- Additional Security Groups

When launching an EMR cluster, one security group for Master node and one for Core & Task node is required.

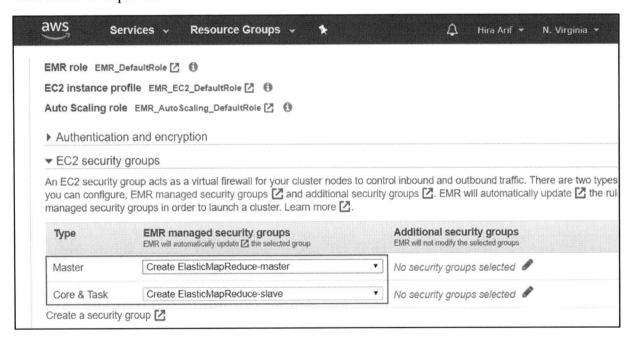

Figure 7-01: EMR Managed Security Groups (default)

Using EMR for the first time, AWS will assign the default security group, i.e., EMR Managed Security Group. EMR automatically updates inbound and outbound rules in these security groups for the proper communication of instances.

The user can specify its security group instead of using the default security group. The advantage for user's security group is that if there are multiple EMR clusters and user wants to provide isolation in terms of security groups; then this will provide separate EMR managed security groups for all clusters.

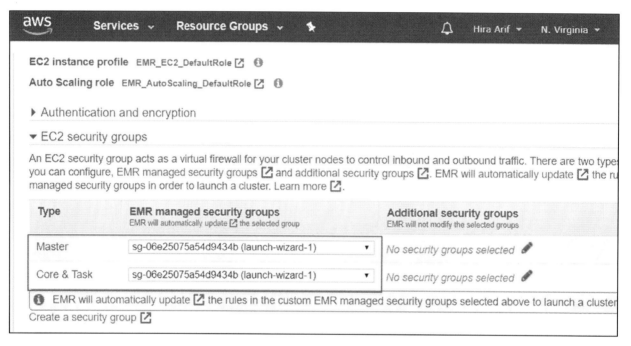

Figure 7-02: EMR Managed Security Groups (Custom)

Additional security groups can be assigned to the master node or core & task node, which will allow the user to create additional rules without changing them, as defined in EMR Managed Security groups. For example, if you want to allow SSH access to the master node

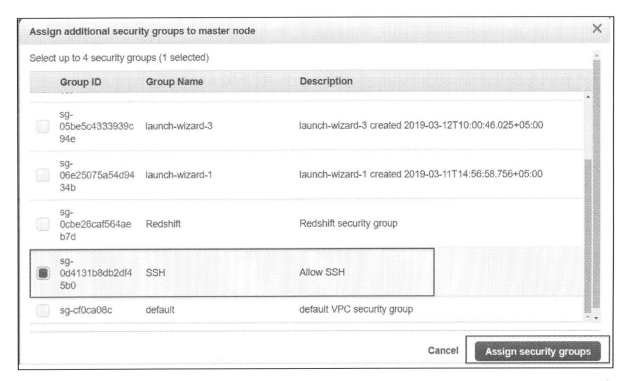

Figure 7-03: Allow SSH

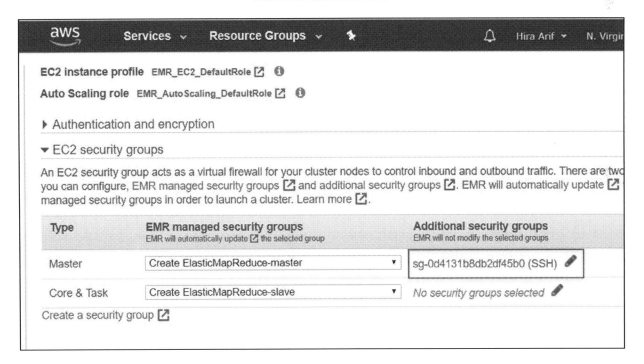

Figure 7-04: Additional Security Groups

Roles

For running EMR cluster, access to several services is required like DynamoDB, S3, CloudWatch, Kinesis, etc, for which Roles should be defined. Roles are not present when

EMR is launched for the first time, but they are automatically created when the cluster is launched.

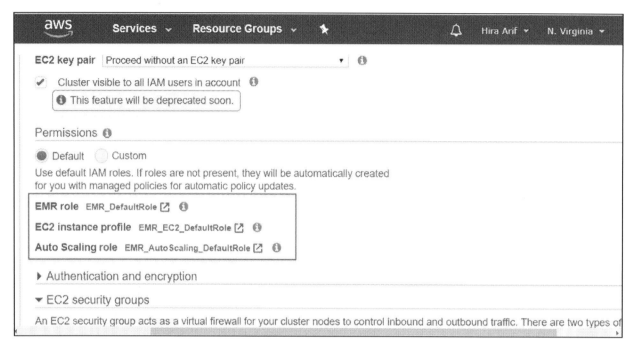

Figure 7-05: IAM Roles

Default_DefaultRole allows EMR services to access the EC2 instance. EMR_EC2_DefaultRole allows EC2 to access other services like S3, DynamoDB, etc. EMR_Auto-scaling_DefaultRole allows Auto-scaling of instances to add or terminate in Core & Task node.

Custom Roles can also be created. For example, to encrypt the cluster, KMS policy should be attached, so a role is defined to ensure that EC2 has a policy attached to generate KMS keys.

Private Subnet

For some security requirements, there might be a need to run the EMR cluster in a private subnet.

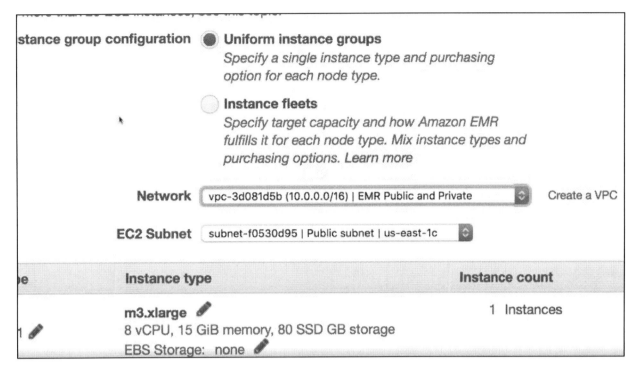

Figure 7-06: EC2 Subnet

Public subnet or a private subnet VPC can be selected

A warning is received when the private subnet is selected that S3 endpoints are needed to communicate via private subnet and NAT instances are required for the communication with DynamoDB, KMS, Kinesis, etc. A link is provided with that warning to add an S3 endpoint or NAT instances. To connect the EMR cluster in a private subnet, the local network should be connected to the VPC, VPN or DirectConnect alternative. A bastion host can be used to connect an EMR cluster in a private subnet.

Encryption At rest and In-transit

For data encryption in EC2 instances, two mechanisms work together to encrypt data on instance-store volumes and EBS volumes. i.e., Open source HDFS encryption and LUKS Encryption.

Encryption at rest can also be applied on EMRFS as encrypted files can be written to S3 and read from S3 by using client-side encryption or server-side-encryption.

By using TLS Encryption, the objects of EMRFS that are in-transit between S3 and cluster nodes are automatically encrypted. In-transit data encryption can also be configured for Spark, Hadoop and Tez.

319

Setup for Encryption At-Rest

Before set up, it should be checked that the policy is attached to the role which is to be used for EMR EC2 instance profile. Access to the KMS master key is not included in the managed policy of both default and custom role; therefore, inline policy should be attached to allow access to customer master key in the key management service.

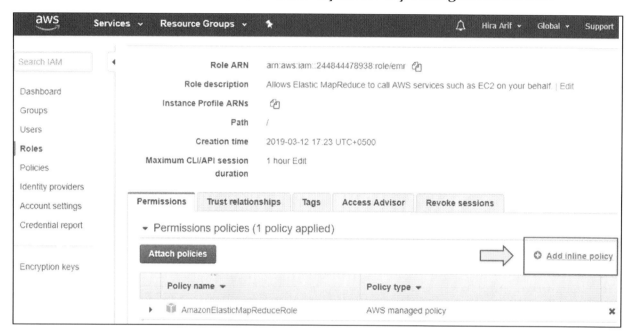

Figure 7-07: Add inline Policy

This is a simple policy, but in a real-world scenario, it would be more complex because it will also provide to those who can access the customer master key.

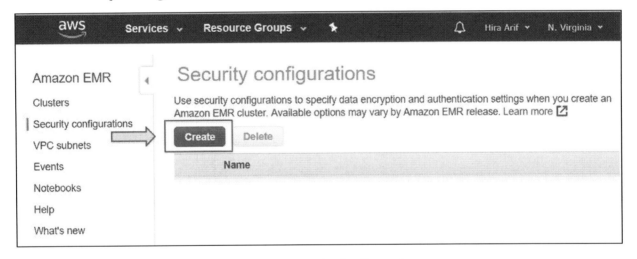

Figure 7-08: Inline Policy

Create Security Configuration in EMR Console

Figure 7-09: Security Configurations

Name the configuration and Select "At-rest Encryption"

Figure 7-10: At-rest Encryption

Select Encryption mode. There are four Encryption modes, which include:

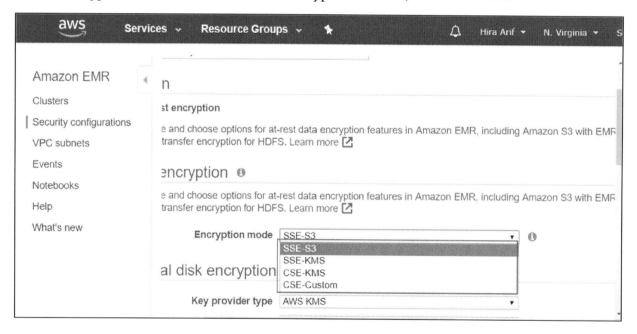

Figure 7-11: S3 Encryption Modes

- SSE-S3 is a Server Side Encryption with S3 managed Encryption keys.
- SSE-KMS is a Server Side Encryption with KMS managed keys in this encryption the data sent from EMR cluster to S3 is encrypted or decrypted by using customer master key that is managed in the key master service before storing it in S3 bucket.

Figure 7-12: S3 Encryption Mode (SSE-KMS)

- CSE-KMS is the Client Side Encryption which is used when data is needed to be encrypted before sending it to S3 with KMS managed keys and decrypts the data after it is downloaded.

Figure 7-13: S3 Encryption Mode (CSE-KMS)

- CSE-Custom is used when data sent to S3 should be encrypted, and the user wants to manage key by himself and wants to use the custom client-side master key. Data is decrypted when it is downloaded. For this, encryption path of the custom key

providing the file is required. The full class name is also required which is declared in your application that implements the encryption material provided with the interface.

Figure 7-14: S3 Encryption Mode (CSE-Custom)

For local disk Encryption, two encryption mechanisms are presently used to encrypt instance-store volumes and EBS volumes. These are open source HDFS encryption and LUKS encryption. Both of these are automatically set when the security configuration is attached, and the cluster is created. Setting local disk encryption provides you the two types of keys provider i.e., by the key management services or custom key. For custom key, enter custom key location and full class name which was declared in your application that implements the EncryptionMaterialsProvider interface.

Figure 7-15: Local Disk Encryption

Automatic Setup for HDFS Behind the Scene

After the Encryption at-rest is selected in encryption mode, security configuration is attached to the cluster that is launching, EMR will automatically update two files:

- Core-site.xml file
- Hdfs-site.xml file

The property that is updated in the core-site.xml file value is updated to "privacy."

In hdfs-site.xml file the property dfs.encrypt.data.transfer is set to true.

Setup for Encryption In-Transit

Select in-transit encryption in security configurations. The security configurations for Hadoop, Tez, and spark are automatically enabled by EMR.

You can use PEM certificates and create a zip file of these certificates and store them in S3. EMR then downloads these certificates at each node and apply encryption in-transit.

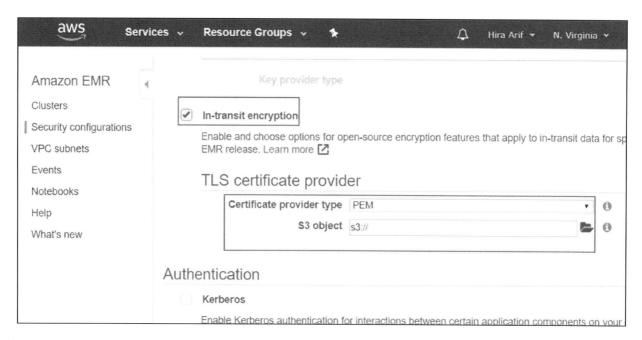

Figure 7-16: TLS PEM Certificate Provider

You can choose a custom key and provide the location of the custom key and full class name.

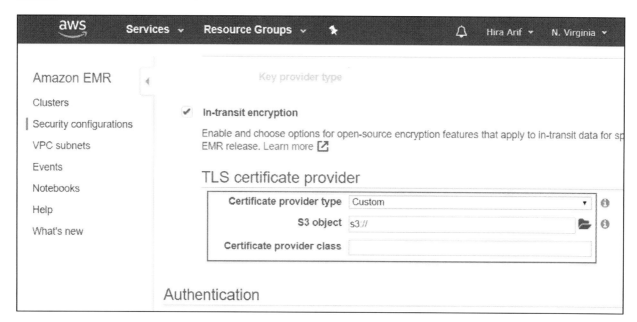

Figure 7-17: TLS Custom Certificate Provider

For the demo, PEM certificates are used. PEM certificates can be created by using open SSL. The example is provided in the EMR documentation of AWS.

Note: using open SSL for demo environment is safer than using self-signed certificates

Here PEM certificates are created

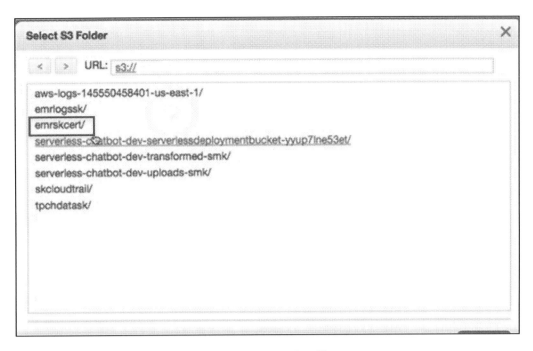

Figure 7-18: PEM Certificate

And the zip file is uploaded to S3 and create a security configuration.

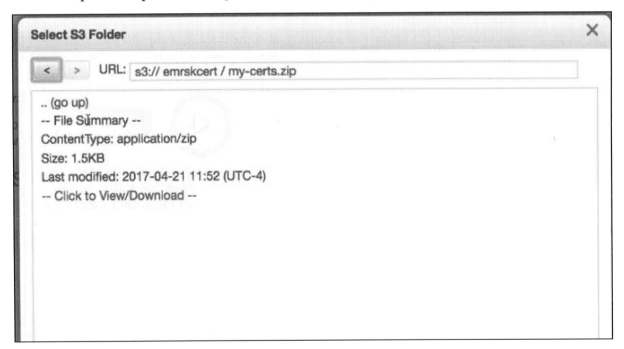

Figure 7-19: PEM Certificate Zip File

EMR setup some configurations automatically for Hadoop, Tez, and Spark.

MapReduce

Transferring of the data from mappers to reducers is known as the shuffle phase. The data is transferred between nodes within the cluster. If data between the nodes have to be encrypted in-transit, then Hadoop encrypted shuffle is used. Encrypted shuffle allows the encryption of MapReduce shuffle using https.

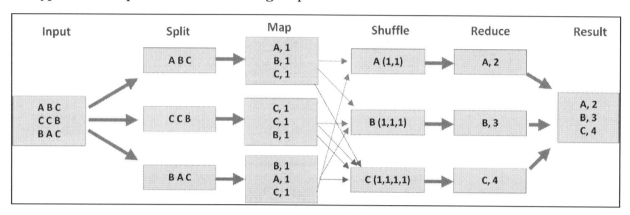

Figure 7-20: MapReduce

Hadoop Encrypted Shuffle

Two files are updated to setup Hadoop encryption shuffle:

- core-site.xml: All the properties in the table are added automatically

Property	Default Value
hadoop.ssl.require.client.cert	False
hadoop.ssl,hostname.verifier	DEFAULT
hadoop.ssl.keystores.factory. class	org.apache.hadoop.security.ssl.fileBasedKeyStores Factory
hadoop.ssl.server.conf	ssl-server.xml
hadoop.ssl.client.conf	ssl-client.xml
hadoop.ssl.enabled.protocols	TLSv1

Table 7-01: Hadoop Properties

- mapred-site.xml: EMR will automatically add mapreduce.shuffle.ssl.enabled property and update its value to "True."

Tez

Tez-site.xml file is updated. tez.runtime.shuffle.ssl.enabled property value is set to "True."

Another property tez.runtime.shuffle.keep-alive.enabled value is set to "True."

Spark

In spark file, i.e., "spark-defaults.conf" security settings are automatically enabled.

This Security has two main purposes

- Authentication
- Ensuring that the data in-transit is encrypted

For handshaking of two endpoints in which data is to be transferred, authentication is required, for which Spark would set two parameters to true, i.e., spark.authenticate and spark.authenticate.enableSaslEncryption.

For Encryption in-transit number of parameters are set up given in the figure below

```
spark.network.sasl.serverAlwaysEncrypt true
spark.ssl.protocol                     TLSv1.2
spark.ssl.keyPassword
spark.ssl.keyStorePassword
spark.ssl.enabled                      true
spark.ssl.enabledAlgorithms            TLS_ECDHE_RSA_WITH_AES_128_GCM_SHA256,TLS_RSA_WITH_AES_25
6_CBC_SHA
spark.ssl.trustStore                   /usr/share/aws/emr/security/conf/truststore.jks
spark.ssl.keyStore                     /usr/share/aws/emr/security/conf/keystore.jks
spark.ssl.trustStorePassword
```

Figure 7-21: In-transit parameters

RedShift Security

For security in RedShift, two types of Encryption are important:

- Encryption in-transit
- Encryption at rest (Key Management Service and HSMs)

Encryption In-Transit

SSL for Encryption in-transit is supported in RedShift.

On each cluster, RedShift creates and installs a self-signed SSL certificate. For setting it, make sure that the parameter group is not set to default because the default parameter group cannot be changed. In the figure below, there is a non-default parameter group.

In parameter group click 'Edit Parameters'.

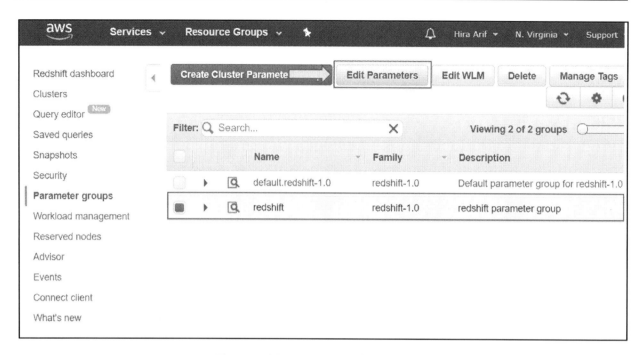

Figure 7-22: User-created Parameter

You have to change "require_ssl" parameter to "true" and then save changes.

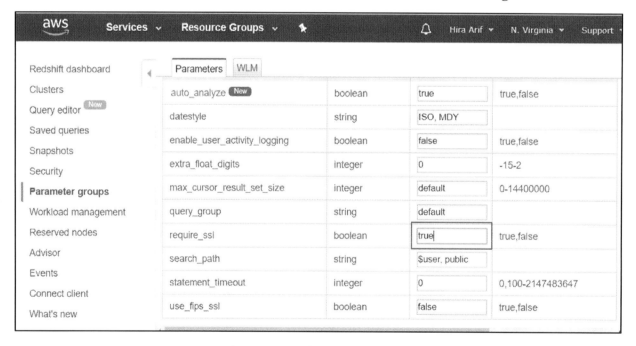

Figure 7-23: Editing Parameters

Associate this parameter group with the cluster.

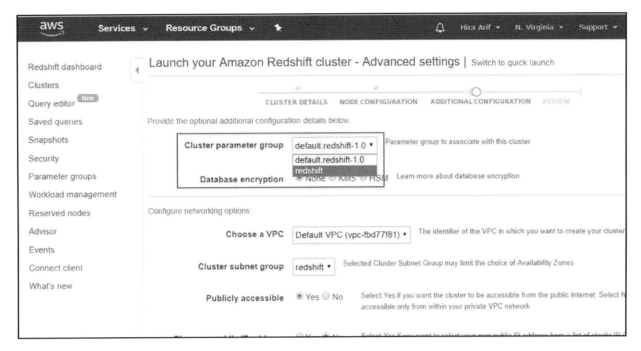

Figure 7-24: Cluster Parameter Group

Parameter group "redshift" is associated with it.

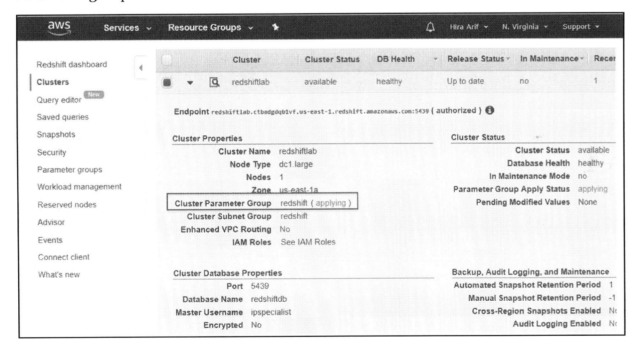

Figure 7-25: Cluster Parameter Group

Moving to the client and connecting to RedShift using SSL.

Figure 7-26: Aginity Login

Note: RedShift supports SSL strictly to encrypt the connection between the client and the cluster.

This illustration shows encryption of connection between SQL client and Redshift cluster. Here the first layer of encryption in-transit is set up.

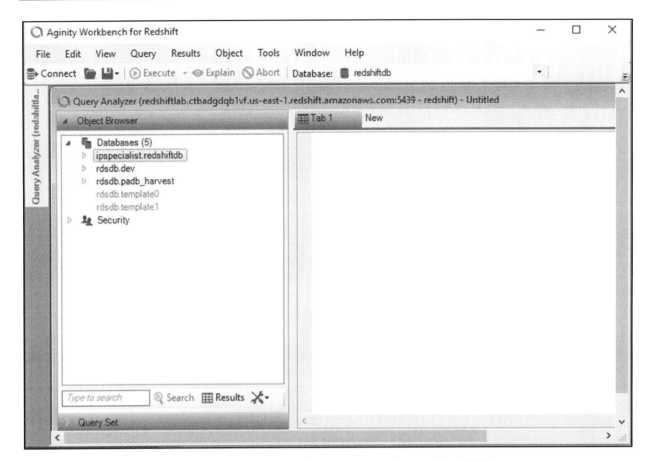

Figure 7-27: Connection between SQL Client and RedShift

The second layer is for an extra layer of security using the certificate by validating the cluster that is connected, is a RedShift cluster.

If you want that, your client verifies your RedShift cluster then install the public key provided by AWS for SSL certificate on your client and use that key to connect to your Redshift cluster.

Encryption At-Rest

For management of Encryption key, RedShift provides two options to use:

- Key Management Service
- Hardware Security Module (CloudHSM and On-Prem HSM)

Data blocks, snapshots, and system metadata are encrypted. Whenever any RedShift Cluster Encryption is enabled, it cannot be changed to the unencrypted form of a cluster. To change the encryption state to the unencrypted state, the data should be unloaded and then loaded into a new cluster.

Encryption At-rest using Key Management Services

This is one of the services provided for the Encryption of data in RedShift. It provides a four-tier hierarchy of encryption keys, which are:

- Master key
- Cluster Encryption key
- Database encryption key
- Data encryption keys

When a cluster is launched, select KMS to encrypt the database

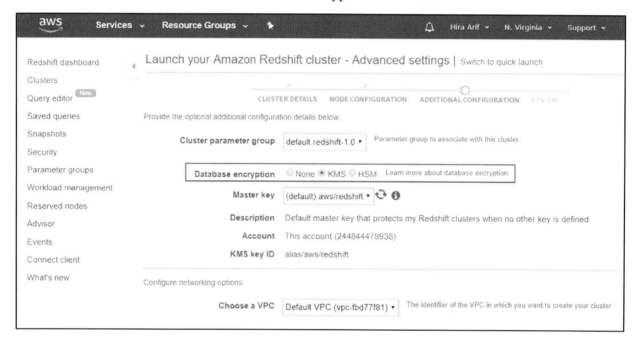

Figure 7-28: Database Encryption Type

RedShift provides a list of customer Master key that can be the default key, the key that you have created, or the key created by others for which you have the permission. The default key is created by KMS in your AWS account when you launch the RedShift cluster for the first time.

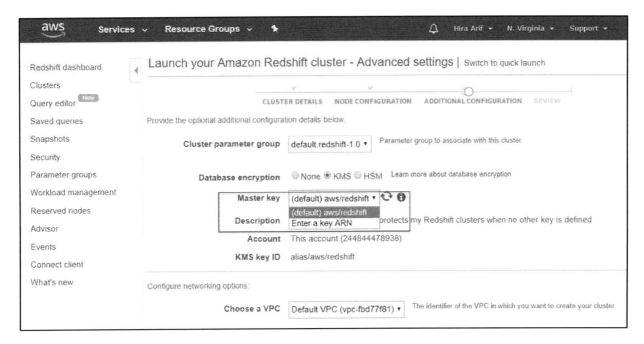

Figure 7-29: Master Key

After the selection of Master key, the encryption process proceeds with the following steps:

- RedShift requests the KMS to generate a data key and encrypt it by using the Master key that you have selected.
- The generated data key is the cluster encryption key.
- The encrypted cluster encryption key is then exported to RedShift by KMS, which is stored internally on a disk in a separate network from the cluster.
- The cluster encryption key is loaded into memory by Redshift.
- Calls KMS to decrypt the encryption key of the cluster and load it in memory
- A database encryption key is generated by RedShift
- The database encryption key is then loaded in memory
- To decrypt the database encryption key, the decrypted cluster encryption key is used.
- This decrypted database encryption key then encrypts data encryption keys for each block in RedShift.

Encryption at-rest using HSM

Hardware security modules are the physical devices used to safeguard and manage digital keys for strong authentication and provide crypto-processing. KMS is perfect for managing the encryption keys in Redshift. When the company have contractual,

regulatory requirements, then the dedicated Hardware Security Modules must be used which helps the organization to control the generation, storing, and management of keys.

For example, a company has a solution that is designed with two CloudHSMs in a single availability zone, and an on-premises HSM is deployed as a backup for storing RedShift encryption keys for which KMS cannot be used.

For the HSM, whether it is CloudHSM or On-premises HSM, a trusted connection should be established between RedShift and HSM, which is used to transfer encryption keys between HSM and RedShift during encryption and decryption operations.

For HSM the steps to be followed are:

- During the initial HSM, configuration obtains HSM's public certificate.
- Create an HSM connection providing the public certificate

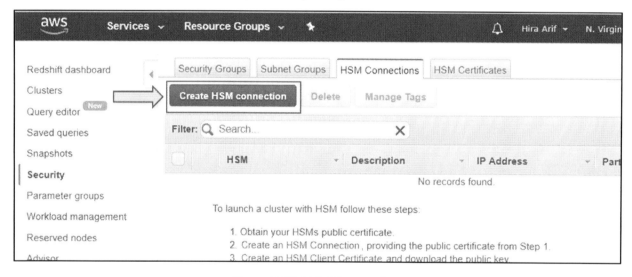

Figure 7-30: HSM Connection

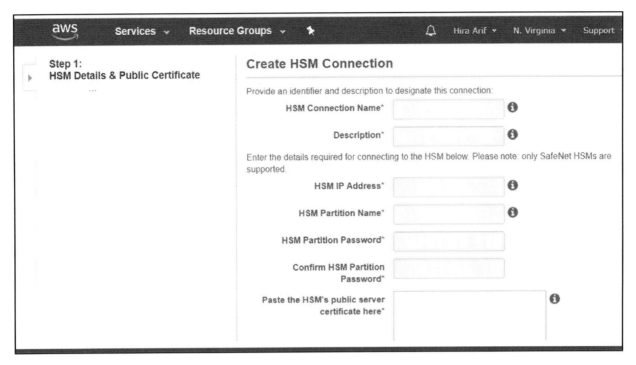

Figure 7-31: HSM Connection

- Create an HSM client certificate and download the public key

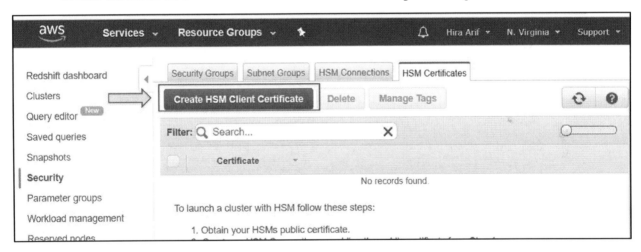

Figure 7-32: HSM Client Certificate

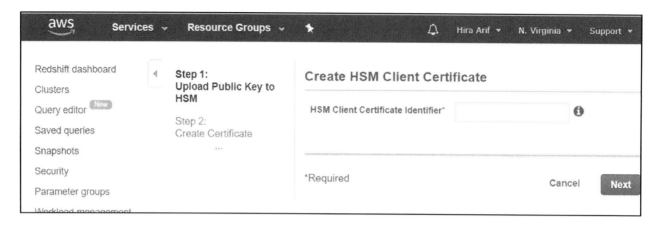

Figure 7-33: HSM Client Certificate

- Upload the public key to your HSM
- Launch a cluster and select the HSM client Certificate

After the HSM is selected to manage the cluster encryption keys, the following are the steps:

- RedShift requests HSM to create a data key and store it.
- This data key is then used as a cluster encryption key.
- The database encryption key is then randomly generated in the cluster by RedShift.
- This key is then passed to HSM to be encrypted by the cluster encryption key.
- HSM then sends the encrypted database encryption key to RedShift.
- RedShift further encrypts this database encryption key by using the randomly generated internal Master key.
- Decrypted version of a database encryption key is loaded into the memory by RedShift so that it can be further used for the encryption and decryption of database encryption keys of individual blocks.

KMS vs CloudHSM

KMS	CloudHSM
Usage-based pricing	Hourly based on Region
Highly available and durable	Need to setup HA and durability
Multi-tenant	Single-tenant access to HSM clients
AWS manages the root of trust	The root of trust is managed by Customer
Auditing	Design to comply with International common criteria EAL4+ and U.S.

	Government NIST FIPS 140-2
Symmetric encryption only	Symmetric and asymmetric encryption

Table 7-02: Comparison between KMS and CloudHSM

Note: In symmetric encryption, same keys are used to encrypt or decrypt while in asymmetric encryption two keys are used, i.e., a public key for encryption and private key for decryption.

Limit data access

To limit the users to access the data in the table follow the given steps:

- Go to the SQL client
- Log in as a superuser

```
[ec2-user@ip-10-0-1-171 ~]$ psql -h viewtest.                          redshif
t.amazonaws.com -U awsuser -d bigdatacert -p 5439
Password for user awsuser:
psql (9.2.24, server 8.0.2)
WARNING: psql version 9.2, server version 8.0.
        Some psql features might not work.
SSL connection (cipher: ECDHE-RSA-AES256-GCM-SHA384, bits: 256)
Type "help" for help.

bigdatacert=#
```

Figure 7-34: Superuser login

After the connection is established with the RedShift cluster. Select some data by using command "select w_warehouse_id, w_warehouse_name from public.warehouse;"

```
[ec2-user@ip-10-0-1-171 ~]$ psql -h viewtest.                          redshif
t.amazonaws.com -U awsuser -d bigdatacert -p 5439
Password for user awsuser:
psql (9.2.24, server 8.0.2)
WARNING: psql version 9.2, server version 8.0.
        Some psql features might not work.
SSL connection (cipher: ECDHE-RSA-AES256-GCM-SHA384, bits: 256)
Type "help" for help.

bigdatacert=# select w_warehouse_id, w_warehouse_name from public.warehouse
;
```

Figure 7-35: Selecting Data from Waarehouse Database

Here are the results

339

```
t.amazonaws.com -U awsuser -d bigdatacert -p
Password for user awsuser:
psql (9.2.24, server 8.0.2)
WARNING: psql version 9.2, server version 8.0.
        Some psql features might not work.
SSL connection (cipher: ECDHE-RSA-AES256-GCM-SHA384, bits: 256)
Type "help" for help.

.bigdatacert=# select w_warehouse_id, w_warehouse_name from public.warehouse
 ;
   w_warehouse_id   |     w_warehouse_name
--------------------+--------------------------
 AAAAAAAABAAAAAAA  | Conventional childr
 AAAAAAAADAAAAAAA  | Doors canno
 AAAAAAAAFAAAAAAA  |
 AAAAAAAACAAAAAAA  | Important issues liv
 AAAAAAAAEAAAAAAA  | Bad cards must make.
 AAAAAAAAGAAAAAAA  | Local, mass universi
(6 rows)

bigdatacert=#
```

Figure 7-36: Results of Selected Data

If you want to limit the user to see the specific details of the warehouse, for example, the warehouse id, then creating a view by using the command "create view whouse as select w_warehouse_id, w_warehouse_name from public.warehouse where w_warehouse_id = AAAAAAAACAAAAAAA"

```
Password for user awsuser:
psql (9.2.24, server 8.0.2)
WARNING: psql version 9.2, server version 8.0.
         Some psql features might not work.
SSL connection (cipher: ECDHE-RSA-AES256-GCM-SHA384, bits: 256)
Type "help" for help.

bigdatacert=# select w_warehouse_id, w_warehouse_name from public.warehouse
;
  w_warehouse_id  |    w_warehouse_name
------------------+--------------------------
 AAAAAAAABAAAAAAA | Conventional childr
 AAAAAAAADAAAAAAA | Doors canno
 AAAAAAAAFAAAAAAA |
 AAAAAAAACAAAAAAA | Important issues liv
 AAAAAAAAEAAAAAAA | Bad cards must make.
 AAAAAAAAGAAAAAAA | Local, mass universi
(6 rows)

bigdatacert=# create view whouse as select w_warehouse_id, w_warehouse_name
 from public.warehouse where w_warehouse_id = 'AAAAAAAACAAAAAAA';
```

Figure 7-37: Creating View

Creating a group by executing the command "create group dwusers"

```
psql (9.2.24, server 8.0.2)
WARNING: psql version 9.2, server version 8.0.
          Some psql features might not work.
SSL connection (cipher: ECDHE-RSA-AES256-GCM-SHA384, bits: 256)
Type "help" for help.

bigdatacert=# select w_warehouse_id, w_warehouse_name from public.warehouse
;
   w_warehouse_id   |   w_warehouse_name
--------------------+----------------------
 AAAAAAAABAAAAAAA | Conventional childr
 AAAAAAAADAAAAAAA | Doors canno
 AAAAAAAAFAAAAAAA |
 AAAAAAAACAAAAAAA | Important issues liv
 AAAAAAAAEAAAAAAA | Bad cards must make.
 AAAAAAAAGAAAAAAA | Local, mass universi
(6 rows)

bigdatacert=# create view whouse as select w_warehouse_id, w_warehouse_name
 from public.warehouse where w_warehouse_id = 'AAAAAAAACAAAAAAA';
bigdatacert'# create group dwusers;
```

Figure 7-38: Creating Group

Creating the user "create user dwuser password 'Dw123456' in group dwusers;"

```
WARNING: psql version 9.2, server version 8.0.
         Some psql features might not work.
SSL connection (cipher: ECDHE-RSA-AES256-GCM-SHA384, bits: 256)
Type "help" for help.

bigdatacert=# select w_warehouse_id, w_warehouse_name from public.warehouse
;
  w_warehouse_id  |  w_warehouse_name
------------------+--------------------------
 AAAAAAAABAAAAAAA | Conventional childr
 AAAAAAAADAAAAAAA | Doors canno
 AAAAAAAAFAAAAAAA |
 AAAAAAAACAAAAAAA | Important issues liv
 AAAAAAAAEAAAAAAA | Bad cards must make.
 AAAAAAAAGAAAAAAA | Local, mass universi
(6 rows)

bigdatacert=# create view whouse as select w_warehouse_id, w_warehouse_name
 from public.warehouse where w_warehouse_id = 'AAAAAAAACAAAAAAA';
bigdatacert'# create group dwusers;
bigdatacert'# create user dwuser password 'Dw123456' in group dwusers;
```

Figure 7-39: Creating a user

Grant selection for the created group by the command "grant select on whouse to group dwusers"

```
SSL connection (cipher: ECDHE-RSA-AES256-GCM-SHA384, bits: 256)
Type "help" for help.

bigdatacert=# select w_warehouse_id, w_warehouse_name from public.warehouse
;
  w_warehouse_id  |   w_warehouse_name
------------------+------------------------
 AAAAAAAABAAAAAAA | Conventional childr
 AAAAAAAADAAAAAAA | Doors canno
 AAAAAAAAFAAAAAAA |
 AAAAAAAACAAAAAAA | Important issues liv
 AAAAAAAAEAAAAAAA | Bad cards must make.
 AAAAAAAAGAAAAAAA | Local, mass universi
(6 rows)

bigdatacert=# create view whouse as select w_warehouse_id, w_warehouse_name
  from public.warehouse where w_warehouse_id = 'AAAAAAAACAAAAAAA';
bigdatacert'# create group dwusers;
bigdatacert'# create user dwuser password 'Dw123456' in group dwusers;
bigdatacert'# grant select on whouse to group dwusers;
bigdatacert'#
```

Figure 7-40: Grant access to Dwusers

Exit from SQL client by using command "\q"

Log in as a dwuser

```
[ec2-user@ip-10-0-1-171 ~]$ psql -h viewtest.                    .redshif
t.amazonaws.com -U dwuser -d bigdatacert -p 5439
Password for user dwuser:
psql (9.2.24, server 8.0.2)
WARNING: psql version 9.2, server version 8.0.
        Some psql features might not work.
SSL connection (cipher: ECDHE-RSA-AES256-GCM-SHA384, bits: 256)
Type "help" for help.

bigdatacert=>
```

Figure 7-41: Dwuser login

By inserting command "select * from whouse" and in result only warehouse id is visible, other data is invisible.

```
[ec2-user@ip-10-0-1-171 ~]$ psql -h viewtest.          ▓▓▓▓▓ edshif
t.amazonaws.com -U dwuser -d bigdatacert -p 5439
Password for user dwuser:
psql (9.2.24, server 8.0.2)
WARNING: psql version 9.2, server version 8.0.
        Some psql features might not work.
SSL connection (cipher: ECDHE-RSA-AES256-GCM-SHA384, bits: 256)
Type "help" for help.

bigdatacert=> select * from whouse;
  w_warehouse_id  |    w_warehouse_name
------------------+------------------------
 AAAAAAAACAAAAAAA | Important issues liv
(1 row)

bigdatacert=>
```

Figure 7-42: Specific information can be viewed

If you will try to select from the main warehouse table, the permission is denied, i.e., there is no access to the table for that user

```
[ec2-user@ip-10-0-1-171 ~]$ psql -h viewtest.          ▓▓▓▓▓ edshif
t.amazonaws.com -U dwuser -d bigdatacert -p 5439
Password for user dwuser:
psql (9.2.24, server 8.0.2)
WARNING: psql version 9.2, server version 8.0.
        Some psql features might not work.
SSL connection (cipher: ECDHE-RSA-AES256-GCM-SHA384, bits: 256)
Type "help" for help.

bigdatacert=> select * from whouse;
  w_warehouse_id  |    w_warehouse_name
------------------+------------------------
 AAAAAAAACAAAAAAA | Important issues liv
(1 row)

bigdatacert=> select * from warehouse;
ERROR:  permission denied for relation warehouse
bigdatacert=>
```

Figure 7-43: Limit Access for specific user

Mind Map

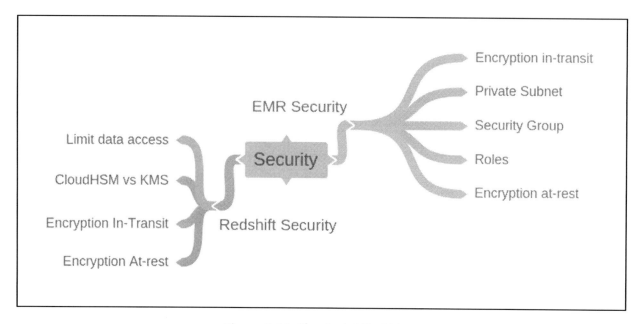

Figure 7-44: Chapter's Mind Map

Practice Questions

1. You can only use CloudHSM when using a RedShift hardware security module. True or False?
   A. True
   B. False

2. What is Hadoop Encrypted Shuffle?
   A. The encryption keys of data at-rest on HDFS are shuffled
   B. Encrypted files in S3 are shuffled before EMR reads them
   C. Data in-transit between node is encrypted
   D. There is no such feature

3. Choose 2 characteristics which do not belong to CloudHSM:
   A. Highly available and durable
   B. Single-tenancy
   C. Supports symmetric and asymmetric encryption
   D. Usage-based pricing
   E. The customer-managed root of trust

4. You have encrypted and loaded 7 TBs of data into the cluster for your RedShift cluster. It turns out that it was not necessary to encrypt this cluster. You want to modify and check that cluster is not encrypted. What options do you have? (Choose 2 answers)
   A. Delete the KMS managed keys
   B. Restore the latest snapshot
   C. Check the decrypt checkbox in RedShift modification options
   D. Create a new cluster that is not encrypted and reload the data
   E. Upload the data into S3 and reload it into a cluster that is not encrypted.

5. To encrypt data at rest on instance store volumes and EBS volumes which of the following mechanism would work? (Choose 2 answers)
   A. LUKS
   B. Open-source HDFS encryption
   C. TrueCrypt
   D. DriveCrypt

6. Both symmetric and asymmetric encryption is supported by Key Management Services. True or False?
   A. True
   B. False

7. Your company with EMRFS will use EMR. However, you need to encrypt all of your data before you send it to S3 and that you maintain the keys. What should be the

encryption option?
- A. SSE-S3
- B. SSE-KMS
- C. CSE-Custom
- D. CSE-KMS

8. An EMR cluster must be launched in a public subnet. If launched in a private subnet, it cannot be used with S3 or other public AWS endpoints. True or False?
- A. True
- B. False

9. Choose two of the security groups provided by EMR
- A. EMR Managed Security Groups
- B. Private Security Groups
- C. Custom Security Groups
- D. Additional Security Groups

10. Roles are automatically created when EMR is launched for the first time. True or False?
- A. True
- B. False

11. Which of the following encryptions can be used for the automatic encryption of the objects of EMRFS that are in transit between S3 and cluster nodes?
- A. Open source HDFS
- B. TLS
- C. LUKS
- D. None of the above

12. SSE-S3 stands for
- A. Server Side Encryption with S3
- B. Service Side Encryption with S3
- C. Support Side Encryption with S3
- D. Support Service Encryption with S3

13. Which of the following is not the encryption mode at rest?
- A. SSE-Custom
- B. SSE-S3
- C. SSE-KMS
- D. CSE-KMS
- E. CSE-Custom

14. For setup Hadoop Encrypted Shuffle, which of the two files are updated?
   A. hdfs-site.xml
   B. core-site.xml
   C. mapred-site.xml
   D. Hadoop-site.xml

15. Choose the two type of encryptions that are important in RedShift security
   A. Encryption between nodes
   B. Encrypted storage
   C. Encryption in-transit
   D. Encryption at-rest

16. Which of the given option is supported by RedShift for Encryption in-transit?
   A. HTTP
   B. SSL
   C. TCP
   D. UDP

17. Which of the two options can be used to manage the encryption keys in RedShift?
   A. Custom management
   B. Key Management Service
   C. Hardware Security Module
   D. Hadoop management service

18. Which of the following is not included in the four-tier hierarchy of Encryption keys in KMS?
   A. Master key
   B. Cluster Encryption key
   C. Database encryption key
   D. Slave Key
   E. Data encryption keys

19. Inbound and Outbound rules are automatically updated by EMR in security groups. True or False?
   A. True
   B. False

20. The user can only use the default security group. True or False?
   A. True

B. False

21. Which of the following role allow EMR services to access EC2 instance?
    A. DefaultRole
    B. EMR_EC2_DefaultRole
    C. EMR_Autoscaling_DefaultRole
    D. Default_DefaultRole

22. A baston host can be used to connect an EMR cluster in a public subnet. True or False?
    A. True
    B. False

23. Which of the following devices are used for crypto processing?
    A. Hardware security module
    B. Software security module
    C. Virtual security module
    D. Hardware authentication device

24. A trusted connection is not necessary to establish between Redshift and HSM. True or False?
    A. True
    B. False

25. Which of the following is not the feature of Key Management Service?
    A. Usage-based pricing
    B. Highly available and durable
    C. Single-tenant
    D. Auditing

Answers:

Chapter 01: Introduction to Cloud Computing

1. A (AWS Region)

Explanation: The region is an entirely independent and separate geographical area.

2. A (IaaS)

Explanation: Infrastructure as a software provide basic building blocks for cloud

3. B (SaaS)

Explanation: Software as a Service provides a complete product as web service provided by service provider that is handled and run by them.

4. B (Hybrid)

Explanation: Hybrid deployment model is mixture of on-premises, private cloud and third part public cloud and it is in between on-premises and cloud.

5. A (Encryption) and **D** (Security)

Explanation: The AWS cloud provides plenty of security and encryption features with governance capabilities that enable continuous monitoring of your IT resources. Your security policy can be embedded in the design of your infrastructure.

6. C (Deploy Quickly) and **D** (Security Increase)

Explanation: Deploy quickly, even worldwide: Deploy applications across multiple geographic areas.

Increase efficiencies: Use automation to reduce or eliminate IT management activities that waste time and resources.

Enhance security: Cloud providers have teams of people who focus on security, offering best practices to ensure you are compliant.

7. C (AWS Virtuous Cycle)

Explanation: The AWS pricing philosophy is driven by a virtuous cycle. Lower prices mean more customers are taking advantage of the platform, which in turn results in further driving down costs.

8. A (Stateless Application)

Explanation: Stateless Applications – An application that needs no knowledge of

previous interactions and stores no session. It could be an application that when given the same input, provides the same response to an end user.

9. **C** (Elasticity)

Explanation: Elasticity - Implement Auto Scaling to horizontally scale up and down automatically depending upon your need to reduce cost. Automate turning off non-production workloads when not in use. Use AWS managed services wherever possible that helps in taking capacity decisions as and when needed.

10. **D** (Spot)

Explanation: Spot Instances - Available at discounted pricing compared to On-Demand pricing. Ideal for workloads that have flexible start and end times. Spot instances allow you to bid on spare computing capacity.

Chapter 02: Collection

1. **A** (They can carry out real-time reporting and analysis of streamed data.)

   D (They can accept data as soon as it has been produced, without the need for batch.)

Explanation: As it is discussed Amazon Kinesis is used to collect and process a large stream of data in real time. Essentially you create a data processing which reads the data from Amazon Kinesis Stream as a data record. The process records can then be sent to the dashboard. They are used to generate alerts and dynamically change the pricing or can be used to change the advertising strategy dynamically.

2. **C** (24 hours.)

Explanation: If your Lambda function invocation is failed for some reasons, firehose retries the invocation for three times and then discard the batch of records if the retry is not succeeded. The retry delivery period is 24 hours. The escape records are treated as unsuccessfully processed records. Invocation errors and records that have the status of processing failed can be emitted to Cloud Watch logs. If data transformation fails, the unsuccessfully process records are sent to your S3 buckets in the processing failed folder.

3. **B** (Aurora.)

   C (Redshift.)

Explanation: It is important to know to which service AWS IoT integrates with. Once a device or a client sends a message to the IoT service, the IoT service triggers the rule action to write data to Elasticsearch service domain, write data to Kinesis Firehose stream, or a Kinesis stream, write data to a DynamoDB table or even send data to Amazon Machine Learning service to makes the product as per machine learning model, so that is the integration with big data services. The IoT service will action and allows you to change the CloudWatch alarm or capture a CloudWatch metrics, write data to S3 bucket, write data to SQS queue, write data to SNS as PUSH notification and finally invoke a Lambda function.

4. **A** (Shard.)

Explanation: Shards are uniquely identified groups of a data record within a stream. A Stream is made up of one or more than one shards, each of which provides a fixed amount of capacity.

5. **B** (Data Producer.)

Explanation: Data Producer puts the data records to Kinesis Stream, and this could be something like the web server, a mobile client. There are three ways by which producers put the data record into the Kinesis Stream. The first one is Amazon Kinesis Streams API, the second is by using the Amazon Kinesis Producer Library (KPL), and the third is by using the Amazon Kinesis Agent.

6. **A** (Data Consumer.)

Explanation: Data Consumer gets a data record from shards in the Kinesis Stream and processes the data. These consumers are also known as the Kinesis Stream application. You can develop a consumer application for Kinesis Stream by using the Kinesis Client Library (KCL).

7. **C** (Kinesis Connector Library.)

Explanation:

Kinesis Connector Library is used to emit data to certain services. The Connector library is Java-based, and you would use it to develop your consumer application along with the Kinesis Client Library.

8. **D** (AWS Kinesis Agent.)

Explanation: The Kinesis Agent is the standalone Java software application that allows you to collect and send data to the Firehose. You can install it on Linux based web servers, log servers or database web servers.

9. **A** (Firehose Data Transformation.)

Explanation: With the Firehose data transformation function, you can now specify a Lambda function that can carry out variations immediately on the flow, when you create a delivery stream.

While you permit Firehose data transformation, Firehose buffers incoming data and invokes the specified Lambda characteristic with each buffered batch asynchronously. The transformed records are despatched from Lambda to Firehose for buffering and then delivered to the destination spot.

10. **A** (All of the Above.)

Explanation: Some parameters are required for the transformation. So, Lambda must contain these parameters. Otherwise, firehose will reject them and treat that rejection as part of the data transformation failure.

11. **A** (To process and analyze a large stream of a data record in real time.)

Explanation: Amazon Kinesis is used to collect and process a large stream of data in real time. Essentially you create a data processing which reads the data from Amazon Kinesis Stream as a data record. The process records can then be sent to the dashboard. They are used to generate alerts and dynamically change the pricing or can be used to change the advertising strategy dynamically.

12. **C** (Kinesis Streams, Kinesis Analytics and Kinesis Firehose.)

Explanation: Amazon Kinesis is a service which is used to process, collect and analyze real-time and streaming data. Through this platform you can gather, process, analyze the data, and helps you to process the streaming of data cost-effectively. Amazon Kinesis contains three different types of services which include Amazon Kinesis Streams, Amazon Kinesis Analytics and Amazon Kinesis Firehose.

13. **A** (AWS IoT.)

Explanation: AWS IoT offers at ease, bi-directional communication among net-linked devices which include sensors, actuators, embedded micro-controllers, or clever home equipment and the AWS Cloud. This enables you to gather telemetry data from more than one device, and store and analyze the data.

14. **C** (AWS Data Pipeline.)

Explanation: Data Pipeline is a web service which helps you to reliably process and move data between different AWS compute and store services as well as on-premise data sources at specified intervals.

15. **D** (All of the Above.)

Explanation: Data Pipeline contains Data Nodes, Activity, Pre-Condition and Schedule as their main components.

16. **A** (Kinesis Producer Library.)

Explanation: The Kinesis Producer Library (KPL) allows and simplifies the creation of producer application.

17. **B** (Kinesis Client Library.)

Explanation: The application that gets data from Kinesis Stream is called consumer application, and these consumer applications can be developed by using the Kinesis Client Library (KCL).

18. **A** (By using the Amazon Kinesis Stream.)

Explanation: By using Kinesis Stream, you can create multiple shards in a stream. The

stream with two shards can give you a total data write rate of 2 MB per second data input and you get a total data read rate of 4 MB per second data output. You get ten transactions per second for read and 2000 records per second for write. If you need to change that, you need to add more shards.

19. **D** (All of the Above.)

Explanation: A Record is the unit of data which is stored in the stream. A record consists of a partition key, a sequence number, and data blob.

20. **C** (Retention Period.)

Explanation: The maximum duration after which the data added in the stream is expired. The default retention period is 24 hours by default, and it can be increased to seven days if required. The retention period can be changed through CLI.

21. **C** (Both A & B.)

Explanation: There are a couple of methods that are used for loading the data into the Kinesis Firehose delivery stream. Firstly, you can use the Kinesis Agent, or you can use the AWS SDK.

22. **B** (Two.)

Explanation: You can use the firehose API to send data to the firehose delivery stream using the AWS SDK. The Firehose API offers two operations for sending data to your firehose delivery stream.

- PutRecord
- PutRecordBatch

PutRecord sends one data record within one call, and PutRecordBatch can send multiple data records within one call.

23. **B** (256.)

Explanation: SQS uses the buffer for storing and producing data. The SQS contains about 256 KB of messages in any format. The components of applications are stored in the queue and retrieved from the queue. Similarly, the message greater than 256 KB is managed using the SQS extended library which uses S3. Any application can be stored or retrieved from the queue.

24. **A** (20.)

Explanation: A queue can be generated in any region and messages can be retained in the queue for up to 14 days. These messages can be sent and read simultaneously. SQS

also provides an option called Long Polling which reduces frequent polling to help you in minimizing the cost while receiving new messages as quickly as possible. So, when the queue is empty long poll request wait for up to 20 seconds for the next message to arrive.

25. **C** (Rule Engine.)

Explanation: The Rule Engine collects the statistics dispatched to the IoT cloud and performs actions based totally on factors which might be a gathered data and routes them to AWS endpoints like Amazon DynamoDB, AWS Lambda, Amazon Simple Storage Service (S3), Amazon Simple Notification Service (SNS), and Amazon Kinesis. It offers message processing and integration with different AWS services.

Chapter 03: Storage

1. **A** (Amazon Glacier.)

Explanation: Amazon Glacieris an exceptionally low-cost service provider that offers secure and sturdy storage for information archiving and backup. To hold expenses low, Amazon Glacieris optimized for the data which is accessed infrequently and for which retrieval instances of numerous hours are appropriate. With Amazon Glacier, clients can reliably store huge or small amounts of statistics.

2. **C** (Vault Locks.)

Explanation: The Vault Lockfeature in Glacier helps in meeting the compliance requirements. GlacierVault Lockfeature is used to deploy and enforce control for a vault with the Vault Lockpolicy. The policies can be locked from editing, and once the policy is locked, it cannot be changed. The idea behind the Vault Lockfeature is to enforce compliance control. The policies are created using IAM.

3. **B** (24.)

Explanation: The first step in locking a vault is to initiate and execute the Vault Lockoperation. This action attaches a Vault Lockpolicy to your vault. The lock is then sent to an InProgress state, and a lock ID is returned. You then have 24 hours to validate the lock. The lock expires after 24 hours if you do not validate it.

4. **D** (All of the Above.)

Explanation: To lock a vault, you can use the Console, API, and CLI. The first step in locking a vault is to initiate and execute the Vault Lockoperation. This action attaches a Vault Lockpolicy to your vault.

5. **A** (Two.)

Explanation: At high- level data is available in two groups:

- Scalar Data Types.
- DynamoDB Data Types.

DynamoDB holds the item such as strings, numbers (positive or negative integer), binary with base 64 encoding, Boolean values (true/ false), null, documents consist of lists and array maps and allowing it to store complex JSON documents and set which is an array data type allowing simple list storage.

6. **C** (Partitions.)

Explanation: Partitions are the underlying storage and processing nodes of DynamoDB. When you create a table with the default settings, DynamoDB allocates your table to one underlying node. By default, until things change all storage and any computation like insert, delete, and that one partition handles update operation.

7. **C** (Both A and B.)

Explanation: To examine an item from the table, you need to specify its Partition Key and sort key value. DynamoDB calculates the hash value from Partition Key, yielding the partition in which the object may be observed.

8. **A** (Two.)

Explanation: DynamoDB offers two main data retrieval operations, Scan and Query. The scan is a very inefficient operation because scans go through the table, returning all the attributes for all items in the given table or index. The query can be used to select a single item by specifying one Partition Key value or a partition and sort key value if the table uses partition and sort keys.

9. **B** (GSI.)

Explanation: The Global Secondary Indexes can be created at any time, and unlike the Local Secondary Index, it allows the use of an alternative Partition Key and Sort key. With GSI you have the number of options for attribute projection.

10. **C** (Three.)

Explanation: With GSI you have the number of options for attribute projection.

- KEYS_ONLY: This includes the new partition, sort key value, and the old Partition Key and the old sort key.
- INCLUDE: This allows you to specify custom projection values.
- ALL: This allows you to project all attributes into the GSI.

11. **A** (Query.)

Explanation: The query operation is used to access one or extra items in a global secondary index. The query has to specify the name of the base table and the name of the index that you want to apply, the attributes to be returned in the query outcomes, and any query situations which you want to use. DynamoDB can go back to the outcomes in ascending or descending order.

12. **B** (Scan.)

Explanation: You may use the scan operation to retrieve all of the records from a global secondary index. You need to offer the base table name and the index call in the request. With a scan, DynamoDB reads all the information within the index and returns it to the software. You may additionally request that just a few of the records return and that the remaining facts get discarded.

13. **A** (KEYS_ONLY.)

Explanation: KEYS_ONLY: In this method only, the key attributes are written to the stream when an item is updated. It applies some limits which impact the functionality of stream.

14. **B** (NEW_IMAGE.)

Explanation: NEW_IMAGE: This stores the entire item to the stream. The entire item post update is written to the stream — means you can create code which reacts on changes and performs an action.

15. **C** (OLD_IMAGE.)

Explanation: OLD_IMAGE: The entire item, as it appeared before it was modified. The entire item is written to the stream pre-update.

16. **D** (NEW_AND_OLD_IMAGES.)

Explanation: NEW_AND_OLD_IMAGES: The pre and post operation state of the item is written to the stream allowing more complex comparison operations to be performed.

17. **D** (Trigger.)

Explanation: DynamoDB Stream is combined with Lambda to allow traditional database triggers.

18. **A** (10 GB.)

Explanation: One partition can cope with 10GB of data indicating a right away relationship among the quantity of data stored in a table and performance requirements. A new partition may be added while more than 10 GB of facts is saved in a table. Then, the records get unfolded throughout those partitions

19. **B** (3000RCU and 1000WCU.)

Explanation:

One partition can cope with 10GB of data, 3000 RCU, and 1,000 WCU, indicating a right away relationship among the quantity of data stored in a table and performance requirements. A new partition may be added while more than 10 GB of facts is saved in a table, or WCUs are greater than 1000, or RCUs are greater than 3,000. Then, the records get unfolded throughout those partitions.

20. **B** (1000WCU, 3000RCU, 10GB of Data Volume.)

Explanation: One partition can cope with 10GB of data, 3000 RCU, and 1,000 WCU, indicating a right away relationship among the quantity of data stored in a table and performance requirements.

21. **A** (Query with GSI.)
    C (Scan against the table with filters.)

Explanation: The query operation is used to access one or extra items in a global secondary index.

You may use the scan operation to retrieve all of the records from a global secondary index. You need to offer the base table name and the index call in the request.

22. **A** (String.)
    B (Number.)
    C (Binary.)

Explanation: DynamoDB holds the item such as strings, numbers (positive or negative integer), binary with base 64 encoding, Boolean values (true/ false), null, documents consist of lists and array maps and allowing it to store complex JSON documents and set which is an array data type allowing simple list storage.

23. **B** (False.)

Explanation: When designing an application anything using Local Secondary Indexes, should assume an element of eventual consistency as the data is copied between the table and indexes. Writing and reading to an index consumes read capacity units and write capacity units of the main table.

24. **A** (1KB.)

Explanation: Write Capacity Units (WCU) is the number of writes of 1KB blocks per second to the table.

25. **B** (4KB.)

Explanation: Read Capacity Unit (RCU) is the number of read of 4KB blocks per

seconds to the table.

Chapter 04: Processing

1. **A (4)**

Explanation: In Spark components, we have 4 modules.

2. **B, C, E, F**

Explanation: In Spark stack, there is Spark core which consists of four modules which are referred to as libraries. These modules are Spark SQL, Spark Streaming, MLlib, and Graph-X.

3. **A (bzip2)**

Explanation: Bzip2 has the highest compression ratio as well as it is splittable.

4. **D (Presto)**

Explanation: Presto is an Open Source in-memory fast distributed SQL Query engine. It is used to run interactive analytics queries against a variety of data source with size ranging from GBs to PBs. It is significantly faster than the Hive.

5. **B (false)**

Explanation: Presto is an Open Source in-memory fast distributed SQL Query engine.

6. **B (Instance store)**

Explanation: Amazon EC2 Instance Storage is generally ephemeral drives that give temporary block-level storage for various Amazon EC2 Instance types. It provides high I/O performance and high IOPS at low cost.

7. **B (Kinesis Client Library)**

Explanation: Spark Streaming uses the Kinesis Client Library (KCL) to consume data from a Kinesis stream. KCL handles complex tasks like load balancing, failure recovery, and check-pointing.

8. **A (EBS)**

Explanation: But when using EBS with EMR then data is lost on termination of the cluster.

9. **B (Batch Processing)**

Explanation: These are cases where avoid using Spark

- It is not a typical database and not designed for OLTP
- Batch Processing

- Avoid using it for multi-user reporting environment with high concurrency

10. **D** (Hue)

Explanation: The Hue is "Hadoop User Experience" which is an open source web interface for Apache Hadoop and other non-Hadoop application. It brings a group of different Hadoop ecosystem projects into a configurable interface. It a browser-based way to run and create a script on Hadoop cluster, manage jobs, view HDFS and manage metastore, etc. by using hue managing of EMR cluster becomes very easy.

11. **A** (task)

Explanation: It is also a slave node but optional. It has no HDFS, and you can add them and remove from running cluster. They have enough extra capacity to manage a high amount of load.

12. **B** (4)

Explanation: Hadoop architecture composes of 4 modules.

- Hadoop Common
- HDFS
- Hadoop YARN
- Hadoop MapReduce

13. **D** (MapReduce)

Explanation: MapReduce module is for processing of large datasets with the parallel distributed algorithm on a cluster. The processing can be done on the file system or in a data set. It also performs processing on the basis of data located, so that transfer distance is reduced.

14. **A** (master node)

Explanation: There is resource manager in the master node which is generally a scheduler that allocates the resources in a cluster among the computing application like if you have two applications, then resource manager is responsible for providing their respective resources.

15. **B** (1)

Explanation:

- Master instance group has only one instance
- Core instance group can have 1 or more core nodes

- Task instance group can have up to 48 instance group

16. **C** (3)

Explanation: In HDFS, there is replication property through which the block is replicated across number of the slave node. By default, replication factor is 3 means initially 3 copy is replicated across the 3 slave node.

17. **B** (EMRFS)

Explanation: EMRFS is such type of Hadoop file system, which stores cluster directly into the Amazon S3. EMRFS helps you to store data for a prolonged period in Amazon S3 for further use with Hadoop.

18. **B** (batch job)

Explanation:

- It is used in the processing of logs and performs analytics on these processed logs.
- For joining large tables
- Batch job
- As-hoc interactive queries against the data in HDFS and S3.

19. **D** (Relational database type feature)

Explanation: Where not to use HBase

- Transactional application
- Relational database type feature
- A small amount of data

20. **A** (true)

Explanation: HBase is used for real-time lookup and Redshift used for OLAP (joins, queries, aggregation

Chapter 05: Analysis

1.   **A** (Supervised Learning)

      B (Unsupervised Learning)

Explanation: The task of supervised learning is to learn a function from labeled training data. The training data are a number of examples. Unsupervised learning is the learning task of a machine which involves the description of the hidden structure from the unlabelled information (the observations do not include a classification or categorization). The other answers are not for machine learning.

2.   **C** (By using COPY command)

Explanation: The COPY is the most efficient and quickest way in which data is loaded into RedShift. Because of the column nature of RedShift, single - line INSERTS are slow. Multi-line INSERTS are better than single - line INSERTS, but they do not still load a large amount of data efficiently into RedShift. Since RedShift is a managed service, data backup files for file restoration cannot be accessed.

3.   **D** (50)

Explanation: The total concurrency level for queries in RedShift is 50.

4.   **A** (All)

Explanation: Tables that change rarely (tables that are not updated frequently or extensively) are appropriate to the ALL distribution type. The whole table is distributed to each node in this distribution style.

5.   **B** (To automatically check files in S3)

Explanation: A manifest is used to ensure that the COPY command loads required files only. It is also used if you want to load files from different buckets, as well as load files that do not share the same prefix.

6.   **A** (EMR/EC2 instances)

      B (S3)

      E (DynamoDB)

Explanation: COPY command can be used to integrate directly S3, DynamoDB and EMR / EC2 instances with Redshift.

7.   **B** (KEY)

Explanation: In this case, the KEY distribution style helps to achieve maximum performance. The rows are distributed in RedShift in one column according to the values.

The leader node will attempt to place matching values on the same node slice. If you distribute a pair of tables on the joining keys, the leader node will collocate the rows on the slices according to the values in the joining columns so that matching values are physically stored together from the common columns.

8.   **A** (Compression, as it helps with performance and provides a lower total cost of ownership.)

       B (They are ideal for Online Analytical Processing (OLAP))

Explanation: RedShift supported compression algorithms help performance and also help to reduce the amount of data stored in a RedShift cluster, thus helping to lower overall ownership costs.

9.   **A** (Create a query user group for small queries based on the analysts' RedShift user IDs, and create a second query group for the large, long-running queries.)

Explanation: RedShift supports workload management, allowing users to create query groups to assign query queues so that short, quick - run queries don't want to wait for long-running queries.

10.   **B** (False)

Explanation: RedShift does not enforce primary key and foreign key constraints. Although they are information - only, these constraints are used by the query optimizer to generate more efficient query plans.

11.   **D** (Use a staging table to replace existing rows or update existing rows.)

Explanation: By first loading your data into a staging table, you can efficiently update and insert new data. RedShift supports no UPSERT. To merge data into an existing table, you can perform a merge operation by loading your data into a staging table and then joining the staging table with your target table for an UPDATE statement and an INSERT statement.

12.   **A** (True)

Explanation: No special actions are necessary if you wish to ensure that S3 files are encrypted automatically by server-side encryption. The unload command generates files automatically using the S3 server-side encryption with SSE - S3.

13.   **B** (False)

Explanation: RedShift is specially designed for applications in the field of Online Analytic Processing (OLAP) and Business Intelligence (BI).

14.   **B** (False)

Explanation: Leader node assists the communication between the SQL clients or BI tools and Compute nodes.

15. **C** (Columns)

Explanation: RedShift is a service that stores data in columns; therefore, it based on columnar databases. Columnar databases directly write and read data to and from disk storage for the fast returning the results of the query.

16. **D** (ODD)

Explanation: There are three types of distribution styles in RedShift, i.e., EVEN, KEY and ALL.

17. **C** (Compound)

Explanation: The compound sort key is the default type. It can be used with JOINS, ORDER BY and GROUP BY operations. It can also be used with PARTITION BY and ORDER BY windows functions.

18. **B** (False)

Explanation: Manual compression requires more steps. Therefore, Automatic compression is recommended.

19. **C** (8)

Explanation: Total of 8 user-defined queues is allowed.

20. **B** (False)

Explanation: UPSERT is used to insert any record or update an existing record. UPSERT are not supported by RedShift. In RedShift, any new data can be inserted into any existing table by using UPDATE and INSERT from staging tables.

21. **D** (VACUUM FULL)

Explanation: VACUUM FULL Execute the vacuum command on all tables in a database. To run the vacuum command on a specific table the command is "VACUUM FULL tablename"

22. **A** (True)

Explanation: Executing vacuum command on large tables is slow, so the recommendation is to perform a deep copy, which involves the recreation and repopulation of tables with a bulk insert that automatically sorts the table.

23. **D** (SageMaker)

Explanation: Amazon SageMaker is a fully managed Machine learning service provided by AWS. This service assists data scientists and developers in building and training machine learning models easily and quickly and then deploy these models into a production-hosted environment.

24.   **C** (Logstash)

Explanation: Amazon Elasticsearch service is connected with the Logstash output plugin that is provided by AWS on GitHub. This plugin is installed on the application instance, which helps to push data from instance to Amazon Elasticsearch service domain.

25.   **D** (R)

Explanation: R is a programming language having a free software environment used for statistical computing and graphics. R is widely used for statistical software and analysis among statisticians and data miners. RStudio is defined as an Open source and an enterprise-ready professional software for R.

Chapter 06: Visualization

1. **C** (Super-Fast Parallel In-Memory Calculation Engine.)

Explanation: SPICE which stands for Super-fast, Parallel, In-memory Calculation Engine. SPICE allows QuickSight to run anything from small to very large queries for fast results. AWS creates a SPICE to use accommodation of storage in memory technology which is enabled using the latest hardware innovation machine code generation and data compression.

2. **A** (Amazon QuickSight.)

Explanation: QuickSight is a cloud-based analytics service that allows you to build visualizations and perform Ad-hoc analysis and allowing you to get better business insights.

3. **B** (Two.)

Explanation: With QuickSight you have a choice of two editions; Standard Edition and Enterprise Edition.

4. **A** (Standard.)

Explanation: In QuickSight Standard Edition you can invite an IAM user and allow them to use their credentials to access QuickSight.

5. **B** (Enterprise.)

Explanation: In Enterprise Edition, you select a Microsoft Active Directory in AWS Directory Service. You use that active directory to identify and manage your Amazon QuickSight users and administrators. In Enterprise Directory, one or more Microsoft AD groups in AWS Directory Service are used for administrative access.

6. **C** (Both.)

Explanation: In both the editions of QuickSight, all data transfers are encrypted. Database connections are secured using SSL and although the transfer is secured using TLS.

7. **B** (Enterprise Edition.)

Explanation: In the Enterprise Edition, data addressed in SPICE is encrypted using block role encryption with AWS managed keys.

8. **A** (Visuals.)

Explanation: Visuals are the graphical representation of your data. In QuickSight you

can create a variety of visuals and then announce using different data sets and visual types.

9. **C** (20.)

Explanation: In QuickSight you can have up to 20 visuals per analysis. Creating a visual is fairly very straight forward. QuickSight can also create a visual for you, you decide the fields you want, and by using Autograph, QuickSight will determine the most appropriate visual type.

10. **D** (Two.)

Explanation: In the field list, you have two categories, the dimension field (blue icon) and the measured field (green icon). In the Fields list pane, dimension fields have blue icons, and measure fields have green icons.

11. **A** (Jupyter Notebook.)

Explanation: Heavy Python user tends to like Jupyter as the front-end interpreter.

12. **B** (True.)

Explanation: QuickSight also supports the creation of Dashboard. You can create a dashboard which is a Read-only snapshot of an analysis that you can share with other Amazon QuickSight users for reporting purposes.

13. **A** (True.)

Explanation: Jupyter Notebook is also a web-based notebook that enables interactive data analysis and collaboration. It contains live code in languages like Python, R, Julia, and Scala.

14. **B** (To generate HTML tables, SVG bar charts, and other visualizations like the real-time dashboard, as well as interactive graph and charts that work in the browser.)
    C (To produce dynamic, interactive data visualization in web browsers.)

Explanation: D3.js is a javascript library uses for producing dynamic, interactive data visualizations in a web browser. D3.js can read data from CSV, TSV or json files and can generate HTML tables, SVG bar charts and other visualization like real-time dashboards, interactive graph and interactive maps that work in a browser. D3 lets in you to bind arbitrary records to a document object model (DOM), and then follow data-driven transformation to the record.

15. **A** (True.)

Explanation: QuickSight is a cloud-based analytics service that permits you to build

visualizations and perform Ad-hoc analysis and allows you to get better business insights. Amazon QuickSight is a fast, cloud-powered business intelligence (BI) carrier that makes it smooth and allows you to supply insights to every person for your company.

16. **A** (10 GB.)

Explanation: SPICE is measured in GB, and each user is initially allocated to 10GB per user. SPICE is highly available and durable because the data imported into it is replicated.

17. **B** (Bar Chart.)

Explanation: QuickSight supports Bar Charts which include horizontal and vertical bar charts. In horizontal bar charts, you have Single Measure bar charts where one measure is for one dimension. You can have Multi-Measure bar charts (two or more measures for one dimension).

18. **A** (Line Chart.)

Explanation: You can use the Line Chart to compare changes in measured values over the period. Line Charts are better suited for date fields. Line Charts can be used for a single measure like Gross sales by month.

19. **C** (Pivot Table.)

Explanation: The pivot table is an essential way to summarize data. Pivot Table is used to show measure values for the intersection of two dimensions. After populating a Pivot Table, you can change the row sort order and also apply statistical function for further analysis.

20. **C** (Scatter Plot Visuals.)

Explanation: To visualize two or three measures in a dimension, scatter plots are used. Bubble on the scatter plot represents items in the dimension.

21. **D** (TreeMap.)

Explanation: TreeMap is a diagram representing hierarchical data using nested rectangles. Each rectangle responds to its numerical value. With QuickSight you can use treemaps to visualize one or more measures for a dimension.

22. **A** (Pie Chart.)

Explanation: Pie Charts are used to compare the values of the items in a dimension. A wedge in a pie chart represents one single item in the dimension.

23. **C** (Heat Map.)

Explanation: Heat Map is the graphical representation of data with individual values contained in a matrix, represented as colors. You can use heat maps to identify trends and outliers.

24. **A** (Stories.)

Explanation: In QuickSight you also have the option of creating a story. QuickSight allows you to preserve multiple iterations of an analysis and then play them sequentially to provide a narrative about the analysis of data. Over time you may use the same chart but apply different filters but still be able to get to the previous chart.

25. **D** (MicroStrategy.)

Explanation: MicroStrategy is the provider of Business Intelligence tools and analytics software. The software help businesses make a better decision and transform the way to your business through the ability to create dashboard, scorecards, reports, queries and more.

Chapter 07: Security

1. **B** (False)

Explanation: You can use either an on-prem HSM or you can use CloudHSM, or even both to ensure high-availability and access to the keys.

2. **C** (Data in-transit between node is encrypted)

Explanation: The process of shuffling data is the transfer from the mappers to the reducers. This process involves data transfer from the node to the node in the cluster, and for the data to be encrypted between nodes, the encrypted Hadoop shuffle must be established. The encrypted shuffle function enables MapReduce to be encrypted using HTTPS. On launching your cluster, the Hadoop Encrypted Shuffle will be automatically set up for the user when the in - transit encryption checkbox in the EMR security settings is selected.

3. **A** (Highly available and durable)
   D (Usage-based pricing)

Explanation: For High Availability and durability, KMS is used and is based on usage-

based pricing

4. **D** (Create a new cluster that is not encrypted and reload the data)

   E (Upload the data into S3 and reload it into a cluster that is not encrypted.)

Explanation: Upon launch, once you enable encryption for a RedShift cluster, you can not turn it into an unencrypted cluster. With your new encryption setting, you will need to unload the data and reload the data into a new cluster. Alternatively, if you still have the data in S3 or other supported source, then load the data into a new cluster with your new encryption setting. When you encrypt a RedShift cluster, data blocks and system metadata are encrypted for the cluster and its snapshots.

5. **A** (LUKS)

   B (Open-source HDFS encryption)

Explanation: For the data stored in instance store and EBS volumes, encryption at rest can be achieved by LUKS and Open-source HDFS encryption.

6. **B** (False)

Explanation: KMS only provides symmetric encryption.

7. **C** (CSE-Custom)

Explanation: In this scenario, CSE-Custom is used because the encryption of data is required before sending the data to S3 and client-side master key management is required. The other options for encryption include SSE-S3 in which S3 manages keys. In SSE-KMS S3 uses a Customer Master Key that is used to encrypt and decrypt data by KMS to save them in an S3 bucket. In CSE-KMS customer master key is used for data encryption before its storage in S3 and data decryption after downloading data by EMR cluster.

8. **B** (False)

Explanation: You may need to run an EMR cluster on a private subnet due to compliance or security requirements. An EMR cluster can be operated in a private subnet with no public IP addresses or an Internet Gateway attached. For running an EMR cluster in a private subnet, your VPC needs an S3 endpoint to access S3 or to create a NAT instance for your cluster to interact with other AWS services, which currently do not support VPC endpoints. To connect to the EMR cluster in the private subnet, your local network should be connected to your VPC using VPN or Direct Connect. Alternately, you can use a bastion host to connect to your EMR cluster in a private subnet.

9. **A** (EMR Managed Security Groups)

   D (Additional Security Groups)

Explanation: Two types of security groups can be used with EMR
- EMR Managed Security Groups
- Additional Security Groups

10. **B** (False)
Explanation: Roles are not present when EMR is launched for the first time, but they are automatically created when a cluster is launched.

11. **B** (TLS)
Explanation: By using TLS Encryption, the objects of EMRFS that are in transit between S3 and cluster nodes are automatically encrypted.

12. **B** (Service Side Encryption)'
Explanation: SSE-S3 that is Service Side Encryption with S3 managed Encryption keys

13. **A** (SSE-Custom)
Explanation: There are four Encryption modes which include:
- SSE-S3 that is Service Side Encryption with S3 managed Encryption keys.
- SSE-KMS that is Service Side Encryption with KMS managed keys in this encryption the data sent from EMR cluster to S3 is encrypted or decrypted by using customer master key that is managed in the key master service before storing it in S3 bucket.
- CSE-KMS is the Client Side Encryption which is used when data is needed to be encrypted before sending it to S3 with KMS managed keys and decrypts the data after it is downloaded.
- CSE-Custom is used when data sent to S3 should be encrypted, and the user wants to manage key by himself and want to use the custom client-side master key. Data is decrypted when it is downloaded. For this, encryption path of the custom key providing the file is required. The full class name is also required which is declared in your application that implements the encryption material provided the interface.

14. **B** (core-site.xml)
    C (mapred-site.xml)

Explanation: Two files that are updated to setup Hadoop encryption shuffle:

- core-site.xml: Number of properties are added automatically
- mapred-site.xml: EMR will automatically add mapreduce.shuffle.ssl.enabled property and update its value to "True."

15. **C** (Encryption in-transit)

D (Encryption at-rest)

Explanation: For security in RedShift, two type of Encryptions are important:

- Encryption in-transit
- Encryption at rest (Key Management Service and HSMs)

16. **B** (SSL)

Explanation: SSL for Encryption in-transit is supported in RedShift. On each cluster, RedShift creates and installs a self-signed SSL certificate.

17. **B** (Key Management Service)
    C (Hardware Security Module)

Explanation: For management of Encryption key, Redshift provides two options to use:

- Key Management Service
- Hardware Security Module (CloudHSM and On-Prem HSM)

18. **D** (Slave Key)

Explanation: This is one of the services provided for the Encryption of data in RedShift. It provides a four-tier hierarchy of encryption keys, which are:

- Master key
- Cluster Encryption key
- Database Encryption key
- Data Encryption keys

19. **A** (True)

Explanation: Using EMR for the first time, AWS will assign the default security group, i.e., EMR Managed Security Group. EMR automatically updates inbound and outbound rules in these security groups for the proper communication of instances.

20. **B** (False)

Explanation: The user can specify its security group instead of using the default security group. The advantage for user's own security group is that if there are multiple EMR cluster and user wants to provide isolation in terms of security groups, then this will provide separate EMR managed security groups for all clusters.

21. **D** (Default_DefaultRole)

Explanation: Default_DefaultRole allow EMR services to access the EC2 instance. EMR_EC2_DefaultRole allow EC2 to access other services like S3, DynamoDB, etc.

EMR_Autoscaling_DefaultRole allow Autoscaling of instances to add or terminate in Core & Task node.

22. B (False)

Explanation: To connect the EMR cluster in a private subnet, the local network should be connected to the VPC or VPN or DirectConnect, alternatively. A bastion host can be used to connect an EMR cluster in a private subnet.

23. A (Hardware security module)

Explanation: Hardware security modules are the physical devices used to safeguard and manage digital keys for strong authentication and provide crypto processing.

24. B (False)

Explanation: For the HSM, whether it is CloudHSM or On-premises HSM, A trusted connection should be established between RedShift and HSM which is used to transfer encryption keys between HSM and RedShift during encryption and decryption operations.

25. C (Single-tenant)

Explanation: Key Management Service is Multi-Tenant

Acronyms:

ANSI	American National Standard Institute
API	Application Program Interface
AWS	Amazon Web Service
AZ	Availability Zone
BI	Business Intelligence
CLI	Command Line Interface
D3	Data Driven Document
DB	Database
DDL	Data Definition Language
DOM	Document Object Model
EBS	Elastic Block Storage
EC2	Elastic Compute Cloud
EMR	Elastic Map Reduce
EMRFS	Elastic Map Reduce File System
ETL	Extract Transform and Load
FIFO	First In First Out
GSI	Global Secondary Index
HDFS	Hadoop Distributed File System
HTTP	Hyper Text Transfer Protocol
HTTPS	Hyper Text Transfer Protocol Secure
HTML	Hyper Text Mark-Up Language
IAM	Identity and Access Management
IDE	Integrated Developing Environment
IoT	Internet of Things
I/O	Input/ Output

JDBC	Java Database Connectivity
KCL	Kinesis Client Library
KMS	Key Management Service
KPL	Kinesis Producer Library
LDAP	Lightweight Directory Access Protocol
LSI	Local Secondary Index
LUKS	Linus Unified Key Setup
Microsoft AD	Microsoft Active Directory
MLlib	Machine Learning library
MPP	Massive Parallel Processing
OBDC	Open Database Connectivity
OLTP	Online Transactional Protocol
RCU	Read Capacity Unit
RDD	Resilient and distributed datasets
RDS	Relational Database Service
SASL	Simple Authentication and Security Layer
SerDe	-Serializer-Deserializer
SDK	Software Development Kit
SNS	Simple Notification Service
SPICE	Super-Fast, Parallel, In-Memory Calculation Engine
SQS	Simple Queue Service
SSD	Solid State Drive
SSH	Secure Shell
SSL	Secure Socket Layer
TLS	Transport Layer Security
VPC	Virtual Private Cloud
WCU	Write Capacity Unit
YARN	Yet Another Source Negotiator

References:

Collection

https://docs.aws.amazon.com/streams/latest/dev/key-concepts.html

https://docs.aws.amazon.com/streams/latest/dev/kinesis-using-sdk-java-resharding.html

https://docs.aws.amazon.com/streams/latest/dev/kinesis-kpl-concepts.html#kinesis-kpl-concepts-batching

https://aws.amazon.com/blogs/big-data/implementing-efficient-and-reliable-producers-with-the-amazon-kinesis-producer-library/

https://docs.aws.amazon.com/iot/latest/developerguide/what-is-aws-iot.html

https://dzone.com/articles/aws-iot-ecosystem

https://docs.aws.amazon.com/iot/latest/developerguide/what-is-aws-iot.html

https://docs.aws.amazon.com/iot/latest/developerguide/aws-iot-how-it-works.html

https://searchaws.techtarget.com/definition/AWS-Data-Pipeline-Amazon-Web-Services-Data-Pipeline

https://docs.aws.amazon.com/datapipeline/latest/DeveloperGuide/dp-concepts-activities.html

https://docs.aws.amazon.com/datapipeline/latest/DeveloperGuide/dp-concepts-datanodes.html

https://aws.amazon.com/blogs/compute/amazon-kinesis-firehose-data-transformation-with-aws-lambda/

Storage

https://docs.aws.amazon.com/amazondynamodb/latest/developerguide/LSI.html#LSI.Writes

https://docs.aws.amazon.com/amazondynamodb/latest/developerguide/HowItWorks.Partitions.html

https://docs.aws.amazon.com/amazonglacier/latest/dev/vault-lock-policy.html

https://docs.aws.amazon.com/amazonglacier/latest/dev/vault-lock.html

https://www.amazonaws.cn/en/glacier/

https://aws.amazon.com/about-aws/whats-new/2017/11/amazon-glacier-select-makes-big-data-analytics-of-archive-data-possible/

https://docs.aws.amazon.com/amazondynamodb/latest/developerguide/GSI.html

https://docs.aws.amazon.com/amazondynamodb/latest/developerguide/SecondaryIndexes.html

https://aws.amazon.com/blogs/big-data/scaling-writes-on-amazon-dynamodb-tables-with-global-secondary-indexes/

https://aws.amazon.com/about-aws/whats-new/2014/11/10/introducing-dynamodb-streams/

https://docs.aws.amazon.com/amazondynamodb/latest/developerguide/Streams.html

https://aws.amazon.com/blogs/aws/dynamodb-update-triggers-streams-lambda-cross-region-replication-app/

Processing

https://docs.aws.amazon.com/emr/latest/ManagementGuide/emr-plan-consistent-view.html

https://d1.awsstatic.com/whitepapers/Big_Data_Analytics_Options_on_AWS.pdf

https://d1.awsstatic.com/whitepapers/Storage/data-lake-on-aws.pdf

https://d1.awsstatic.com/whitepapers/Migrating_to_Apache_Hbase_on_Amazon_S3_on_Amazon_EMR.pdf

https://media.acloud.guru/aws-certified-big-data-specialty/resource/dec42f32-9121-3b6d-3dbd-e6882a53acbd_da25b325-b5a3-6f28-38a7-293267c46f14/aws-certified-big-data-specialty-cc61a9eb-8e86-4e1c-af35-17ca9e92ffe1.pdf?Expires=1550635792&Signature=CJzhWAKcoZydcTReDyFiXQJViNIBDca+2EQ4dl/tf6IW4ufEHaZWgs55t2OhEDKIyh703eNd2mnXngK35w2NolkRQ6P9tjH5pNOZ5NxRX8ynd98Hoc6ic1OB6KR/t56QxMzBYF5f50QD6W8S4Cg/oqjBIW+D6oS7TFEDXiIq1ANX/Qb1lYP/59UTQvXh/cE+B7TTICQNHIDaZJeU/us6fIiyrLKnFvHB5oL9LVcODKQIxHRMolD3fRbEXLk1Gs+OCpmZNTEQVSjAiFrvkp6HtsdLbf2E/IKm6Wb4Ewi43SklWLNk7YKDtE5T8fjasA7/a+RdKENujwYMPCEKQCVbnA==&Key-Pair-Id=APKAISLU6JPYU7SF6EUA

https://docs.aws.amazon.com/emr/latest/ReleaseGuide/emr-hue.html

https://docs.aws.amazon.com/emr/latest/ManagementGuide/emr-web-interfaces.html

https://docs.aws.amazon.com/emr/latest/ReleaseGuide/hue-ldap.html

https://docs.aws.amazon.com/emr/latest/ReleaseGuide/emr-hive.html

https://aws.amazon.com/blogs/big-data/using-spark-sql-for-etl/

https://aws.amazon.com/blogs/big-data/a-zero-administration-amazon-Redshift-database-loader/

https://aws.amazon.com/blogs/database/indexing-metadata-in-amazon-elasticsearch-service-using-aws-lambda-and-python/

https://docs.aws.amazon.com/lambda/latest/dg/with-Kinesis.html

https://aws.amazon.com/blogs/compute/implementing-a-serverless-aws-iot-backend-with-aws-lambda-and-amazon-dynamodb/

https://media.acloud.guru/aws-certified-big-data-specialty/resource/dec42f32-9121-3b6d-3dbd-e6882a53acbd_da25b325-b5a3-6f28-38a7-293267c46f14/aws-certified-big-data-specialty-cc61a9eb-8e86-4e1c-af35-17ca9e92ffe1.pdf?Expires=1550895695&Signature=dP+ACR6k9iggDTow47iUFwqhErWl65d05nbGotGkdXn5vhDVoRULq/t6LIVcVqX/cfj7u/aY3YWb/SIc8tNg2rPP2oYV12WPupF5g7nwicVwn5xbyRT4BgLYlXmFsIoyew+X4OAnYnU+bAC4Xo1Jc8OuvvVzKPxCSVMtmIkwS+bwPLReMN3zfxwuDSXpIF2dM8WiGLq+ScXQGBExE3E7wcJQVehF+EeQOM1Q7kYFnNxCuYHidA9wHr6XHhDker/syBHng2Rn+4jZOojgLdbmvr8odQnzMnrJea+AtlmMpeGKozroix3VKVw717pKzY4mS1ZRj2zeecOMLnAWHBAdVA==&Key-Pair-Id=APKAISLU6JPYU7SF6EUA

https://aws.amazon.com/blogs/compute/amazon-Kinesis-firehose-data-transformation-with-aws-lambda/

https://docs.aws.amazon.com/lambda/latest/dg/with-ddb.html

https://aws.amazon.com/blogs/big-data/using-aws-lambda-for-event-driven-data-processing-pipelines/

Analysis

https://docs.aws.amazon.com/RedShift/latest/mgmt/welcome.html

https://docs.aws.amazon.com/RedShift/latest/dg/c_RedShift_system_overview.html

https://www.intermix.io/blog/amazon-RedShift-use-cases/

https://docs.aws.amazon.com/elasticsearch-service/latest/developerguide/es-managedomains.html

https://aws.amazon.com/blogs/security/how-to-visualize-and-refine-your-networks-security-by-adding-security-group-ids-to-your-vpc-flow-logs/#more-3559

https://aws.amazon.com/blogs/big-data/connecting-r-with-amazon-RedShift/

https://aws.amazon.com/blogs/big-data/statistical-analysis-with-open-source-r-and-rstudio-on-amazon-emr/

https://aws.amazon.com/blogs/big-data/crunching-statistics-at-scale-with-sparkr-on-amazon-emr/

https://aws.amazon.com/blogs/big-data/running-r-on-aws/

Visualization

https://docs.aws.amazon.com/quicksight/latest/user/working-with-visuals.html

https://docs.aws.amazon.com/quicksight/latest/user/viewing-visual-data.html

https://docs.aws.amazon.com/quicksight/latest/user/changing-visual-fields.html

https://docs.aws.amazon.com/quicksight/latest/user/creating-a-visual.html

https://docs.aws.amazon.com/quicksight/latest/user/autograph.html

https://docs.aws.amazon.com/quicksight/latest/user/bar-charts.html

https://docs.aws.amazon.com/quicksight/latest/user/pivot-table.html

https://docs.aws.amazon.com/quicksight/latest/user/working-with-dashboards.html

https://aws.amazon.com/blogs/big-data/running-jupyter-notebook-and-jupyterhub-on-amazon-emr/

https://aws.amazon.com/blogs/big-data/analyze-realtime-data-from-amazon-kinesis-streams-using-zeppelin-and-spark-streaming/

Security

https://hadoop.apache.org/docs/r2.7.1/hadoop-mapreduce-client/hadoop-mapreduce-client-core/EncryptedShuffle.html

https://docs.aws.amazon.com/redshift/latest/mgmt/working-with-db-encryption.html

About Our Products

Other products from IPSpecialist LTD regarding AWS technology are:

 AWS Certified Cloud Practitioner Technology Workbook

 AWS Certified SysOps Admin - Associate Workbook

 AWS Certified Solution Architect - Associate Technology Workbook

 AWS Certified Developer Associate Technology Workbook

 AWS Certified DevOps Engineer – Professional Technology Workbook

 AWS Certified Advanced Networking – Specialty Technology Workbook

 AWS Certified Big Data – Specialty Technology Workbook

Upcoming products from IPSpecialist LTD regarding AWS technology are:

 AWS Certified Security – Specialty Technology Workbook

Note from the Author:

> Reviews are gold to authors! If you have enjoyed this book and helped you along certification, would you consider rating it and reviewing it?

Link to Product Page:

Made in the USA
San Bernardino, CA
04 September 2019